PRISONER OF CONSCIENCE

PRISONER OF
CONSCIENCE

FRANK WOLF

with **ANNE MORSE**

ZONDERVAN.com/
AUTHORTRACKER
follow your favorite authors

ZONDERVAN

Prisoner of Conscience
Copyright © 2011 by Frank Wolf

This title is also available as a Zondervan ebook. Visit www.zondervan.com/ebooks.

This title is also available in a Zondervan audio edition. Visit www.zondervan.fm.

Requests for information should be addressed to:

Zondervan, *Grand Rapids, Michigan 49530*

Library of Congress Cataloging-in-Publication Data

Wolf, Frank R.
    Prisoner of conscience / Frank Wolf with Anne Morse.
      p. cm.
    ISBN 978-0-310-32899-5 (hardcover)
    1. Wolf, Frank R. 2. Legislators—United States—Biography. 3. United States.
Congress. House—Biography. 4. Human rights workers—United States—Biography. 5.
Human rights advocacy—United States—History. I. Morse, Anne. II. Title.
    E840.8.W63A3 2011
    328.73'092—dc22
    [B]   2011012856

Published in association with the literary agency of Alive Communications, Inc., 7680 Goddard Street, Suite 200, Colorado Springs, CO 80920. www.alivecommunications.com.

Cover photography: by Daniel Scanding, staff of Congressman Frank Wolf
    by Edward Newberry, staff of Congressman Frank Wolf
    U.S. House of Representatives photograph
    by the National Republican Committee
    by World Vision, Bob Latta
    Shutterstock®
Interior design: Matthew Van Zomeren
Interior photography: credit listed next to each image

Printed in the United States of America

11 12 13 14 15 /DCI/ 23 22 21 20 19 18 17 16 15 14 13 12 11 10 9 8 7 6 5 4 3 2 1

For Carolyn, my beloved wife,
my anchor and truest friend.

CONTENTS

FOREWORD

IN EVERY GENERATION, God chooses a handful of courageous leaders to defend the truth and promote righteousness — often against the prevailing currents. Frank Wolf is such a man for our times. As the patron saint of unpopular causes, Frank is a modern-day William Wilberforce.

The parallels between their lives are amazing. Wilberforce, a great hero of mine, was the nineteenth-century British parliamentarian remembered mainly for his decades-long battle against the slave trade. Frank Wolf, an American congressman, has fought long and hard against modern slavery, as with Sudanese Christians.

Wilberforce also declared war on dozens of other social evils of his time, promoting everything from prison reform to the prevention of cruelty to animals. One of the sponsors of the Prison Rape Elimination Act of 2003, Frank Wolf also fought for prison reform, and he's fought against the social scourges of gangs and gambling interests and led efforts to keep "blood diamonds" from being sold in the U.S.

Other parallels: Wilberforce worked closely with a small group of friends known as the Clapham Sect — men and women who met in one another's homes and prayed together as they fought their political battles. Frank Wolf has for decades been part of a congressional small group, both Republicans and Democrats, who pray for one another as they fight great humanitarian battles, from world hunger to the persecution of Iraqi Christians to the slaughter of innocents in Darfur. And like Wilberforce and his colleagues, they get together with their wives to socialize outside the halls of Congress.

Wilberforce, father of six, gave high priority to his family, often, as one biographer noted, excusing himself "from important deliberations with fellow MPs to go out on the lawn and have a race with the children."[1] Frank, father of five, also vowed not to sacrifice his family. He reserves Sundays for church and family and installed a special phone line in his office for the exclusive use of his wife and kids. If the phone rings, no matter what he's doing or how important his visitors, he answers that phone.

In 2000, Frank and I both worked on the issue of the sexual trafficking of more than two million women and children around the world — another tragic form of slavery. Frank was one of the first people to speak out on this issue, and he was absolutely relentless against the fierce opposition of the Clinton administration, which wanted to help women find "work" by allowing certain prostitution rings to flourish.

This is just one more example of Frank's determination to promote righteousness. The administration relented, and the law was passed to prosecute traffickers.

During his thirty-year career, Frank has dared to go where few members of Congress have gone before — often in defiance of the authorities, and frequently in disguise. As one reporter wrote, "His is the ubiquitous, not-famous face that pops up in places where bullets fly, babies starve, and thousands of people suffer in obscurity."[2]

While other congressmen and congresswomen take "fact-finding tours" to Bermuda or Paris, Wolf has traveled to Soviet gulags, to rebel-held Sierra Leone, and to the bombed-out villages of Sudan and Chechnya.

His life story reads like a fiction thriller, but it is all true.

Frank has steadfastly spoken truth to power, whether that power was Ronald Reagan, Bill Clinton, George W. Bush, or the world's most ruthless dictators. Frank is the conscience of the House.

There is no one in American public life I admire more than Frank Wolf. Like the late Mother Teresa, he measures himself by faithfulness, not success. Political and religious freedom fighters around the world, and advocates for the world's poor, consider Frank Wolf a hero. So do I. This humble, self-effacing man has earned the grateful thanks of everyone from Romanian defectors to Darfurian rape victims to the Dalai Lama.

Frank's passion for justice is the reason he became the second person to whom Prison Fellowship awarded the Wilberforce Award, given annually to an individual who has made a difference in the face of formidable societal problems and injustices. Frank is the living embodiment of the biblical command "to act justly and to love mercy and to walk humbly with your God" (Mic. 6:8). I am proud to call him my friend.

— *Chuck Colson*
February 21, 2011

THOUSANDS OF BABIES WAILED under the blazing Ethiopian sun, desperately seeking nourishment from their mothers' breasts. Three-year-olds were so severely malnourished, they could not stand, much less crawl or walk, their pencil-thin legs so frail, they could be snapped like twigs. Drinking water was nearly nonexistent — a four-hour walk each way. Crops had failed in the scorched fields, and the sun had so thoroughly baked the hand-dug collecting ponds, that the earth had cracked.

It was 1984, and nearly one million Ethiopians had already perished in the famine. I was sitting in a feeding station, holding a dying baby in my arms, surrounded by thousands of desperate, starving people. I looked around at the squalid camp conditions, at the bloated bellies of the children, at the suffering faces of their mothers. Disease and despair stalked everyone there.

How did a guy who had scarcely ever been out of the United States, a congressman who had run on transportation issues, the son of a Philadelphia policeman, end up in a place like this?

Earlier that year, the BBC had broken the story of a terrible famine ravaging Ethiopia, which the Mengistu government had tried to keep secret. Record low rains were in large part responsible for the famine, and the problem was exacerbated by the cost of fighting off various rebellions. As well, the Ethiopian government did not prepare well for famine relief.

I had spent a lot of time campaigning that year, and one day in October I was at the Department of Motor Vehicles at Bailey's Crossroads. A young woman working for World Vision came up to me. "Have you seen on television what's going on in Ethiopia?" she asked.

"Yes, I have," I replied.

"Would you go to Ethiopia and see for yourself?" she asked.

I said I would like to. I was reminded of that conversation two months later, after the election, when my friend Tony Hall, a Democratic member of Congress from Ohio, called me up. "I just got back from Ethiopia, people are dying all over the place, you gotta go, too," he said. "I won't be able to help them unless I have a partner, and I need you to be my partner."[1]

The reality of life in Congress is that if you want to get anything substantive done, you have to partner with someone on the other side of the aisle. Before deciding what could best be done, I wanted to see for myself how dire the famine was, and how deep the suffering. Members and senators frequently take trips like this when they involve issues important to them or their constituents. In addition, America gives billions in foreign aid around the world, including in Ethiopia; those who authorize it have a responsibility to keep an eye on how the money is being spent — or misspent, as the case may be.

I had just gotten on the Appropriations Committee, which appropriates money for foreign aid. I naively went to the ranking Republican member, Silvio Conte, who approved my trip. Without a second thought I jumped on a plane all by myself — no staff — and flew to Rome. There I spent the night and then flew out to Addis Ababa, Ethiopia. I'd never been outside of the United States except for trips to Canada and Germany, and I really had no idea what I was getting into.

CHAPTER ONE

A FEARFUL FAMINE: ETHIOPIA

"I was hungry and you gave me something to eat, I was thirsty and you gave me something to drink...." Then the righteous will answer him, "Lord, when did we see you hungry and feed you, or thirsty and give you something to drink?" ... The King will reply, "Truly I tell you, whatever you did for one of the least of these brothers and sisters of mine, you did for me."

Matthew 25:35–40

This was still the time of the Cold War, and, following the overthrow of Emperor Haile Selassie a decade earlier, Ethiopia was being run by a Communist dictatorship. An embassy staffer drove me to my hotel, directly across from which was the Cuban military post, where I saw Cuban forces wandering around with their guns.

After checking into my room, the first thing I did was to go to the hotel's restaurant and order some pizza. A *Washington Post* reporter named Blaine Harden was there, covering the famine, and he spotted me. He proceeded to write an article mentioning that the congressman from northern Virginia was, in the midst of a famine, "cooling his heels in the Addis Ababa Hilton" and "eating a pizza in the Hilton's pizzeria."[2] Well, Italy used to control Ethiopia, and so it wasn't surprising that you could find pizza there. But Harden made it sound like I was on vacation! We later got to know each other, and he wrote a very nice piece about my human rights work.

The next morning, I went to see the deputy chief of missions, from the U.S. Embassy. "I want to go to the hunger area," I announced. The embassy people hadn't been up there, and they didn't seem particularly interested in helping me visit, either. They were quite unfriendly and a little arrogant. The deputy chief of missions said, "Well, you're going to have to fly in, and it's going to take a private plane."

"Okay," I said. "I'm game to fly. Tell me how."

He said, "Well, it's going to cost you five thousand dollars to rent a plane."

"I don't have that kind of money," I told him. "I'm not wealthy; I live on my pay. I still haven't paid my retirement back the money I took out to run for Congress. Can't we just drive?"

"No, you can't drive," he said.

I was pretty frustrated and walked around Addis Ababa for a while by myself, trying to figure out what to do next. I got in touch with World Vision, which was running a big relief camp in Alamata. One of their guys said, "We're flying up to the famine area tomorrow; you want to come?"

So early the next morning I jumped on their airplane along with someone from the embassy staff. It first stopped briefly in Korem. I climbed out of the plane — and was met by the most terrible sight I'd ever seen. Some fifty thousand people were living on an open plain or, at best, in tents or huts. Children, covered in flies, were dying all over the place, just as Tony had warned me. It was awful.

We then flew to Alamata. Below us, scorched fields, sun-baked holding ponds, and cracked earth told of a total crop failure. World Vision and the Missionaries of Charity, the order founded by Mother Teresa, were running feeding camps adjacent to each other. I was there to observe and ask questions, and the plan was for me to return to Addis Ababa with the plane that night. But as we walked out to board the plane, I suddenly turned to Bob Latta, the guy from World Vision, and said, "I think I want to stay." I wanted to pick up the rhythm of a full day there.

"If you spend the night, I'll spend the night," he replied.

The embassy guy overheard us. "No," he said. "You can't stay."

"I'm going to stay," I announced.

So the plane left and Bob and I went back into the camp, and a hospitable Ethiopian aid worker told us, "You can spend the night in my hut."

That night torrential rains poured down onto the corrugated tin roof. I thought, "Wow, isn't this amazing? This is great! They have a drought, and now it's raining."

But I got up the next morning to see the most unbelievable sight. There was no vegetation, so the rainwater had just come down out of the hills and swirled around and made everything extremely muddy.

At daybreak I went out with a Dutch doctor named Peter, who was volunteering with World Vision. Outside the camp fence the women were wailing, holding out babies with distended bellies, and the men who ran the World Vision camp were beating them back to keep them from overrunning it. Dr. Peter would examine the children, and if a child was really dying, and there was hope for survival, the doctor would give the mother a little paper authorizing medical treatment and entrance to the feeding camp.

Because of the shortage of medical supplies and food, the doctor could treat only a limited number of children every day, nursing them back from the brink of starvation. The mothers knew this, which is why they fought so hard to get to the doctor. Many of the untreated children would probably die within a short time, as the mothers knew full well. We sorrowfully watched as aid workers dug graves for those who had died the previous night.

Later that day I helped feed the kids who were in the camp, handing them bowls filled with porridge specially formulated for their nutritional needs. I picked up one terribly emaciated little boy, whose sagging, wrinkled skin bore evidence of his starvation and who was clearly close to death. I couldn't help thinking of my own five healthy children. It was heartbreaking.

Next door at the Missionaries of Charity camp, one of the white-robed nuns came up to me and asked, "Do you want to see our generator room?"

"Sure," I said.

She opened the door to a hut. When I stepped inside, I realized her "generator" was a dirt-floored chapel. A simple crucifix hung on the wall. The sisters would come here every day to recharge their batteries, so to speak, in order to continue their difficult work.

I had given away all my granola bars the night before because the plane was coming the next day to take me back to Addis Ababa. But because the weather turned bad, the plane didn't come after all, so I had to live on those high-calorie United Nations biscuits, which didn't taste bad. I took a lot of pictures to show people back home. Otherwise they might not have believed how bad things were.

When I arrived back in America, Tony and I supported legislation increasing funding for African aid. Tony also joined me in authoring a letter to President Mengistu of Ethiopia, which was cosigned by 130 of our House colleagues, urging him to consider all available means of expediting donations to the people of Eritrea and Tigre, which were part of Ethiopia at the time, and to begin development of a "safe passage" policy to ensure that famine relief efforts reached all areas of Ethiopia.

I wanted to make sure President Reagan was aware of how bad the situation was. Washington was emptying out as residents left to go home for Christmas, but I called up the White House in hopes of an immediate audience with the president. Ed Meese, who was chief of staff, had a lot of influence over who got to see Reagan, and he got me an appointment.

A few days later I met with President Reagan, Vice President George Bush, and Peter McPherson, head of the Agency for International Development, in the Oval Office. I told Reagan about what I'd witnessed in Ethiopia and how important it was to get the people some food. He was very interested and very supportive of doing something to help. I'm sure he must have heard from many others about the famine, too, because within days he authorized the shipping of food to Ethiopia.

Reagan was always willing to meet with members of Congress and would follow through on the issue — one of the reasons why I've always admired him.

* * *

The 1984 – 85 famine killed nearly a million people, and I never thought I would see such terrible suffering again. But I did, nineteen years later, when I returned to Ethiopia in January of 2003. A severe drought had destroyed most of the harvest the year before, even in parts of the country that normally provided surpluses of food. Not only that year's crops had been destroyed but also the seeds needed to plant the next year's crop.

Once again the country was embroiled in a horrific famine. The population had increased from forty-five million in 1984 to sixty-nine million. Whereas eight million Ethiopians had faced starvation in 1984, eleven million faced it now.

To make matters worse, HIV/AIDS was spreading throughout the country, and Ethiopia's two-and-a-half-year border war with neighboring Eritrea had drained precious resources and led to thousands of displaced individuals and families, particularly in remote areas of the country. Water for drinking and bathing was almost nonexistent, and what water was available was putrid. There was no medicine, not even so much as an aspirin. Disease was rampant. Ethiopian prime minister Meles Zenawi told a BBC reporter, "If [the 1984 famine] was a nightmare, then this will be too ghastly to contemplate."[3]

An elderly woman at a feeding station in the northern part of the country showed me her monthly allotment of wheat, which would have fit easily into a bowling ball bag. I watched an Ethiopian working under the hot African sun with fellow villagers, digging a massive rain-collecting pond, carrying fifty-pound bags of dirt up from the bottom of the pit, over and over again. The man told me he had not had a drink of water all day and didn't know if he would eat that night. It would depend, he said, on whether his children had food.

I visited villages in both the north and south and talked with farmers who had already begun to sell off their livestock and with mothers who did not know where or when their children would get their next meal. Tragically, many Ethiopians have little memory of any other way of life. As Tony Hall notes in his book *Changing the Face of Hunger*, "The sequence of drought, famine, hunger, and starvation had been repeated in Ethiopia for centuries."[4]

I later met, along with U.S. State Department officials and NGOs (nongovernmental organizations), with Prime Minister Zenawi and several relief officials in his government.[5] The Ethiopian government's decision not to establish large feeding camps was a wise one; such camps would only have exacerbated the crisis, because they allow diseases to spread much more quickly, and take people away from their homes and (albeit limited) support systems. In 1984 many families had traveled great distances to reach the camps. By the time they arrived, they were often near death. Moreover, villagers who left for the camps and somehow managed to survive had nothing to return to, because they had lost their homes and sold their livestock.

With each new crisis — drought, war, disease — more families became desperate, dependent on others for their welfare and their very survival. The repeated droughts made more people vulnerable to hunger and hunger-related diseases, sharply increasing the danger of outright starvation among groups that may have been able to survive previous crop failures and livestock losses.

This was also a tough neighborhood, with border countries Sudan to the west and Somalia to the east both struggling to overcome internal turmoil of their own. Refugees from each country had crossed into Ethiopia and were now living in camps. But perhaps the greatest difficulty was getting the world to respond to this humanitarian crisis. This time, nearly two decades after the first famine, Ethiopia's leaders were out in front, trying to draw attention to the crisis. But in 2003 the world's capitals were deeply focused on the war on terror, on Iraq, and on North Korea.

As I once again saw hundreds of hungry, crying children covered in flies, I wondered where the world's press — so helpful in publicizing the 1984 famine — was now. The disaster had been building since the fall of 2002, yet there had been scant mention of it in the Western media, let alone any in-depth reports. Without graphic photographs and video, foreign governments would not feel the pressure to act. Before I left for Ethiopia, a number of well-read Washingtonians looked at me quizzically when I told them where I was going. "Why?" they all asked. When I told them the country was facing another famine, rivaling the scale of the 1984 famine, they were dumbfounded.

When a famine strikes, time is of the essence. A village can slip dramatically in just a matter of weeks. Many of the children I saw in January would, I knew, be dead by early February. Those who did by some miracle survive would, tragically, be severely mentally handicapped by the malnourishment.

In addition to visiting Ethiopia in 2003, I also traveled to Eritrea. The situation there was not much better. Widespread crop failures were the result of the drought, and compounding the situation were the lingering effects of Eritrea's war with Ethiopia, which ended in December 2000. While nearly two hundred thousand refugees had been reintegrated into society following the truce, almost ten thousand were unable to return to their homes because of the presence of land mines, unexploded ordnance, security issues, or the simple fact that the infrastructure near their homes had been completely destroyed.

When I returned to the States and tried to get the media to focus on the situation, one television producer told me he would not be interested in covering the story until hundreds of children were dying on a daily basis. That's exactly the kind of situation worldwide attention would prevent — a point the producer seemed to be missing.

At the time, hundreds of journalists were embedded with coalition forces in Iraq, and hundreds more were scattered throughout the Persian Gulf region. But how many journalists visited the Horn of Africa? I'd be surprised if more than a handful did.

It would also have been helpful if Hollywood and the music industry had taken notice. In 1985 Western rock stars raised almost $150 million for Ethiopian famine relief through their Live Aid concert. But in 2003 they were noticeably absent when the new crisis unfolded.

It seemed that American news outlets were giving more attention to the dust-up involving the Baseball Hall of Fame canceling the commemoration of baseball film *Bull Durham* (because stars Susan Sarandon and Tim Robbins were noisily opposing the war in Iraq)[6] than to the crisis in Ethiopia. While Americans tried to satisfy their insatiable appetite for reality shows, the starving people of Africa were living the ultimate "reality show" in the most stark and grim terms.

But is not the value of an Ethiopian child the same as that of any other child in the eyes of God? In Matthew 25 we are admonished regarding our obligation to feed the hungry — to treat them as we would treat Christ himself.

From August 2002 to January 2003, the United States provided approximately 430,000 metric tons of food, valued at $179 million — an amount that constituted approximately 25 percent of the total need.

Will there ever be an end to the suffering of Ethiopians? Not unless something is done to develop long-term strategies to tackle the root causes of the food shortages — such as improving irrigation, drilling wells, developing drought-resistant crops, and teaching Ethiopian farmers about sustainable agricultural practices. Because 80 percent of Ethiopians make their living off the land, the government must develop a ten- or fifteen-year plan designed to help end the constant cycle of massive food shortages. Such a plan would go a long way toward reassuring the international community that the country wants to end its dependence on handouts.

A veterinary missionary named Fred Van Gorkom, who recently returned to the U.S. after twenty-five years working in Ethiopia through Christian Veterinary Mission, has this to say about Ethiopia's future: "The Ethiopian government has done some irrigation projects, but has little capacity to do much on its own; they need outside funding. SIM (Serving in Mission) Ethiopia has an irrigation project using simple windmills, manufactured in-country on the Omo River in the southwest corner of Ethiopia. SIM has also done an irrigation project on Lake Langano, for a famine area, and I know that other NGOs have irrigation projects. But these are only a start — nowhere near enough."

Regarding drought-resistant crops, Van Gorkom says, "The government research station seems to me to do pretty good work. They have developed some drought-resistant sorghum that we tested in the southwest with success. A big challenge is farmer acceptance. Subsistence farmers are not quick to risk their lives to try something that will mean they and their family starve to death if it fails. Can't blame them. We did some pilot plots. The local people were very impressed, but in the end, what was most easily acceptable to them was an improvement on their current system of survival rather than a whole new thing."

Transplanted American ingenuity has also improved the lot of subsistence Ethiopian farmers.

"During certain times of the year the people we worked with in southwestern Ethiopia are always reduced to eating weeds and tree leaves," Van Gorkom explained. "So I introduced the Moringa tree — a healthier, more palatable tree leaf at no risk to their current survival system. It really took off! We also introduced fruit trees. I felt that they would survive and maybe even bear fruit even in years where the rainfall was insufficient for a crop of corn or sorghum. That worked well. With all the highlands in Ethiopia, many fruit trees do surprisingly well and have tons of potential. We also introduced (from other parts of Ethiopia) a type of peanut and a type of sweet potato that do well on low rainfall. That was also a success. These things all taken together, holistically, are what make a community more able to weather cycles of drought — which is why they've been nomads for hundreds of years."[7]

The Ethiopian government also should do more to help diversify its economy. Its largest export — coffee — is subject to huge price fluctuations in the world market, and its exports of hide and leather to Italy and China are simply imported back into the economy as belts and purses. The government should work to attract business that will allow these products to be made on Ethiopian soil.

Ethiopia's leaders should also consider a sweeping land-reform policy that would allow farmers to own their property rather than the government owning most of the country's land, a vestige of the country's socialist days.

Sad to say, government-to-government foreign aid money can sometimes be a problem. According to *Dead Aid* author Dambisa Moyo, 97 percent of the Ethiopian government's budget is attributed to foreign aid, much of it from the U.S.[8] But how much of this money actually benefits the Ethiopian people?

The aftermath of the 1985 Live Aid concert illustrates how difficult it is to help the poor even when our motives are good. There were allegations by many, including Human Rights Watch, that the corrupt Ethiopian government stole much of the money that Live Aid raised.[9]

Because the same sort of thing happens with government-to-government assistance, "aid has been, and continues to be, an unmitigated political, economic, and humanitarian disaster for most parts of the developing world," Moyo writes. The best long-term solution, for Ethiopia and the rest of the developing world, Moyo maintains, is economic development, not aid.[10] She's right.

In the short term, when lives are immediately at stake from famine, the Ethiopian government should take its case to capitals around the globe, sending representatives armed with photographs of dying children to donor nations in order to put a face on the crisis. Regrettably, if they do not ask, they will not receive.

The squalid condition of the refugee camps and the faces of thousands of Ethiopians begging for help are sights I will never forget. The hunger problem today is, tragically, not confined to Ethiopia. There are eight hundred million people worldwide for whom chronic hunger is a way of life and, too often, a way of death. In Africa alone, thirty million people are at risk. There are reports of widespread hunger in North Korea as well. We need to do more to refocus American attention on this issue and reenergize the global community. At stake are the lives of millions of mothers and children around the world.

·   ·   ·

Had I not traveled to Ethiopia in 1984, and to Romania the following year, I would probably not have become interested in human rights. These two trips were the seeds of everything that came afterward — my concern for people suffering under China's one-child policy, for political prisoners languishing in the Soviet gulags, for Tibetans suffering under the brutal control of the Chinese government, and for Christians in Muslin countries being persecuted for their faith. What I saw and experienced in Ethiopia, and later in Romania, fully awakened me to the suffering of other people. And as both a U.S. congressman and a Christian, I knew I had to do something about it.

CHAPTER TWO

ROMANIAN
RESCUE

Human rights are indivisible. They are God-given, not
man-made. Respect for the human rights of their citizens by the countries of the world isn't optional.

Rep. Chris Smith

PEOPLE ARE SOMETIMES SURPRISED to learn that one of my greatest friends is Tony Hall, a Democrat from Ohio.[1] We don't always see eye-to-eye on political issues, but we agree very strongly on many moral ones. More than any other person, Tony opened my eyes to human rights and religious freedom violations around the world. Until he did, these matters were simply not on my radar screen.

Not long after my first trip to Ethiopia, Tony suggested that we, along with Congressman Chris Smith of New Jersey, travel together to Romania, then in the grip of one of the most vicious men in the world: Nicolae Ceausescu.

During the days of Communist rule over much of Europe, Romania was darker than Moscow, darker and more evil than any other Soviet bloc country. Tony, Chris, and I wanted to look into alarming reports we'd been hearing from groups like Amnesty International, Helsinki Watch, Christian Response International, and our State Department about the persecution of Christians there and other massive human rights violations. We'd all read the book *Tortured for Christ* by Richard Wurmbrand, an evangelical pastor who had endured many years in Romanian prisons for refusing to give up preaching the gospel.[2]

In the mid-1960s Wurmbrand was granted amnesty from prison and later moved to the United States, where he founded the Voice of the Martyrs, an organization "dedicated to assisting the persecuted church worldwide."[3] He testified before the Senate Internal Security Committee in 1966, and for years had been appealing to all people of faith to speak out on behalf of Christians behind the Iron Curtain, who were at that time among the most persecuted people on earth.

It was the kind of book you could not just put down and forget about. So Tony, Chris, and I decided to travel together to Romania under the auspices of Christian Solidarity International (which paid for our trip), visit with religious believers and government officials, and find out for ourselves just how bad things were.

I flew to Bucharest in July of 1985 with Tony and his wife, Janet, Chris and his assistant, Mary, and my daughter Virginia, who was then a Wheaton College student.[4] As soon as we landed, we were hustled off to the U.S. Embassy. The embassy's Romania Country Team took us immediately into the embassy's "bubble zone," a tiny room where it was impossible for the Romanian government to listen in on our conversation.

"The Securitate will be spying on you every minute," embassy staffers warned us. "They will follow you everywhere you go. Even your hotel rooms will be bugged."

We made something of a joke of it. That evening at our hotel, when we were discussing our plans for the following day, one of us would yell, "Did you get that?" Just to let them know we knew they were listening — and perhaps watching us, as well.

Of course, it was not so funny for the Romanian people, who paid terrible consequences if they were overheard criticizing the government, or if it turned out a neighbor, or even a family member, was reporting them to the Securitate, one of the most dreaded secret police organizations behind the Iron Curtain. The oppression was so intense, it could be felt even by outsiders like us. People on the street, seeing the government handlers around us, avoided eye contact.

We spent a few days in Bucharest, meeting with government officials and visiting churches. After that we flew to Oradea in Transylvania to visit the Second Baptist Church, where Billy Graham had once preached and where we had been asked to speak. The Romanian government, of course, was not keen on our doing this, and the Securitate and government officials kept holding us up at various meetings. They also went ahead to the church and told the congregation they might as well leave because we weren't coming. They held us up for four hours, hoping the congregants would give up and go home. They didn't; in fact, they were singing lustily when we finally arrived.

The church was packed, with people filling the balconies and sitting in the windows — young women wearing colorful hats and headscarves, older women in black, men in suits, and smiling children. Coincidentally, members of the Wheaton College soccer team were also visiting the church. Our Romanian handlers, who never let us out of their sight, sat directly behind us.

A men's choir began singing a powerful hymn in Romanian, and as I listened, I began to sense the overwhelming holiness of that church. I had never seen a congregation so full of the Holy Spirit as I did among those suffering believers, and I was deeply moved by their faith in the face of such persecution. I couldn't help wondering if our hard-eyed handlers could feel it, too.

After the service, as we wandered outside, our fellow worshipers told us how grateful they were that we'd come. A number of them approached us and, while shaking our hands, furtively slipped notes into our pockets. When I had a chance to read them later, I was deeply saddened.

"My son is in prison, please help him," one of them read in English. "My husband disappeared, please help me find him," read another. And, "Help my daughter get out of Romania."

They pleaded with us to tell the West about the oppressive reality and wretched poverty that was daily life under Ceausescu. My daughter was especially affected by these notes, and both Virginia and I gave our Bibles away to people who approached us. (Bibles were not prohibited, but they were hard to come by.)

We visited three more churches in and around Bucharest, and with each visit, the Securitate delayed us and tried to get the congregation to disperse before our arrival. At all three houses of worship, however, the people stayed until we arrived, and joyfully worshiped with us. Simply by showing up, they risked beatings, torture, and prison. Everywhere, people pressed notes into our hands. And away from the prying eyes and ears of the Securitate, they told us stories of persecution, oppression, and misery.

We were horrified to learn that two years before, as an energy-conserving measure, the government had ordered the heat turned off in hospitals, leading to the deaths of Romanian babies in their incubators. Thanks to Ceausescu's ill-conceived financial policies, the Romanian people were enduring food shortages and rationing, little or no heat during the winter, and little or no electricity during the night.

We learned that ethnic minorities — particularly Hungarians and Gypsies — were being cruelly repressed, and that the Romanian government was selling Jews to Israel and ethnic Germans to West Germany for up to fifty thousand dollars per person, depending on his or her level of education and profession.

We also found out what had happened to some twenty thousand Bibles that had been sent to Romanian believers by the Hungarian Reformed Church. Romanian leaders had given permission for the delivery of these Bibles, but they feared their influence. So they seized all twenty thousand of them and recycled the pages into toilet paper. But the words of Scripture were still clearly legible. I brought a roll back with me and later displayed it in a House Committee hearing where Tony, Chris, and I testified about what was going on in Romania.

We learned about Father Geza Palfi, a Roman Catholic priest, who said in his Christmas Day homily of 1983 that Christmas should not be a day of labor, as Ceausescu had declared it, but a holiday. The Securitate arrested him on charges of "agitating against the government" and put him in prison, where he was badly beaten. He died a short time later, at age forty-eight, of severe internal injuries. The Romanian government falsified his death certificate, but a human rights group noted that "it is common knowledge that his liver and his kidneys were completely crushed and shattered due to the beatings he received while in custody."[5] All because he said that Christmas should be a holiday.[6]

We also met with pastors of fourteen denominations (or "cults," as the government called them), including Baptists, Evangelicals, and Orthodox believers; churches were significantly restricted by the government. We met both with pastors who were spouting the government line and with those who bravely refused to do so. The Romanian Orthodox Church was the largest of the denominations, and there were many in that church who remained true to the faith, as well as those who had been co-opted.

One person we didn't meet on our Romanian trip was Nicolae Ceausescu. We had asked for a meeting with him, but because Chris, Tony, and I had so strongly criticized Ceausescu's human rights violations, we didn't get the kind of access given to congressmen and senators who had taken a softer line. You didn't get to see Ceausescu if you weren't kowtowing and saying gratuitously nice things about him and his wife.

However, we did meet with a number of people under him, including Foreign Minister Stefan Andrei, which was an infuriating experience. Tony and I knew perfectly well that the government officials were blatantly lying to us, because we had plenty of evidence regarding what was really going on. They knew we knew they were lying, but we also suspected that some of them, at least, were afraid to tell us the truth about the extent of Ceausescu's repression.

Recalling those tense meetings, Tony notes, "Oftentimes Frank and I would play good cop/bad cop. He was mostly the one that pressed and pushed and fought. He really came down hard on them. It didn't matter to him that we were in a Communist country and that we could have been thrown out — or something else. When he believed in something, he spoke out. Frank was pushing them to release a particular prisoner, a pastor. Frank really pushed and pushed and pushed for them to release this guy. And the pastor said that if it wasn't for Frank's perseverance, he would never have got out of prison — that Frank actually saved his life."

We pressed them to stop the repression and brought up cases of citizens who had been sent to prison for their faith, but they refused to listen. We did have one hold on them, however: most favored nation status (MFN), whereby the United States allowed the products of Romania to pay the lowest duty we charged. We resolved to do something about that when we returned home.

Chris, Tony, and I also visited a church the government had bulldozed, which gave us a sense of how anti-Christian Ceausescu truly was. Still, the people continued to hold services at that site as an act of divine protest, notwithstanding the fact that nothing was left of the building but rubble.

We worshiped with them there under a tent they had put up to keep out the weather. Their church building had been destroyed, and they lived in great fear, yet these Christian followers remained so faithful. (When we asked government officials why such churches had been bulldozed, they said that the buildings violated building codes.)

We also met with Pastor Buddy Cocar, his brother, and others who had been in and out of prison and endured torture for their faith. We were not able to meet with Father Gheorghe Calciu-Dumitreasa, a Romanian Orthodox priest who'd spent twenty-one years behind bars, because he was then living under house arrest. Calciu was considered an "enemy of the state" because he criticized Ceausescu's religious repression. He had become world famous, and there was great pressure to release him. Ceausescu was between a rock and a hard place; he couldn't kill Calciu for fear of how the West would react, and he couldn't let him go, for fear the heroic priest would immediately resume his antigovernment protests. So for two decades Ceausescu kept him locked up. As Calciu told the *Washington Post* about his time in prison, "Ceausescu saw me as his personal enemy. For this he applied to me special methods of torture."[7]

Calciu later visited me in Washington. He told me these "special methods" included beatings, being confined to an unheated cell, and being deprived of food and drink. Guards urinated on him and subjected him to psychological torment designed to break his will. None of it succeeded. Finally, prison officials decided to kill the priest in such a way that the government would not be blamed. They went to two hardened inmates — real criminals, not political prisoners. Kill the priest, they promised, and we will make sure you get more lenient treatment.

These inmates — who were now Calciu's cellmates — subjected the priest to even worse treatment. Openly telling him they planned to kill him, the two subjected Calciu to severe beatings and forced him to stand for long periods without rest. They made him ask their permission before he could eat, drink, or use the chamber pot. This treatment went on for weeks. But, ever the preacher, Father Calciu spoke to them about Christ and the gospel message of love.

Then something miraculous happened. The two criminals were taken to see the head of the Securitate. When they returned, Calciu recalls, they were in a subdued mood. The men took Calciu to a small prison yard and ordered him to stand in a corner while they talked between themselves. Believing this was the end, Calciu prayed, confessed his sins, and asked God's blessings on his family.

As Calciu recalled for the *Washington Post*, some fifteen minutes later the men approached him. "And the youngest one said, 'Father,' — and that was the first time they called me Father — 'we have decided not to kill you.'"[8] And then they knelt with him in prayer. The incredible faith of this gentle man had turned the hearts of these hardened criminals to God. They repented for what they had done to Calciu — and went off to serve a more severe sentence — but they went with joy in their hearts. It was a modern-day version of the story of the apostle Paul, who converted his jailer to Christ while locked behind bars.

Father Calciu was ultimately set free thanks to pressure from President Reagan and others. After Calciu left Romania, he settled in northern Virginia and pastored a church there until his death in 2006 from pancreatic cancer at age eighty.

· · ·

Back home — with the memory of those Romanian Christians we'd worshiped with fresh in our minds — Tony, Chris, and I began publicizing their plight and engaging in letter-writing campaigns, including sending a letter to Ceausescu insisting that he free Father Calciu and intervene in several other cases of religious persecution. Ceausescu ignored us. We also put in a bill to take away most favored nation trading status (now called normal trade status) from Romania — a bill which, if passed, would cost Romania around a billion dollars a year.

During my testimony, I described the oppression I had witnessed, and pointed out that we were not asking the Romanian government to break with the Soviet Union and allow NATO forces to be placed in Bucharest. We were simply asking that they respect human rights. And by that we didn't mean token concessions, such as releasing a high-profile prisoner of conscience or two when the heat was on, and then resuming abuses once America's attention had shifted elsewhere.

"These people understand only one thing: strength," I warned. "Verbal slaps on the wrist will not alter domestic policies in Romania."[9] I reminded them of the words of former Soviet dissident and prisoner of conscience Natan Sharansky, who said, "Weak agreements only make those suffering behind the Iron Curtain despondent. They are taking a tough line on the front. The least Western diplomats can do is remember them between the caviar and cocktail parties."[10]

I told them that things were so bad that — according to Nestor Ratesh, the senior Washington correspondent for Radio Free Europe — many Romanians thought a return to direct control of their country by Moscow would be an improvement over life under Ceausescu.[11] "The citizens of Romania are looking to Premier Gorbachev as the great liberator, the champion of human rights, because they see the continuation of MFN by the United States as support of President Ceausescu," I said.

I reminded my colleagues that Romania had recently bulldozed a Seventh Day Adventist church while worshipers were still inside, injuring a number of them. "How can you give a government like that MFN?" I asked. "We have a responsibility not only to the constituents we represent but also to the broader constituency of freedom-loving people around the world." Many people will tell you how things have improved, I warned; they will tell you they have allowed people to leave, and that is important.

"But what about allowing them to stay in Romania, to stay with their husbands, their wives, their children, in their own homes with their families? What about allowing them to further their religious beliefs and continue to stay in their homeland?" Taking away MFN would force the Romanian government to "put up or shut up," I concluded.

There weren't many Romanians living in America, so I knew that members of Congress would not be bombarded by people pleading with them about their husbands, wives, sons, and daughters back home. But Tony, Chris, and I tried to convince them that by canceling Romania's MFN status, they would be helping a lot of people.

We received a fair amount of press coverage over our testimony, mostly in religious media. The business community was instantly up in arms, and the Reagan administration came out against us, as did the State Department and leaders of both parties of Congress. And we were right about the attitude of certain members and senators who had traveled to Romania, where they had attended receptions and were treated very well; they received a false impression that everything was going swimmingly in Romania. Sadly, they did not visit the places that Chris, Tony, and I visited, nor did they speak with the people we spoke with — those suffering terribly under the Ceausescu brutal dictatorship. Many of them, no doubt, remembered the state dinner Jimmy Carter had given Nicolae Ceausescu in 1978, hailing this monster as a "great leader."[12]

We had a long, hard fight to pass our bill. Every year, when MFN came up for renewal, the lobbyists hired by companies doing business in Romania would say how wonderful everything was and how much freedom the churches had. To Ceausescu, MFN status was the be-all and end-all; it gave him standing with other Eastern bloc and European countries and led other countries to say, "Look at Ceausescu; he's got this wonderful relationship with the United States."

I met with President Reagan in November of 1987 to discuss the issue, and I gave him an autographed copy of *Red Horizons*, an expose of the Ceausescu regime by Lt. Gen. Ion Mihai Pacepa, former head of Romanian Intelligence, who became, in 1978, the highest-ranking intelligence official ever to defect from the Eastern bloc.[13]

Pacepa's explosive memoir exposed the fact that Ceausescu (whom Pacepa refers to as a "two-bit Dracula") was using U.S. tax dollars to "demolish churches, persecute religious believers, [and] promote international terrorism." According to Pacepa, Carter was completely fooled by Ceausescu; both Nicolae and his wife, Elena, mocked the Carters in private. As Pacepa recalls, "After I was granted political asylum by the United States, President Carter was so afraid that ... he had offended Ceausescu that in September 1978 he sent a ranking State Department counselor, Matthew Nimetz, to Bucharest to apologize to the tyrant, saying he would do his 'utmost to assure that publicity on the Pacepa case is avoided completely, or kept at a bare minimum.' "[14]

Pacepa also wrote that the West's support of Romania had not brought about any improvement economically, nor regarding human rights, nor in terms of raising Romania's standard of living. He noted that Romania's secret police was the most oppressive in the entire Soviet bloc, described assassination operations against defectors and dissidents, and told of Ceausescu's close friendship with Palestinian Liberation Organization leader Yassir Arafat.

But despite all our testimony and evidence, there were still members insisting that "now is not the right time" to deny MFN status to Romania, because doing so would "complicate our ability to influence further decisions in Bucharest"[15] — as if we had any real influence *then*. They claimed that MFN status prompted greater civil liberties — despite the fact that human rights violations and religious persecution had *increased* during the eleven years Romania had enjoyed MFN trade benefits. They wanted to pass resolutions expressing concern over Romania — nothing more. It was unbelievably frustrating.

Thanks partly, I believe, to *Red Horizons* and partly to our making our case face-to-face, Reagan changed his mind about Romania's MFN status. As he wrote in his diary on November 12, 1987, "After lunch a meeting with Rep. Frank Wolf, Sen. Helms & others about removing 'Most Favored Nation' status from Romania. I can do that on basis of violation of human rights. We have given them that status because of their apparent independence from Soviet U. Apparently that is a sham and their violations of human rights are worse than in the Soviet U. I'll take this up with Geo. S. [George Schultz] tomorrow."[16]

The president was as good as his word. His diary entry the next day read, "I've proposed ... to drop Romania's most favored nation status until they clean up their human rights act."[17]

Reagan stuck to his guns over the objections of the business community and members of his own administration. He was so strong on human rights, and he was never afraid to speak truth to Communist power (although his staffers often tried to stop him). He believed until the end of his days that tyranny would one day be conquered across the globe.

Most people remember Reagan's electrifying speech in Berlin, in which he said, "Mr. Gorbachev, tear down this wall!" And they remember his "evil empire" speech to the National Association of Evangelicals that so outraged journalists on the Eastern seaboard, who never stopped thinking of him as a cowboy who was going to set off a nuclear war with the Soviets. Fewer people remember a speech Reagan delivered to students at Moscow University in 1988, one that was every bit as important as the other two speeches, because by refusing to pull his punches, Reagan gave hope to prisoners of conscience rotting away in Soviet gulags.

In that speech, delivered as Reagan stood beneath a huge and grim-faced bust of Vladimir Lenin, the American president linked progress to "freedom of thought, freedom of information, freedom of communication." He defined freedom as "the right to question and change the established way of doing things," to "follow your dream or stick to your conscience." And he talked about the need for nations to "renounce, once and for all, the right to an expansionist foreign policy."[18]

During the question-and-answer session with students following his address, Reagan said he had "brought lists of names that have been brought to me from people that are relatives or friends that know that — or that believe that this individual is being mistreated here in this country, and they want him to be allowed to emigrate to our country — some are separated families."[19]

Former prisoner Natan Sharansky has written that Reagan's words, delivered in the heart of the "evil empire," gave great hope to those who languished in the gulags.[20]

In the end, we wore down our congressional colleagues; both the House and Senate finally approved a six-month suspension of MFN in 1988.

The minute Reagan announced his decision about withholding most favored nation status for Romania, Ceausescu claimed he no longer wanted MFN status and complained about America interfering in Romania's internal affairs — just as the Soviets did in 1973 when the Nixon administration and the Congress refused to sell them grain unless they allowed 35,000 Jews to emigrate. Romanian goods would now be subject to higher tariffs, costing Romanian exporters about a billion dollars a year.

Some scholars think America's decision to drop Romania's MFN status helped bring about the Romanian revolution. I'm not sure about this, but regardless, it was the right thing to do. Efforts to deny Romania MFN status were supported even by many Romanians.

I told my congressional colleagues what happened in Romania after we passed the MFN amendment: "The night after we and this Congress passed the MFN amendment, this went out over Radio Free Europe, and millions of Romanian citizens hovered around their radios — they are hidden sometimes — and listened to the fact that the U.S. Congress, the people's body, passed this resolution, and millions of Romanian citizens knew for the first time, after twelve long years, that finally the U.S. Congress cares very deeply about them."[21]

The battle over MFN showed that at least some people in the West recognized Ceausescu's true colors — and that the Romanian people were willing to sacrifice this economic advantage even if it hurt them in the short term. Dissidents later told us that knowing we were on their side, fighting on their behalf, greatly encouraged them. And as Tony notes in his own account of our Romanian adventures, freedom-seeking people always remember if you stood with them — or stood with their oppressors.[22]

I continued to keep an eye on what was going on in Romania from Washington, D.C., and wrote letters to Romanian officials, including Ceausescu, asking for the release of political prisoners and better treatment of churches and various individuals.

Ceausescu's repressive regime defiantly continued to restrict free speech, free assembly, free association, and the freedom to worship. Among its outrages was the bulldozing of the last remaining Sephardic synagogue in Eastern Europe, Bucharest's Spanish synagogue, and Bucharest's main Adventist church.

Then, suddenly, I had a new and compelling reason for returning to Romania. When he defected in 1978, General Pacepa had been forced to leave his daughter, Dana, and her husband behind. In *Red Horizons*, Pacepa writes that when Ceausescu learned of his defection, the outraged dictator sent murder squads to the U.S. to hunt him down and assassinate him. Failing in his efforts to do this, Ceausescu revenged himself on Pacepa's daughter, keeping her under house arrest for many years and subjecting her to weekly, terrifying interrogations by the Securitate. Pacepa was now assisting the CIA with various projects, ultimately making, as the CIA put it, "an important and unique contribution to the United States."[23]

Just after his defection, Pacepa wrote his daughter an open letter published in the French newspaper *Le Monde*. He told Dana that he had decided to defect when Ceausescu personally ordered him to murder Noel Bernard, director of Radio Free Europe's Romanian program, and blow up the Munich headquarters of Radio Free Europe. "I had to ultimately decide between being a good father and being a political criminal. Knowing you, Dana, I was firmly convinced that you would prefer no father to one who was an assassin," Pacepa wrote.[24]

One day in 1987, Pacepa came to my office, wearing a disguise — a fake nose and wig — for fear of being assassinated. He was accompanied by his wife (his former CIA caseworker, with whom he had fallen in love) and Bill Geimer, chairman of the Jamestown Foundation. Pacepa and I had met previously, and he knew about my trip to Romania and of my ongoing efforts to help the Romanian people. The general gave me a copy of his ten-year-old *Le Monde* letter to Dana, written two years before I entered Congress. I was moved by the letter, thinking of my own young daughters.

Shortly after Pacepa's visit, the State Department told Pacepa that Dana had asked for political asylum in the United States, as her father had urged her to do. Then-congressman Dick Cheney and I immediately wrote a letter to Ceausescu, cosigned by more than three hundred other members, asking him to permit Dana to leave. He refused to do so.

Pacepa was also upset at hearing that the Securitate had spread rumors in Romania that he had been found dead in a New York subway station — which meant that Dana would have no idea if her father was dead or alive. And he was distraught over the fact that Dana had been kept isolated, under house arrest, for a full decade. Pacepa asked me if I would be willing to travel again to Romania to find out if his daughter was all right and speak to her, if possible, to let her know that her father was alive and well.

"I'll try," I told him.

A short time later Congressman Chris Smith and I boarded a flight to Bucharest. Once again we went straight to the U.S. Embassy for a briefing in the bubble zone. We told the embassy people that, in addition to visiting churches and government officials, we planned to try to locate Dana and speak with her. We were concerned, we said, that Dana would eventually have an "accident," falling down the stairs or getting hit by a car.

"They aren't going to put a bullet in her head," Chris told them. "They're going to make it look like an accident, just like every dictatorship does. You fall down fifteen flights of stairs, straight down, and they'll say you just tripped. It's what they do."

The idea was to attempt to visit Dana, knowing we would probably not be allowed to see her. But we would broadcast to the world that she was being watched and that if she had an accident, we would let the world know it was murder, a direct assassination of this young woman.

The embassy staff was apoplectic. "No, don't do it," they warned.

Chris and I asked them to leave us alone for a few minutes. After they left the room, I turned to Chris. "Why are we here?" I asked him. "We're here to visit Dana. Yes, we're here to raise the issue of human rights in general, but our specific mission is to provide at least some protection for Dana — at least as much as we can — and to find out exactly what is going on here. Besides, Pacepa asked us to do this."

Then we prayed together in the bubble zone, where no one but God could hear us. In the end, we decided to try to see Dana. When we told the embassy staff, they didn't like it, but they were helpful and even sent a staffer who spoke Romanian along with us to help us find the street where Dana lived with her husband and his parents.

Later that evening, we walked together in the darkness to the street where Dana lived under house arrest. The front of Dana's apartment building was guarded by armed men. We showed one of the guards our cards, which identified us as members of Congress, and the embassy staffer translated for us. The guards refused to let us in. Before we left, Chris looked one of the guards straight in the eye and said, "We know she's in there. Don't let anything happen to her. We are watching; the world is watching."

And then we left.

The embassy staffers weren't kidding when they said the Romanian government would not care to have us calling on the daughter of its most infamous defector. Here is how Chris recalls that night: "It was very dark, because Bucharest did not have many streetlights. We were walking along, and I kept checking my back. A police car filled with four burly policemen, or Securitate members, was following us. And on one occasion, just as I turned around, the car's headlights were switched off. I thought, 'They're going to run us down.' And all of a sudden the car started racing towards us. I pushed Frank up against the wall, and the car went up on the sidewalk, just a few feet from us, and then roared down the street. We were all pushed up against the wall, and if we hadn't been aware, we would have been hit from behind. They might have broken our legs or something. Who knows what would have happened. If they had really wanted to take us out, I think they would have backed up and done it. So maybe they were just sending us a message: 'We can run you down anytime we want.'"

Another carload of secret police openly followed us back to our hotel and never let us out of their sight during the whole time we were in Romania; they were the most indiscreet "secret" police I ever encountered. That night, I wedged a chair under my hotel room doorknob, fearing that someone would barge in. At least, I thought, I would wake up if they tried.

The next morning, we met with the Romanian foreign minister. His men had reported to him our escapade of the night before, and he blasted us for what we had done. We left Romania later that day, disappointed that we had not been able to fulfill our mission.

· · ·

Over the following two years I occasionally wondered what was happening to Dana. I was to find out, in fairly dramatic fashion, just before Christmas in 1989. I was wandering through an electronics shop in Vienna, Virginia, shopping for a television set for my wife, when suddenly the news flashed on TV sets all over the store: the Romanian people were rising up against their brutal Communist leaders, aided by the Romanian army. My chief of staff, Charlie White, and I jumped on a plane on December 30 and flew over there. The revolution was still going on, and bullets were flying all over the place.

We stayed with the U.S. ambassador at his residence, and except for Ambassador Alan "Punch" Green Jr. and a handful of embassy staff, we were almost the only Americans there; most of the others had been evacuated.

The word was that the Securitate was shooting people in the head. The news turned out to be grimly accurate: Charlie and I walked into a hospital and saw men lying on beds with bandages on their bleeding heads. We had planned to hold a TV interview on the front steps of the hospital, but we were warned not to because the television camera lights would draw attention to us, and we ourselves might be shot. And there were rumors swirling all around that the Securitate were hiding in tunnels under the city and on rooftops, searching for targets. So we moved the TV interview to a location where the lights would not attract attention.

On December 31, the day after I arrived, Ginny Young, the U.S. consul in Romania, told me the news I'd been waiting for: Dana was alive, but she'd had a rough ten days. Her apartment was located in downtown Bucharest, near the U.S. Consulate, which meant her home was in the middle of a battle zone. Securitate agents had come to the building where Dana and her husband worked, and told them they needed to relocate the couple for a time.

"You will come with us in our cars," they told the frightened couple.

As helicopters roared overhead, filled with soldiers firing on civilians, Dana, her husband, Radu Damaceanu, and her parents-in-law were driven to the Bulgarian border. Securitate agents told the family that they would all be executed and their bodies left along the border to give the impression that they'd been shot while attempting to leave Romania illegally. After driving for several hours, the Securitate took the family to a newly constructed, unoc-cupied apartment building. Dana and her family were put into one apartment, and the agents who had brought them there, along with those who had followed in several additional cars, took possession of a second one.

As Dana recalls of that terrifying day: "It was all very tense; we strongly believed it was our last day to live. We didn't know what had happened; we didn't know which side had won. I decided — okay, at least I'm going to take a hot shower and be clean before I die! My husband turned on the radio, which was able to catch two Romania stations. That's when we heard that Ceausescu and his wife had fled the country by helicopter. Outside the apartment building, people began waving flags and screaming, 'We're free! We're free!'

"I told my husband, 'We need to leave this apartment, now!' But when we opened the door, we found one of the men who brought us there — a high-ranking Securitate member. He was very pale. He said, 'You know, things have changed.'

"'You bet they have,' I thought.

"'We won't leave you here. I came to take you back to Bucharest,' he said.

"'Don't worry about that,' I said, 'I'll take a train.'

"He started to smile a little. 'It will take you two days to get there by train in this situation. After all we've been through together, I'll make sure you get back safely to Bucharest.'

"I said, 'Okay, I'll take a chance.' During our return, the cars that followed us started to pull away, one by one, so that in the end, when we got back to our apartment in Bucharest, there was no security car following me for the first time in eleven years. I couldn't believe I was alone on the street."[25]

Dana discovered that the Securitate car that had sat in front of her home for more than a decade had been abandoned. But the agents had left behind not only their weapons and uniforms but also their operational file on Dana.

Dana found her front door broken down. She later learned that colleagues who had witnessed the Securitate taking her and her husband away had feared the couple had been taken home and shot, and had broken in to check on them.

It was too dangerous to stay at their apartment; people were randomly shooting at buildings, and Dana could hear bullets hitting the roof. Fires had broken out everywhere. The decision was made to split up and attempt to find secure places to hide.

"I jumped fences I never knew I could jump, and went through back streets," Dana recalls. She decided it would be best to try to get shelter from a stranger — someone the Securitate would not know.

"I knocked at a front door and begged to be allowed to stay the night." The owner — an eighty-year-old woman — agreed to take her in. The next morning, Dana awoke to the smell of fresh coffee, and her hostess smiled at her and said, "Oh, darling, everything is fine! We have a new president; we are free! Everything is okay!"

"She was the sweetest person in the world, and I owe my life to her," Dana says. The family gathered at their bullet-scarred apartment on Christmas Eve and heard the news that Nicolae and Elena Ceausescu had been put on trial. The next day, they saw the tape of the executions on TV.

"It was unthinkable that they were finally gone. If you live most of your life under one president who is the terror of your life, you can't believe he's gone," Dana recalls. A few days later Ginny Young and the embassy's vice-consul arrived on Dana's doorstep. Ginny helped Dana and her husband visit the U.S. Embassy two days later, apply for passports and exit visas, and arrange to relocate to America. She also arranged for Dana to call her father — the first time she had spoken with him in more than a decade.

"We applied for passports. And then we found out that somebody was coming to pick us up," Dana says. "It was Congressman Wolf. It was the first time I met him, the first time I knew he was working with my father to get me out of Romania. I wasn't aware of the times he'd tried before to contact me."[26]

We met at last at the U.S. Embassy. I found myself shaking hands with a petite, slender young woman in her midthirties. I also shook hands with Dana's husband, Radu. On January 6, Dana, Radu, his parents, and I boarded a plane to Frankfurt, where we spent the night. The CIA took Dana away to a secret location to interview her.

The next day, we headed for Washington, D.C., where we held a press conference at Dulles Airport. Dana's arrival made international headlines and was broadcast in dozens of countries.[27] Agents from the FBI or CIA hustled us through the crowd, taking us to a room where we could talk privately. Later, at a secure location, Dana and her father had a joyous reunion.

A few weeks after beginning their new life in the U.S., Dana's husband, who is a sculptor, finished a bust of me, done from memory, and presented it to me.

The bust now sits in my family room at home. My younger grandchildren yell, "Pop Pop!" whenever they see it, and rub the nose.

"It was certainly not the most faithful portrait of the congressman," General Pacepa notes, "but for Dana and her husband, however, it was the symbol of their freedom."

CHAPTER THREE

MY JOURNEY TO CONGRESS

Why don't you get out of this town? You're halfway decent.

Mr. Smith Goes to Washington

IF YOU HAD KNOWN ME sixty-odd years ago, your first thought would probably not have been, "That boy is going to grow up to become a congressman." As far back as grade school, I was earning some of the lowest grades in my class, and I also suffered from a terrible stutter.

I was born on January 30, 1939, into a pretty tough neighborhood: the south side of Philadelphia. My father worked as an electrician at the Philadelphia Public Ledger building, across from Independence Hall, and then enlisted in the navy during World War II. While my father was away, my mother found work in a helicopter factory and later worked at the Philadelphia Baltimore Stock Exchange, making sandwiches in the cafeteria.

I was six when my father came home for good. We hadn't seen each other for about two and a half years, and my dad was so anxious to get to us that he knocked down a lamp as he fought his way through the crowd at the naval station in Bainbridge, Maryland.

After leaving military service, my father became a Philadelphia policeman, and our family moved into a row house in a working-class neighborhood in southwest Philadelphia.

My younger brother Joseph and I attended John Bartram High School, where I earned pretty poor grades, mainly because I never studied. The one thing I loved was reading history and biography. I used to go to the library a lot and read biographies of Washington, Jefferson, Madison, Monroe, and Lincoln. Anything in school not related to history — well, I didn't pay much attention to it.

I also got into fights pretty often. And yet, even as a small boy, I had a lot of determination and a certain vision. As early as the third grade — despite the stutter — I began dreaming of becoming a congressman one day.

An old friend from the neighborhood, Bill Pepe, recalls of those days, "Frank and I met in 1946 when I was nine years old and he was seven. His family lived right behind us in a row house. A bunch of us would meet on the corner and walk to school together every day. Frank was always late, and he always had this Brill Cream rolling down the side of his face. Frank stuttered a lot when he was young. There was a gang from another area of southwest Philly that was made up of mostly Italians. They would sometimes make fun of Frank because of his stuttering, and we would tell them to shut up and leave him alone.

"When we were teenagers, everybody cursed — not in the house, of course, but to each other. Not Frank. He didn't use profanity, and he didn't drink. His father and mother never drank or cursed. His mother was a very sociable person. If she saw you on the avenue, no matter who you were, she would stop and talk to you. I think Frank has gotten a lot of his values from his mom and dad.

"Frank didn't start fights. But if somebody egged him on, he wouldn't know when to back down. If someone were verbally attacking him, Frank would give it right back. I don't think it's in his vocabulary to back down on anything. I remember when he wanted to vote during a break from college, he had to get an absentee ballot. We went to city hall in Philly, and he asked for the absentee ballot. The clerk said, 'No, you can't have one.' Frank said, 'Who is your supervisor?' He ended up trying to see the mayor to get his absentee ballot. That was an indication of his perseverance."

Perseverance was something I would certainly need in Congress, where I learned early on the impossibility of getting anything done quickly or easily. And Bill was right: I did get a lot of my values from my parents. My mother's faith was very strong, and she made sure my brother and I were in Sunday school every week at Southwest Presbyterian Church of Philadelphia. She also warned us very strongly against drinking and smoking, because she saw the effects of these vices on people she knew. Neither Joe nor I ever did. I never drank even during my college years when I lived in a fraternity house.

My friends John and Don Federico moved into the neighborhood when we were all teenagers. Here are John's memories of those days: "When we moved into that neighborhood, my brother and I started palling around with Frank until we all got out of high school. We went to Saturday night high school dances together and played those native Philadelphia games stepball, halfball, and stickball.

"We lived on Seventieth Street, and back then, if you went down to west Philly, outside of your own neighborhood, you could have a little bit of a problem. Someone you ran into would ask, 'Where you from? Seventieth street? Waddaya doin' here?' That could lead to throwing punches at each other.

"Whatever we could do for each other, we would do. That's just how we were raised. You have a friend, and your friend needs help, you help him. And Frank is the same way today."

Many years later I learned to appreciate not only friendships with people just like me, with similar upbringing and values, but also colleagues on the other side of the aisle, whose background and values were sometimes a little different from mine.

Early in my congressional career, I joined a bipartisan congressional small group, modeled after the little band of friends who had encouraged a personal and political hero of mine: William Wilberforce, the eighteenth-century British member of Parliament who is remembered as the Great Abolitionist. More than any other single person, Wilberforce is credited with ending Great Britain's slave trade in 1807, after two decades of hard work, and with ending slavery itself in 1833. Wilberforce, who was very critical of party politics, succeeded in part because he was willing to join forces with members of the British Parliament from across the political spectrum. He was known for his friendships with those with whom he disagreed.

In our original congressional small group were Tony Hall, Dan Coats, from Indiana, Bob McEwen, an Ohio Republican, and me. We worked on many issues together and developed lifelong friendships. Tony contributed financially to my 2008 and 2010 campaigns and always puts in a good word for me. He even offered to write a letter of endorsement to the Democrats in my district.

Despite all you may have heard about congressional gridlock and about how hostile members are to people on the other side of the aisle, the fact is that there are members of both parties who are committed to reconciliation and to working together the way Wilberforce and his colleagues did. The members of my small group have changed over the decades in which I have taken part, but the group remains bipartisan. We meet in the House chapel every Tuesday afternoon for fellowship, Bible study, and prayer and try to put our faith into action, working together as brothers on issues like human rights, hunger, religious freedom, and blood diamonds.

The friendships that have formed and the respect gained have, in an extraordinary way, changed how we treat one another outside the chapel. When colleagues meet together respectfully and begin to listen to each other and work toward reconciliation, it changes the nature of the way they conduct their business on the floor of the House and in committee meetings. After all, if you pray with and for a fellow congressman and he prays for you, it's hard to turn around and attack him on the House floor or in the press.

. . .

I was so eager to get out of my high school classroom that I took a bunch of art classes in order to get my ticket punched, graduating at age sixteen in 1956. I still can't draw a straight line. As I recall, out of a class of 190, I was 176th.

I got a job as a mail boy with the Curtis Publishing Company, located in Philadelphia, across the street from Independence Hall. Often, on my way to work, I would cut through Independence Hall and go past the Liberty Bell, which at that time was located on a wooden platform, not encased in glass as it is today. I would touch the bell as I passed by.

After a year at Curtis, I began to think seriously about attending college, but there was no way any college would accept me with my grades and lack of credits in serious subjects. In the end, I took the necessary classes in order to complete the coursework demanded by most colleges, and then applied to both Penn State and the University of Mississippi. Ole Miss accepted me; Penn State did not. So I packed up and moved to Oxford in the fall of 1957.

Mississippi was quite a culture shock. Here I was, a kid born in south Philly, attending a school that would shortly make headlines for the violence that ensued after its refusal to admit James Meredith, the school's first African American student. I tasted catfish and hush puppies for the first time in Oxford. It was a different world.

I supported myself waiting tables at a sorority house — not bad work at a school that had two future Miss Americas enrolled while I was there.[1] But I never really felt at home at Ole Miss, and after one year I transferred to Penn State.

During the summer of 1958 I found employment with the McCloskey Construction Company, working on the Schuykill Expressway in Philadelphia. The story behind that job is one of the great lessons of my life. I worked hard all summer, but in the end I kind of tapered off and wasn't doing a very good job one day. In fact, I was goofing off. The foreman finally confronted me. "You used to be one of the best workers I had," he told me, "but I'd never hire you again." I asked him to give me another chance.

For the rest of that week I really hustled. I worked concrete and plywood, and at the end of the week the guy said, "If you ever need a job, I'd hire you again." I thanked him, but privately thought I would never need another construction job, because I was planning to go to law school. Little did I know that within a few years I would drop out of law school and be looking for another construction job.

In 1962 the McCloskey Construction Company happened to be building the Rayburn House Office Building. And guess who one of the foremen on the project was? He hired me on the spot. It was my first job on the Hill — pushing a broom and cleaning up.

During and after my college years, determined to lose my stutter, I took every speech and therapy course I could find. I would force myself to get up and speak in class. I finally conquered it, although I still stutter occasionally when I'm tired. But I realize now that my stuttering was something of a gift from God, because it gave me the drive and determination I would need to accomplish my goals. Had I not stuttered, I would never have been elected to Congress. Most people don't run for Congress a third time after failing twice, as I did; people would laugh and say, "Are you running *again*?" But my stutter had taught me to deal with laughter and ridicule.

I occasionally speak to students about my stutter. Sometimes, I tell them, something we view as a handicap can end up being a very good thing.

In September of 1958 I began my sophomore year at Penn State and pledged a fraternity, Alpha Sigma Phi — a bad idea for someone who was not a gifted student. The party atmosphere was not conducive to studying, to put it mildly. It was a pretty wild place.

I probably would have flunked out eventually had it not been for an attractive, brown-haired girl who caught my eye one day at the campus hub. I'd been in a fight the night before and had bandages all over my face. The girl, whose name was Carolyn Stover, sat down at a table next to mine and, despite my disreputable appearance, let me introduce myself and talk to her while we ate. And then she let me walk her back to her dorm.

Carolyn came from a family that was very different from mine. My dad was a policeman; her father was a Harvard-educated banker. I was from southwest Philly; she grew up in Marblehead, Massachusetts. Carolyn's mom was a Radcliffe alum; my mom never got beyond the seventh grade. So we came from totally different worlds.

Carolyn and I began going to the library every Friday night to study together. I also moved out of the fraternity house and buckled down. Under Carolyn's tutelage, my grades began to rise. I did much better in my junior and senior years partly because by then I was taking courses that interested me — history and political science.

I graduated from Penn State in June of 1961, with a major in political science and a minor in history and with grades good enough to get me accepted at the law schools of American University, Emory, and Georgetown. In April I hitchhiked to Massachusetts to ask Carolyn's parents' blessing to marry her. They thought we should wait to marry until I had finished law school and performed my military service. But Carolyn and I didn't want to wait that long. We tied the knot on September 9, just two weeks after Carolyn's August 26 graduation. I started classes at Georgetown Law School the following week.

I disliked every moment of my time at Georgetown and dropped out after just one semester. I then began a season of lightning-fast career changes.

First came the construction job working on the Rayburn House Office Building. Next came another construction job, with the Blount Construction Company, helping to build the entrance ramp to the Teddy Roosevelt Bridge. I then went to work at the old brick Smithsonian museum that housed military exhibits. My job was cleaning the antique weapons up in the tower. The museum smelled revoltingly of the dead rats that had crawled behind the walls after ingesting a fatal dose of rat poison. I don't think I spent more than two weeks working there.

I then got a job at the State Department, and as I awaited my first day on the job, I had romantic visions regarding what I'd be doing there. Would I be invited to share my views on foreign policy? No indeed; they assigned me to the passport division in a dingy little room in the basement where they kept the file cabinets. By 11:30 a.m. on my first day, I'd decided to quit. Somebody came up to me and asked, "Do you want to take early lunch or late lunch?"

"Early," I replied. I left for lunch and never came back.

I was pretty sure my new in-laws were less than pleased at my career choices. I couldn't blame them. They thought their daughter had married a future lawyer, and instead he's wearing steel-tipped construction boots to work every day. They were extremely nice people, and they never actually said anything to me, but I could imagine they were thinking, "What's going on here?"

My father, on the other hand, left me in no doubt as to how he felt about the first college-educated member of the Wolf family working in construction. "What will Carolyn's parents think of you?" he asked me.

I decided to take another stab at law school, but the minute I walked into Georgetown's admissions office, I turned around and walked out again. Carolyn was waiting for me in the car. "I'm not going to go," I told her. I just couldn't stand going back to law school. So we drove home.

I enlisted in the army in November of 1962, spending six months on active duty at Fort Knox, Kentucky, and Fort Gordon in Augusta, Georgia, and then going into the reserves. I then reenrolled in law school, and this time I stuck it out. I worked part-time during the day at the National Canners Association (now the Grocery Manufacturers Association). It was the first job I'd ever had that I really liked. I later switched to night school so I could work there full-time, because on March 15, 1964, Carolyn gave birth to our first child, Frank, whom we called Bud.

I graduated from Georgetown in 1965 and continued working at the National Canners Association. I spent five years there altogether. The job involved contacting legislators and tracking state and federal legislation that had anything to do with canning.

In the spring of 1968 I attended a reception fundraiser for a guy running for the Senate, Richard Schweiker. I met a congressman there, Pete Biester, from Bucks County, Pennsylvania. Pete invited me to consider a job working with him, but I decided not to pursue it.

But something happened a few weeks later to make me change my mind: Bobby Kennedy was assassinated. I watched the funeral on television and listened to Ted Kennedy giving the eulogy. He read the words of George Bernard Shaw, which Bobby Kennedy had frequently quoted: "Some men see things as they are and ask, 'Why?' I dream things that never were and ask, 'Why not?'"

All of a sudden a lightbulb went on, and I said to myself, "I should go after that job." I remembered my old dream of becoming a congressman someday and being able to make a difference in the world.

I went to work for Congressman Biester in December of 1968. I left in 1970 when I was offered a job at the Department of Interior in Congressional Relations. I spent five years there, and then, in August of 1975, at age thirty-six, I decided the time had come to fulfill my dream of becoming a congressman.

I lived in the Tenth District of Virginia, which was then held by a Democrat named Joe Fisher. I announced my candidacy at a good friend's house. There were exactly seventeen people in attendance. Leaving out me, my wife, our five kids, my friend and his wife, and a reporter, only seven people showed up to support me — not exactly an encouraging start. Despite campaigning from September of 1975 until the June 1976 Republican primary, I got beat by a Virginia state legislator named Vince Callahan, who has since become a good friend.

In 1978 I ran for Congress again and lost to Rep. Joe Fisher, the incumbent Democrat, earning about 46 percent of the vote. Following this defeat, I pretty much decided not to run again. Carolyn and I were broke, with five children to support. In the years after my second losing campaign, I had begun to build up a pretty good law practice. But then a man named Guy Vander Jagt, a congressman from Michigan who was head of the Republican Campaign Committee, wrote me a note saying, "You did a great job. I hope you'll run again."

So I ran again in 1980. I took money out of my retirement account, cashed in all my insurance policies, and basically spent all of 1980 running for Congress. I ran on transportation issues, including stopping night flights at National Airport.

There was no group too small for me to speak to. Wherever two or three were gathered together, you'd find me there shaking their hands. I think I was the first congressional candidate to campaign at the Washington Metro, at the Rosslyn station. I went to bus stops, office buildings, supermarkets, beauty parlors, and trash dumps almost full-time for a whole year. I would stand outside movie theaters and greet people waiting in line. It was a long, hard campaign.

On Election Day, I thought I had lost again. It was a cold, dark night, and I was standing on the sidewalk near my polling booth. People were rushing in to vote, and hardly anybody would shake my hand in my own precinct. But I managed to grab Ronald Reagan's coattails, and he pulled me across the finish line, 51 percent to 49 percent.

And so now, at the age of forty-one, I was a member of the 97th United States Congress. That was the beginning of a whole new era of my life. My mother had died of cancer several years before I started running for Congress, but my father — who had only a sixth-grade education — came to my swearing-in ceremony. I don't think he ever thought I'd get into Congress. He used to carry a picture of me and Ronald Reagan together and show it to everyone he knew. He died just two years later.

I never forgot the example my parents provided regarding how to treat people, and those early lessons came into play decades later when I became a member of Congress. In 2003 I was working on a bill to outlaw prison rape, the Prison Rape Elimination Act, which was a pretty significant piece of legislation that has since become law. It was my bill in the House, and Senator Edward Kennedy's bill in the Senate.

Kennedy was going through a difficult time then — I don't recall what it was about. This was before he became ill. A colleague had told me, "Kennedy really feels abused by some of those Republicans who've been publicly attacking him."

My good friend Joe Pitts, a member from Pennsylvania, and I went to see Kennedy to discuss the bill with him. We sat down in his office, which was filled with family pictures and mementoes of a half century in politics. But before we starting talking about the bill, we had something we wanted to say to him.

"Senator," I said, "I know we don't agree on a lot of issues. But we know you have been hurt by the attacks against you, so Joe and I want to apologize for all of the attacks that came from the Republican side of the aisle against you over the years."

Kennedy was dumbfounded, and he got very, very emotional. Maybe nobody had ever said anything like this to him before. Personally, I'd never said anything bad about Kennedy, and I know Joe Pitts never did, either. But I think the fact that we both went in there and apologized kind of took him aback a little bit.

We discussed our bill, and then Kennedy began talking with us about other things. He brought out a book that he was working on for children and showed it to us, and he chatted about his Portuguese water dogs and showed us around his office. Joe and I were in there for a long while listening to him.

A few days later I received a letter from Kennedy:

Dear Frank and Joe,

As you could tell, I was deeply touched and humbled by your visit to my office this morning and by the extraordinary words of you both about my family. There are many stones in my own life I certainly should not have cast, and with God's help I hope I can do better as well.

In the words of the old Irish blessing, may God hold you both in the palm of his hand.

> With great respect and appreciation,
> Your friend,
> Ted

. . .

While I believe in supporting my Republican friends and colleagues, I don't think we're meant to sacrifice what we believe to be right in order to march in lockstep with our party. But if you vote against your party, sometimes you may have to pay some unpleasant consequences.

On opening day of a new Congress, the vote for Speaker is the first vote held, and it is always by voice vote. Each member's name is called out, and he or she shouts out the name of their party leader.

On January 7, 1997 — the opening day of the 105th Congress — we were voting on the reelection of Newt Gingrich as Speaker of the House. Newt was then under investigation by the House Ethics Committee. The House Democratic whip, David Bonior, had filed most of the eighty-four ethics charges against him, which ranged from accusations that Newt had misused tax-exempt funds to criticism over a lucrative advance he was offered by HarperCollins to write two books. (Eighty-three of the eighty-four charges were later dropped.)

The Ethics Committee report had not yet been published. I felt that I could not, in good conscience, vote for Newt as Speaker until

I had seen the report. This turned out to be a very controversial decision. Members are not supposed to vote against the leaders of their party; it simply isn't done. If for no other reason, it gives the other party ammunition to use against your party.

My friend Dan Coats knew what I planned to do, and he came over and stood beside me during the forty-five-minute vote. He knew that when you break with your party, it's not a very comfortable situation, and he wanted to provide moral support. So we stood at the back rail, waiting for my name to be called. And when the House clerk called my name, instead of saying, "Gingrich," I answered, "Present." I later issued a statement explaining why:

> I voted present and withheld my support today on the election of the Speaker of the House because I believe that the vote for Speaker should have been held after the House received the Ethics Committee's full report on Mr. Gingrich. I felt that the formal process should have been completed first and therefore I could not vote in good conscience any other way.
>
> I am not saying that my colleagues in the House should have reached the conclusion I did. In serving in Congress, this was clearly a vote of conscience, and I respect those who came to a different conclusion.
>
> I am reminded of a scene in Robert Bolt's play *A Man for All Seasons*, when Sir Thomas More was asked by the Duke of Norfolk to go along with him and others out of fellowship and publicly agree with the king. More says, "And when we stand before God, and you are sent to Paradise for doing according to your conscience, and I am damned for not doing according to mine, will you come with me, for fellowship?"

I was one of just eight Republicans to vote against Gingrich. For a couple of weeks my life was very uncomfortable. I was immediately disinvited to several Republican fundraising dinners. A number of people told me, "Your political career is over, you're finished, you're dead," because a Speaker can pretty badly damage your political career. I received a comforting letter from my friend Chuck Colson, who told me that I'd shown good political judgment.

Many of my colleagues were certain that Newt Gingrich, who was now Speaker, would lose no time in punishing me. But Newt, to his credit, never did. He understood why I'd voted the way I did. I have always appreciated that he took that position when he didn't have to. Never once did he express any anger or bitterness. We got along very well and ended up becoming good friends.

CHAPTER FOUR

FROM GLASNOST TO THE GULAG

I was in prison and you came to visit me.

Matthew 25:36

I WAS BOUNCING ALONG a rutted dirt road in one of those ubiquitous Soviet government Volga sedans, headed for the most infamous prison camp in the Soviet Union. It was August of 1989, and Chris Smith and I had decided it was time to investigate the condition of political prisoners — especially those in Perm Camp 35, located in the foothills of the Ural Mountains, one thousand miles east of Moscow.

Perm 35 was a Stalinist-era camp known for its severe conditions and mistreatment of prisoners. Among the camp's famous alumni were Natan Sharansky, Alexander Ginsburg, Deacon Vladimir Rusak, Father Alfonsas Svarinskas, and many other dissidents.

Bumping along for two hours from the city of Perm to the camp, we wondered what to expect. The Soviets had never before allowed any Western government official to set foot inside a Soviet "political" labor camp. Even my friend Chuck Colson, who had founded Prison Fellowship and gone into hundreds of prisons around the world, was denied entry into the Soviet gulag. But I was determined to speak with as many prisoners as possible, find out how they were being treated, and tell the world what was happening to them.

A few years earlier, between 1986 and 1988, we had begun to see the first signs of a thaw regarding human rights — a thaw that was labeled *glasnost* (openness) — as part of larger political reforms known as *perestroika* (restructuring). Soviet leader Mikhail Gorbachev had declared, prior to the signing of the Vienna Concluding Document in 1988, that there was no longer anyone in prison "sentenced for their political or religious convictions."

However, addressing the release of all remaining political prisoners was made a condition of the Vienna agreement — to schedule a follow-up conference of the Helsinki Commission (formally known as the Commission on Security and Cooperation in Europe) in Moscow in 1991. Chris and I were members of the Helsinki Commission, which monitors the condition of human rights in thirty-five Eastern and Western bloc nations.[1]

The Soviets subsequently agreed to a process of review for most of the nearly one hundred prisoners remaining on U.S. political prisoner lists. Many of these "disputed cases" were the cases of those we wanted to meet in Perm 35. They were being held under basically three charges: attempting to flee the country, war crimes, and espionage. Many languished under Article 64 of the Soviet criminal code, "treason," in combination with more clear-cut political offenses such as Article 70, "anti-Soviet agitation and propaganda."

The American Embassy in Moscow told us that, over the past few years of perestroika, political prisoners were being released from camps all over the Soviet Union, many making their way to Moscow. Some came to the U.S. Embassy, often still in their camp overcoats and with shaved heads, so embassy staffers knew something different was going on. Gorbachev had told Andre Sakharov, a Soviet nuclear physicist (the "father" of their hydrogen bomb), dissident, and human rights activist who had been awarded the Nobel Peace Prize in 1975, that he could return to Moscow from his banishment to internal exile in the closed city of Gorky.

Our embassy also knew that citizens felt safe enough to gather in apartments and discuss political issues. Religious groups were proselytizing more openly, and new publications were coming out featuring articles that for the time were quite forward leaning.

Clearly, citizens were beginning to fear the Communist government less. Various groups would call our embassy and say they were holding a demonstration somewhere, and staffers would show up to observe. They'd see plainclothes KGB operators, sometimes with briefcase cameras photographing the demonstration, and sometimes breaking it up. But there was much less of a sense that you were going to be hauled off to the camps or the psychiatric wards for speaking out. On the other hand, participants still knew there would be a price to pay, such as the loss of a job or a place at a university.

Glasnost, however, had failed to penetrate into the gulag, either to change the evil conditions in the labor camps or to impact penal procedures that led to systematically cruel and unusual punishment. Lingering fears of being tossed into the gulag threatened to hold hostage any meaningful reforms in Soviet society.

Chris and I had been working to help bring glasnost to the gulag, trying to ensure that prisoners of conscience were included in the reforms sweeping dramatically through the Soviet Union. Bringing glasnost to the gulag was also an important step the Soviets could take to deal with concerns that Gorbachev's reforms might be reversed or undermined.

Accompanying us to Perm 35 and serving as our interpreter was Richard Stephenson, a U.S. State Department official assigned to the Soviet desk, who a year earlier had been assigned to the U.S. Embassy in Moscow as a second secretary in the political section.

It had taken a year to get permission from the Soviets to visit and to work out the details of the trip. Helsinki Watch (now Human Rights Watch), Amnesty International, and former inmates of the gulag provided important background information for us. Our being allowed to visit Perm 35 was clearly a political decision made at the highest levels, probably in the Politburo. A couple of weeks before our trip, they had opened up Perm 35 to a French news team and allowed in *New York Times* editor Abe Rosenthal, but we were the first group of political leaders from a Western democracy being allowed to visit.

The Soviets were clearly sending a signal. Perm 35 was one of the last, if not *the* last, political prisoner camps. In effect, the Soviets were saying, "Look, we've released all our political prisoners. Go ahead, visit Perm 35, walk around and talk to people. We have no political prisoners left, so stop criticizing us." It wasn't true, of course, but it was clearly an effort to relieve the pressure the West was putting on them.

We knew, thanks to groups such as Helsinki Watch, that there were still some one hundred remaining suspected political prisoners in the Soviet Union. Some were well known because various human rights groups and the U.S. government had publicized their plight and loudly advocated for their release. This practice — which we continue today regarding the plight of Chinese prisoners of conscience — is rooted in American values recognizing the inherent dignity and rights of each human being.

Richard Stephenson, who had gone to Moscow a couple of days ahead of us, contacted various human rights leaders in Moscow to line up interviews for us. Richard told us that many of those with whom we were interested in talking had no phone service, or if they did, it could be mysteriously cut off at any time. So in order to set up interviews, Richard had to traipse all over Moscow to locate the apartments of human rights representatives, trying to catch them at home.

On August 6, 1989, Chris and I touched down at Sheremyetevo International Airport in Moscow and took a cab to a hotel reserved for Westerners. We spent the next few days talking with government officials about Soviet progress toward legal reforms that served to advance the rule of law in Soviet society. Our discussions focused on the need to institutionalize the positive changes occurring in Soviet human rights practices, open up the Soviet prison and labor camp system to greater scrutiny, and establish due process. We met with Ministry of Foreign Affairs officials on legal reforms, including the critically important draft laws on freedom of conscience, whose principal impact would be upon religious communities. We talked about emigration reform and met with representatives of the procurator general and Ministry of Internal Affairs regarding the Soviet penal system.

Chris and I emphasized that our interest in proposed Soviet legislation was to find indications that changes were systematic and permanent, not arbitrary and temporary. "The American people place great importance on fundamental human rights like freedom of speech, peaceful assembly, the right to publish, and to organize independent groups," I told them. We spoke about the lasting impression such changes would make on the American people. For religious believers especially, a well-written law on conscience would offer legal recourse should local authorities decide to be heavy-handed. We stressed that the adoption and implementation of laws guaranteeing freedom of conscience would have a direct bearing on U.S. support and enthusiasm for the upcoming 1991 Human Rights Conference in Moscow. Our Soviet government interlocutors were noncommittal in their responses but attempted to assure us that human rights were fully respected in the Soviet Union, as underscored by their willingness to meet and discuss such matters with U.S. congressmen.

Next, Richard had been successful in arranging for us to meet with a number of human rights activists and political dissidents in the religious communities. Over tea, they told us what they thought about the present situation and the future for churches and synagogues in the U.S.S.R. While expressing optimism about some of the changes they were experiencing, and of the less repressive measures being taken against those speaking out publicly, they noted that the changes were occurring mainly in Moscow and Leningrad, where large numbers of Westerners were present. They expressed skepticism about the depth and scope of changes taking place across the Soviet Union outside of a few major metropolitan areas. Nevertheless, in their voices and expressions, there was a sense of the positive energy building in the nonconformist communities with which we spoke. Clearly, this was a period of change, but how permanent and how pervasive that change would be was still an open question.

Meetings finished, we embarked on the most important part of the trip: going into the gulag and speaking to the prisoners.

The Soviet government arranged for us to fly out to the airport at Perm, where we were met with what were pretty clearly some local KGB, judging by their demeanor and command of the activities arranged for us. They took us to a hotel, and the next day we traveled in a little caravan of two or three cars out to the camp. Despite it being August, the day was chilly. Along the dirt road through the evergreen trees of the Ural forest, we passed simple wooden homes, some of which appeared to be in derelict condition. We drove for hours.

When we arrived at the Perm 35 labor camp, the oppressive atmosphere was manifest in the high, barbed wire – topped walls around the camp. Within the camp itself was a high-voltage electrified fence surrounding the white, two-story barracks. As I walked into the first one, one of the first things I noticed was a framed picture of Vladimir Lenin, a standard feature in Soviet government offices.

We were greeted by camp officials and taken into the office of the camp commandant, Colonel Osin, a big, unsmiling guy. "We will take you on a tour; you can see everything," he told us. We were pretty sure that wouldn't be the case, but we started walking together through the camp, accompanied by our KGB escorts and uniformed camp guards. Richard was lugging a big video camera and filmed our entire visit through the camp.

We wanted to speak with the prisoners, but the camp officials were more interested in showing off their camp, which had, we later learned, been freshly repainted just before our visit. The camp officials were especially proud of their dining facility. Huge, hand-painted posters listed all the dietary requirements — how many grams and calories of bread and soup and chicken each prisoner was supposed to get each day. "We follow these rules so no one starves here, and no one is abused," prison officials told us. We later found out from prisoners that these posters had been put up for our benefit.

We were also shown the rooms where rows of beds stood, each with a mattress and blanket. There was even a potted plant on a windowsill. I saw no personal possessions — just white walls and rows of bunks.

We kept trying to bring our hosts back to the reason why we'd come: to speak to the men imprisoned there. Finally, we were taken out into the prison courtyard, where there were perhaps a couple dozen prisoners, each wearing a dark blue prison overcoat, shirt, and pants. "We're U.S. congressmen! Chris Smith and Frank Wolf!" I called out. "I represent the Washington, D.C., area. We want very badly to speak with all of you!"

"We've given a list to the gentlemen," Chris added. "We want to speak with everyone who wants to speak with us."

As we slowly moved toward a building where we were told we could meet with the prisoners one-on-one, suddenly one prisoner ran up and slipped me a note. One or two of the guards immediately tried to get it out of my hands, and one of them started shouting at Richard. "Mr. Stephenson! This is against protocol! You must tell him to give it to me! Give back this note!"

It was a tense moment, because the prison camp guards didn't know how far to go. Their natural instinct would have been to kick us, throw us on the ground, and grab the note. But they knew we were U.S. congressmen. At one point the KGB escorts were all but pleading with us to give them the note, saying that it was a security breach, and they threatened to shut down the visit.

I finally handed the note to the guard, who opened it up, read it, said it was all right, and handed it back to me. As I recall, the note said something along the lines of "I want to get out of here, please help me, I'm innocent." The KGB escorts demanded that the guy who'd written the note be brought in for us to interview along with the others who expressed an interest in meeting with us.

It was an ironic little episode. Here the Soviet officials were, attempting to make everything seem open and above board, while at the same time they were doing their level best to control the entire interaction. They wanted to convince us that they were not holding people who were being punished for their political views but instead holding people who had committed serious offenses against the state.

Whenever a prisoner said he wanted to meet with us, he was brought into a sort of rec room area, where he had to sit on a little bench, facing us, the guards, and Colonel Osin. They would tell us who they were, why they were in prison, and anything else they wanted to say. Some of them said they were treated well and had enough to eat and warm clothes in the winter; others complained of the harsh treatment and rotten herring they were often fed. Many denied they had committed any crime. One told us he'd been in a KGB psychiatric hospital, and three of them said they'd been locked up after the authorities discovered they were working for the CIA.

Clearly, among these men were political prisoners. One man told me he'd been locked up because he wished to emigrate to Israel; another found himself behind bars because he'd criticized the government. One prisoner, whose face was badly scarred and who had bandages on his ear and nose, told us, "For the last sixteen years I have not had a normal life. I don't have a family or children. I lost all the relatives I had because of the KGB."

"Do you get any meat?" I asked one man.

"I wouldn't call it meat," he replied. "Animal by-products and fat and maybe a little meat."

A common theme running through the men's stories emphasized the dreadful conditions and treatment of prisoners at Perm 35: long periods of isolation, severe cold used as torture, and being cut off from family and friends because of routinely intercepted mail and arbitrarily canceled visits. Prisoners told us their stories boldly and bravely, several of them condemning the abuses of the KGB and camp officials in their very presence. Many expressed thanks to those in the West who had written letters to Soviet officials on their behalf, and letters to the prisoners themselves. They had been overjoyed when they learned that President Ronald Reagan had spoken out against the abuses of the Soviet system, a system that would punish individuals for exercising their human rights.

We had sought and received assurances beforehand from Soviet officials that no retribution would be brought against any prisoner. We repeated this Soviet promise loudly during meetings with many prisoners. The men told us that there had indeed been reprisals against some who met with Rosenthal during his visit; others said they understood reprisals were a possible consequence of speaking to us, as well. Nevertheless, we continued to stress that assurances had been given by the Soviet officials that there would be no retaliation.

Tragically, the nature of their everyday lives made reprisals almost superfluous. As I stressed the Soviet promises to one inmate, he sadly told me, "There is nothing more they can do to us."

We later handed out some Russian Bibles, wondering if the guards would stop us. All they did was check through them to be sure they contained no contraband. I asked each prisoner, "Would you like a Bible?" until we ran out. And as we met with the prisoners, we took pictures and videotaped the interviews until our camera's batteries died.

Surprisingly, when we asked to see the infamous *shizo* punishment cell, the Soviet officials agreed. The shizo was sort of a prison within a prison. Veterans of the Soviet gulag had given vivid accounts of this notorious four-by-eight-foot cell, and now we were seeing it for ourselves.

I walked up to the shizo's solid door, and the guards opened up a tiny, six-inch window. I peered inside. From inside the dimly lit room, three men with shaved heads peered back at us. They were Oleg Mikhailov, Ruslan Ketenchiyev, and Aleksandr Goldovich, who had been placed in the punishment cell for organizing a work stoppage in protest of the camp's dangerous working conditions.

The smell emanating from that tiny room was overwhelming. There was no ventilation, and the only plumbing was a bucket. We talked with those prisoners for a minute or two through the window and snapped pictures. As they talked (and Richard translated), I glanced around the cell. It was every bit as bad as we'd heard. Fastened to the wall were wooden planks on which to sleep, with no bedding or blankets. There was a rough cement stump on which to sit. The cement walls had a sharp, rough surface, which meant that if a prisoner pressed up against it while sleeping, the protrusions would poke him.

The cell is designed to make the cold of a Soviet labor camp that much more severe, turning the unbearably low temperature of a Siberian winter into a torture device. The prisoners told us they previously were fed only once every two days, later changed to once a day.

I later learned Goldovich's background. He'd been living in Odessa with his girlfriend, and the two decided to leave the Soviet Union, escaping in a little rowboat across the Black Sea to claim political asylum in Turkey. They gathered some provisions, got their hands on a rowboat, checked the tides, and figured the trip would take them about three days.

They pushed off one night, and the next morning some Soviet fishermen passing by in trawlers saw them and radioed a report to the border patrol. Goldovich and his girlfriend were arrested and charged with treason for attempting to illegally leave the U.S.S.R., and with "anti-Soviet propaganda" because the authorities found in Goldovich's wallet a picture of their apartment. Because the apartment was rather dilapidated, he was accused of planning to show it to the West to complain of how impoverished and badly treated he was under the Soviet system. In other words, he was planning to engage in anti-Soviet propaganda.

After they'd been picked up, Goldovich and his girlfriend found out that, because of the currents, they would never have made it to the Turkish shore in three days, as they'd expected. They would most assuredly have died of thirst or exposure, so their lives were actually saved by their arrests.

The Soviets got Goldovich's girlfriend to testify against him in exchange for more lenient treatment. He, however, ended up with a twenty-year sentence, to be served in Perm 35.

Goldovich now lives in northern Virginia, works for a company that improves network securities for the Department of Homeland Security, and attends a Russian-speaking church. He recently recalled for me what life was like in the Perm. "They'd give you food, very limited food. A normal ration in the prison would be about 1,800 calories, which is not enough even for teenagers, let alone adults working hard. But in prison you will have one day nothing, another day not even 1,000 calories, very thin soup. About a pound of bread, and that's it. So people are starving, and some of them literally were starving to death.

"They wouldn't give us warm clothes, so we were constantly cold in that punishment cell, and you cannot even sit down because there is no chair.

"I would sleep on bare boards. In the middle of the night you wake up cold. I usually quietly put my bunk bed to the wall and started exercising for about an hour until I warmed up. Then I prepare my bunk and climb again to the upper bunk because it's warmer.

"Anytime somebody was expected into prison, they would improve our conditions. And if you don't behave like you are supposed to, praising the humanity of the guards and the benefits of the Soviet system, they will punish you somehow."

Tragically, not all prisoners of conscience survived Perm 35.

· · ·

We were able to interview twenty-three of the thirty-eight declared prisoners in the camp. The guards ostensibly allowed anyone who wanted to meet with us to do so, but we had good reason to believe we might not be allowed to visit all the men we'd come to see. One of the prisoners we most wanted to speak to was a young physicist from Leningrad named Mikhail Kazachkov. He'd been arrested for treason, allegedly meeting with CIA officers. He was also a very outspoken human rights advocate and was, I think, considered particularly threatening to the Soviet government because he was highly educated and connected with all their science groups. The fact that someone who had enjoyed a very favored life position would speak out against the Soviet government — well, that particularly rankled them.

At the camp, when we asked to meet with Kazachkov, we were told that he had violated a camp rule and had been transferred to the Perm city prison a day or so before we arrived. Chris and I were convinced that they had deliberately pulled him out of Perm Camp 35 because he spoke excellent English and would be a compelling witness to the reality in the camp. We kept insisting that we be allowed to meet with him but were told he was back in Perm and no arrangements had been made for us to visit that prison. As the afternoon wore on, our KGB escorts became agitated about concluding the camp visit, saying that it was late and if we didn't depart immediately, we would not have time to drive back to Perm without arriving in the middle of the night. "You don't want to do that," they told us. "Driving on these roads is dangerous enough just during the day, with all the trucks. You don't want to try it after dark."

But we were still interviewing prisoners who wanted to speak with us. By this time I'd had enough. "Well, that's fine," I said. "We'll just stay here."

"Oh no," they said. "There's no place for you to stay."

"Well, we'll stay in a cell, then," I retorted. I noted that if we remained at the camp overnight, Kazachkov could be brought back so we could meet with him.

I think that made an impression on them. They couldn't imagine two U.S. congressmen and a U.S. State Department official being willing to spend the night in one of their cells, even though they'd just spent a lot of time telling us how wonderful it was in the camp and how delicious the food was. So they finally relented and agreed to let us speak to Kazachkov the next day — but at the Perm city prison.

By this time it was too late to drive safely back to Perm, so the KGB escorts took us to a hotel on the outskirts of the prison camp (so much for there being no place to stay). It was dark by the time we got there and checked in.

In those days there was a floor maid (*dezhurnaya*) on each floor of every Soviet hotel. You'd tell her which room you'd been given, and she would open a drawer and pull out a key with a huge fob on it, so you couldn't put it in your pocket and easily take it away. Whenever you left the floor, the floor maid was right there, and you had to give your key back to her. Nobody could go down the hall without passing the floor maid, so she always knew which guests were in their room. As experienced travelers in the U.S.S.R. knew, this made it easier for the KGB to go into the rooms and snoop through the guests' possessions.

Richard had an amusing experience that night at the hotel — or at least as amusing as anything involving the KGB can be: "One of the things I would typically do when traveling in the Soviet Union would be to put water glasses on the doorknob. That way, if anybody opened the door, they would knock the glasses onto the floor and wake me up with the noise. That night, about three o'clock in the morning, I happened to be lying awake when I heard the doorknob jiggle. The door was quietly opened, and of course the water glasses fell down and made a huge racket.

"One of the KGB escorts — a short little guy — hopped into my room, was surprised by the noise, and oddly dashed into the bathroom right by the room's entrance. I heard him flush the toilet; then he dashed back out of the room and closed the door. I'm convinced the guy came in the middle of the night, figuring I was asleep, in order to grab the videotape we'd taken at the camp that day. They probably didn't like us filming there, but they didn't stop us. It's entirely possible that they were surprised by our filming, but they didn't put up any objections when we taped people talking to us. In any case, I was keeping that videotape close to me the whole time.

"The next morning, I told the congressmen, 'I think the KGB has the B-team on this detail here,' because they weren't very professional."

This was confirmed to us when we returned to Perm and went directly to the city prison, where they had taken Kazachkov. Almost without stopping, we entered the prison from the street with our KGB escorts and walked briskly through security doors directly to the warden's office. After a few minutes they brought Kazachkov into the warden's office, and he sat down with us, the warden, other prison officials, and our KGB escorts. As soon as Kazachkov found out we were U.S. congressmen, he started talking in his impeccable English. The KGB immediately objected. "No, no, we don't want this interview in English," they said, because they didn't understand English and wouldn't know what he was telling us. They were very adamant on that, and so we conducted the interview in Russian.

The same little KGB agent who had barged into Richard's room the night before was there, and as we were speaking with Kazachkov, we suddenly heard beeping noises coming from him. He evidently had a small tape recorder concealed on his person, and it had run out of tape, or maybe the batteries were running down. The guy jumped up, red-faced, and ran out of the room. It was just comical, and yet it was tragic, too.

Political theorist Hannah Arendt coined the phrase "the banality of evil," a concept the Soviet dissident Aleksandr Solzhenitsyn explored in his books about the Soviet system of repression, particularly in the gulag. Solzhenitsyn meant that the Communist government was not an all-knowing, all-seeing state filled with crack professionals who never made a mistake. Instead it was made up of ordinary people doing ordinary jobs and screwing up in ordinary ways — oppressing people every day in unremarkable, routine, and ordinary ways.

At any rate, Kazachkov's analytical mind had lost none of its sharpness as he related interesting details about life in the camp. Arrested in 1975 after applying to emigrate, he had spent nearly two hundred days of his fourteen-year incarceration in punishment cells. Some things, he said, had changed over that time in the camp. Kazachkov's arm had been injured when he tried to resist a forced head-shaving — something he said was done to prisoners as a way of humiliating them — but general-purpose beatings were no longer a regular occurrence in Perm 35.

I learned later that just three weeks after our visit, Kazachkov was singled out for his role in a protest against working conditions in Perm 35. He was put on trial for "refusal to work" and sentenced to serve the next three years of his term in the more severe regime of Chistopol Prison. After serving his sentence, he was finally allowed to emigrate from the U.S.S.R. and eventually settled in New England. Over the years since his arrival in the U.S., I have met with him a number of times.

.   .   .

When we returned to Washington, we called on the Soviets to close Perm Camp 35 permanently. We also encouraged other members of Congress and humanitarian groups to visit Perm Camp 35 and other Soviet prisons to ensure that, as the Soviet thaw continued, no individuals were left stranded. Only by bringing the Soviet prison system into the open could we put pressure on the Soviet government to undertake lasting reforms.

We pointed out to the Soviets that — regardless of conflicting definitions of political prisoners — most of the current prisoners would not be prosecuted for their "crimes" today, or would have their offenses treated far less severely. In view of the excessive punishment already endured by these men, we called on Soviet leaders to reexamine their cases in the context of "new political thinking" — and to release the men on humanitarian grounds.

·   ·   ·

I didn't forget about those prisoners who had claimed to work for the CIA, and back in the U.S. I called the agency to ask someone about this. They denied that any of the Perm Camp 35 prisoners had been working for them, but I wasn't sure what to believe.

Several months later, however, sitting in my family room one day, I was watching the videotape of the trip when suddenly something caught my attention — something I had not noticed while I was there. The tape showed Chris and me standing in the prison yard talking with the inmates. One of the prisoners stood in the background, smiling at us. After a few moments he moved forward so that he would be in full view of Richard's video camera. Then he made a peculiar gesture, placing a finger from one hand between the thumb and forefinger of his other hand, forming a cross. He held it that way for several seconds as he stared hard at the camera. It was clearly a signal of some kind.

I went back to the CIA and reminded them of the tape — which I had already provided them — noting the gesture. They finally acknowledged that the three prisoners had worked for them, although they fudged on whether the gesture by the man on the tape was indeed a signal. And so we began the long and difficult task of trying to get the men out.

I also launched an inspector general investigation, asking for an explanation regarding why I hadn't been given all the relevant information at the time. The report confirmed my suspicion that the CIA had not been truthful with me. I recently asked for the IG report to be declassified, but it hasn't happened yet.

All three of the prisoners at Perm 35 who had spied for the CIA had been compromised either by Aldrich Ames or Robert Hanssen. Ames was the CIA counterintelligence officer who was responsible for the deaths of ten agents spying on behalf of the U.S. and for the suffering of more than a dozen others. Ames lived in my congressional district in Arlington, and Hanssen lived near my home in Vienna. Hanssen was an FBI mole who also exposed several of our sources in the Soviet Union.

One of the Perm 35 prisoners in the film — the guy making the gesture — was Vladimir Potashov, a senior military analyst for a Soviet think tank who "volunteered his services to Defense Secretary Harold Brown at a Carter-era arms control meeting and began spying for the U.S. on disarmament matters in 1981," according to the *Chicago Tribune*.[2]

After his arrest on treason charges in July of 1986, Potashov spent eighteen months in a KGB dungeon and then was sent to Perm 35. Thanks to the greed of Aldrich Ames, Potashov endured torture, beatings, bad food, solitary confinement, the loss of all his teeth (because of radioactive drinking water), and severe cold before being released in 1992 by Boris Yeltsin. His wife, out of fear of the KGB, had divorced him. Potashov escaped into Poland and was eventually granted political asylum in America.

The visit of two U.S. congressmen to Perm 35, Potashov said, so encouraged the prisoners "that we started doing unthinkable [things] in [the] gulag," such as filing complaints with human rights groups, giving interviews to journalists, and treating KGB agents with insolence.

Years later, after moving to the U.S., Potashov decided to petition for assets forfeited by Aldrich Ames, who had grown rich betraying Potashov and others. But first Potashov had to prove that Ames had indeed betrayed him.

Potashov recently sent me a copy of a letter written in 1994 by U.S. attorney Helen Fahey, who confirmed that she had "been advised by a Special Agent of the F.B.I. with supervisory responsibility for the Ames case that Vladimir Potashov was, in fact, betrayed by Ames's espionage."

Potashov is now living in California on what they call a 110 — a citizenship and a pension that the U.S. government provides to former spies in acknowledgement of their service to the United States. A few years ago he asked me to serve as godfather for his son. After his son's baptism, which unfortunately I was unable to attend, in a letter to me he wrote,

> Dear Mr. Wolf:
>
> A wonderful Thanksgiving. Let me thank you for my new life, a new life you helped to plant here when your efforts first opened the gulag door, then a door to U.S.
> Resettlement November two years ago. I came back here one year ago, got married, and this year we had our son, Elias, baptized. It was a real great harvest for us. We wish you were there at the church to share our joy.

Alexandr Goldovich served several more years at Perm 35 before being released. While he was there, a fellow prisoner, a Pentecostal minister, witnessed to him, which led to his conversion to Christianity in the camp. When I found out how near he lived to me, we arranged to get together and talk. He told me how much it meant that two U.S. congressmen would travel all the way to the Soviet Union and come into the gulag to see him. At that point he knew, he said, that the West had won and that Communism was going to crumble.

· · ·

It's been more than twenty years since I entered the gulag to speak with political prisoners and spoke out on their behalf. Clearly, our government needs to do a better job helping non-Americans who risk their lives spying for our country.

Soviet camps for prisoners of conscience are now mercifully closed; Boris Yeltsin, the first president of the Russian Federation, released the last ten Perm 35 political prisoners in 1992.[3] But sadly, the battles to protect those who speak out against their government or worship God in defiance of the law never end. We are constantly having to refight them in other gulags around the world in such places as China, North Korea, Tibet, and Iran — anyplace where speaking out against government policy can get you thrown in prison, tortured, executed, or turned into involuntary organ donors.

CHAPTER FIVE

BEIJING PRISON NUMBER ONE

Silence in the face of evil is itself evil: God will not hold us guiltless. Not to speak is to speak. Not to act is to act.

Dietrich Bonhoeffer

MORE THAN TWO DECADES AGO an astounded world watched as hundreds of thousands of Chinese rose up against their Communist leaders, demanding economic and democratic reforms, symbolized by the Goddess of Democracy erected by students on Tiananmen Square, facing the portrait of Chairman Mao. Although we had witnessed the fall of Communism in Europe, we never expected to see it happen in China.

Nor did we, as it turned out. Tragically, a few weeks after the protests began, China's leaders ran out of patience. On June 4, 1989, they sent army tanks smashing into Tiananmen Square, killing unarmed student protesters and crushing vehicles. Other protesters were finished off with AK-47s or beaten to death by soldiers, their bloody bodies left in the streets. Estimates of the slaughter ranged from a few hundred up to three thousand. Many more were wounded, and untold numbers were executed in the aftermath.[1]

In the months following the Tiananmen Square massacre, I often wondered what had happened to those who survived their brief, ill-fated bid for freedom. Almost two years later, during my first visit to China, I discovered the fate of some of them, at least:

they were in Beijing Prison Number One, making golf socks for export to the West.

Congressman Chris Smith and I decided to visit China in March of 1991 to meet with pro-democracy activists, look into the treatment of political prisoners (who officially do not exist), bring up family reunification cases, and discuss religious liberty (which definitely does not exist). We wanted to tell China's leaders what we thought about their human rights abuses — especially Premier Li Peng, who had ordered the use of deadly force against the young Tiananmen Square demonstrators.

We arrived in China on March 24, accompanied by Steve Snyder of Christian Solidarity International, and Dorothy Taft, one of Chris's staffers. Stepping off the plane, I couldn't believe I was finally there, visiting a country that had been closed to most Westerners for so many years. On the drive to the hotel, I was struck by the crowds, the huge number of people riding bicycles, and the nonstop activity of the city.

Over the next few days, we had meetings with government officials ranging from Premier Li Peng to Peng Peiyun, minister of the State Family Planning Commission, to Zhu Rongji, the mayor of Shanghai (later premier of China), to Ren Wuzhi, director of the Religious Affairs Bureau. We were polite, but we were brutally honest and didn't mince words. We told these leaders that the Tiananmen Square massacre had awakened many Americans to the fact that human rights and freedom were nonexistent in the People's Republic of China. We said we were disturbed about the detention of thousands of pro-democracy activists — students, intellectuals, and ordinary workers — and about the unfair sentences meted out to them.

"You are mistaken," our hosts smoothly replied. "There are no political prisoners in China."

That was true, in a way. Chinese leaders were continuing the charade carried on by other Communist countries when the West pressured them about political prisoners: when they arrested political activists, the Chinese simply charged them with other, nonpolitical crimes. As for the Tiananmen Square massacre — that was "merely an incident," they told us.

We told the Chinese we were alarmed over reports of religious leaders being harassed and thrown into prison, and disturbed by the approximately three thousand Chinese families forced to live apart because the Chinese government refused to allow its citizens to emigrate to the country of their choice. Many husbands and wives had not seen each other for years.

And we were appalled, we told them, at China's coercive population-control measures, which included many forced abortions, involuntary sterilizations, mandatory insertion of intrauterine devices, and female infanticide, practiced by parents who, forced to limit their families to one child, chose to have a boy, even if it meant killing their baby girls.

"These policies are crimes against humanity," we told our unsmiling hosts. The U.S. Congress had twice declared them such, just as the Nazi atrocities committed against Polish women were declared crimes against humanity during the Nuremberg war trials. China's own laws prohibited the government from unlawful detention, we reminded them, and the right to freely practice one's religion is recognized by the United Nations Declaration of Human Rights.

Their response to all of this was either to ignore the questions, offering no answers, or to simply deny the accusations.

Before flying off to Beijing, Chris and I had compiled a list of seventy-seven Protestant and Catholic leaders known to be in prison or under house arrest. We wrote a letter we planned to hand to Premier Li Peng, signed by 110 members of the House, urging that the cases of these religious leaders be reviewed and that they be freed. "As long as such arrests and imprisonments continue, it will be very difficult for the United States to improve relations with the People's Republic of China," we wrote. This kind of thing was done quite effectively during the time of the Soviet Union.

Members would take lists of dissidents with them and raise their cases to Soviet officials.

On the day we met with the premier, after talking at length about China's human rights violations, I got up, crossed the room, and tried to hand the letter to him. (It probably wasn't a wise idea to do this, any more than it would be smart for someone to get up and approach the American president; I probably alarmed Li's security people, who were undoubtedly armed to the teeth.) Li refused to accept my letter. So I just set it next to him on an end table, but Li wouldn't even look at it.

Then Chris spoke very eloquently about human rights and China's one-child policy. Premier Li didn't want to deal with Chris, either; he simply ignored him as well.

A handful of other members of Congress were there at the meeting, and I sensed that they were a little upset with us. They were there to talk about trade and business, and Chris and I were the skunks at the party, raising issues the Chinese leadership didn't like to hear about, and making the Chinese angry. But Chris and I wanted China's leaders to know that releasing religious and political prisoners would greatly help to improve U.S.-Chinese relations.

The next day we asked to be taken to Beijing Prison Number One. Although it was early spring, it was a very cold day, with snow falling. As we walked through the dank gray prison, we saw a sign that read, Hosiery Factory.

"Can we go in there?" I asked.

We were given a tour of the prison's textile and plastic ("jelly") shoe factories. We spent a few minutes watching the prisoners making socks on machines in the crowded factory area. I picked a pair of them off the line for a closer look. The warden, who was leading the tour, noticed our interest. "If you want some of those socks, I'll give you the socks," he said.

I brought home several pairs of different-colored socks, including a white pair with a little golf logo on them. There was no doubt they were made for export to the West, because in those days the

Chinese didn't play golf. (The U.S. Department of Commerce later acknowledged that the socks were exported to the West.)

We were startled to learn from Warden Zhou that there were forty inmates in this prison because of the part they had played in the pro-democracy demonstrations in June of 1989. Not even our own embassy knew this.

"We'd like to speak to them," I said.

"No," our guide replied. He claimed this was a day of rest and that the prisoners were scattered throughout the prison. We also asked for a list of the prisoners' names and the alleged crimes they had committed. Again the answer was no.

Chris and I then asked to meet with Xu Wenli, a pro-democracy activist who was serving a fifteen-year sentence for "counterrevolutionary activities." Xu had been in solitary confinement for five years, and Warden Zhou refused to allow us to see him, claiming that Xu didn't want to meet with foreigners.

"Let us judge that for ourselves," Chris demanded. "Let us pass him our business cards, and let him make that decision."

Warden Zhou shook his head. "No," he said. It appeared to be his favorite word.

We knew that China used forced labor for much of its manufacturing and textile production. Now that I'd seen a prison factory close-up, I had no doubt that at least some of these goods were making their way to the West.

While Chinese leaders try to prevent details about convict-made products from reaching Western ears, among themselves they boast about the quality of what amounts to slave labor goods. Shortly after Chris and I returned from Beijing, Asia Watch released a report titled "Prison Labor in China," which quoted a journal for Chinese prison and labor officials. One of the journal's authors bragged that "our indigo-blue denim [made in Chinese prisons] ... won the title of 'quality product' awarded by the Ministry of Textiles. ... We won goodwill and praise from customers in such developed countries as Japan, the United States, and West Germany."[2]

Many Americans have no idea that the plastic flowers, toys, wines, ceramic mugs, and mandarin oranges they purchase are made in some three thousand slave labor camps spread out over the Chinese countryside. These slave laborers are, moreover, often imprisoned for such crimes as speaking out for democracy or worshiping in a house church.

The conditions in which they labor rival anything faced by prisoners held in Soviet gulags. According to Harry Wu, a dissident who spent nineteen brutal years in Chinese labor camps before emigrating to the U.S., Chinese prisoners — miners, factory workers, and farm laborers — are forced to work up to sixteen hours a day, seven days a week, with only a few days off each year. They are "forced to handle toxic chemicals with no protective clothing, or work in asbestos mines without adequate safety precautions," Wu writes.[3] Prisoners, including some one hundred thousand religious believers, often die from malnutrition, overwork, exhaustion, torture, and suicide. I was horrified to learn that even children were being forced to labor in Chinese prisons, making goods for export.

It is hard for me to understand why there is so little Western outcry against the millions killed in Mao's Cultural Revolution and the Chinese prisons compared with the outrage Westerners expressed about the Soviet gulags after Aleksandr Solzhenitsyn exposed them in his bestselling book *The Gulag Archipelago*.[4]

Harry Wu refers to this vast network of prison camps as the Laogai ("reform through labor") Archipelago. The savings in labor costs have greatly contributed to China's economic status — and greatly harmed competitors who must pay their workers. The late Abe Rosenthal of the *New York Times* was right in reporting that China today is a "vast, organized slave camp, where daily 16 to 20 million men" toil, and where "prisoners failing to meet quotas are beaten, tortured, fed starvation diets, and can have their sentences lengthened."[5]

And you and I buy the products they are forced to make.

Importing gulag-made goods into America is against the law,

but it's a law that is rarely enforced.[6] Even if the U.S. were committed to turning away all ships carrying convict-made goods, the Chinese make it difficult to identify them. American companies often place orders with Hong Kong agents, who then work with Chinese shippers and suppliers. The supplier then contracts out work to subcontractors. Guess who comes up with the lowest bid? That's right: prison factories. Slave labor is cheap — and America's factories are paying the price, forced to close as a result of China's unfair and immoral trading practices.

Unfortunately, since many prison-made products are also manufactured in nonprison factories, it's difficult for American consumers to be sure they are purchasing goods that do not exploit convicts — especially since the Chinese government goes to great lengths to cover its tracks. The Laogai Research Foundation, which Harry Wu founded, makes an effort to let consumers know which goods are slave-made, so that Americans can avoid them.[7]

When Chris and I returned to America, we raised Cain with the George H. W. Bush administration about the hosiery factory in the middle of Beijing Prison Number One. Bush, who had been an ambassador to China years before, declined to do anything substantial about it. President Clinton didn't want to hear about it, either, and for a long time refused to do anything about it.

On the House floor, I held up a pair of those prison-made golf socks. "How would you like to learn that our socks were made by Tiananmen Square demonstrators who are in jail for expressing democratic ideas?" I asked. "Why should Americans unwittingly contribute to a system which enslaves political prisoners, workers, and even children to earn hard currency — through exports — for the Chinese government?

"If I had to write a book telling the Chinese government how to mess up trade relations with the United States," I declared, "I would probably tell them to do just what they're doing: use forced labor to make export goods [and] lock up protesters."

Since 1980 China had been forced to undergo a yearly waiver

in order to maintain free trade status. Year after year, members of Congress concerned with human rights introduced legislation disapproving the president's waiver in an effort to link free trade to human freedom. Because of China's massive and undeniable human rights violations, I (and others) also urged members to take most favored nation status away from China unless certain conditions were attached to it.

Some members argued hard against taking away MFN, claiming that it would take away any influence we had over China, undermine America's economic and foreign policy interests, serve as an attack on U.S. companies doing business in China, and abandon one billion Chinese to a bleak future. Taking away MFN was "illogical" and "not well thought out" and would be a "crippling blow" to the cause of political reform in China. Keeping the channels of trade open, they argued, is the best way to communicate democratic ideals. Yes, we all share human rights goals, they agreed, but we must be reasonable. After all, important progress was being made on the human rights front.[8]

I couldn't stand it anymore.

"Give me a break," I said. "This place has not improved. These are the same arguments used when we brought up the amendment when we suspended MFN for Romania. The first time we brought it up, everyone said, 'No, do not do it. You take it away, Ceausescu will get angry and it will hurt the people.'

"Yet as they were bulldozing churches, bulldozing synagogues, putting people in prison, all the people in Romania when I went there said privately, 'Take MFN away, because it is the only thing that will send a message to Ceausescu.' We took MFN away, and Ceausescu is no more.

"I would hope and pray that on behalf of the prisoners that we have met and their families, if we could pass [this] amendment with a 100 percent vote ... the gates in Beijing and throughout China would open up, and it would be a message. Those that listen on shortwave radios in China, Tibet, and places like that would know that the people's body, the United States Congress, has sent a message. And that will make a great difference."

Unfortunately, my speech didn't do much good. Nobody wanted to hear about forced labor in China. Nor, going by letters I received, were the American people up in arms over this. In 1991 the vote to take away China's MFN status failed, 308 to 118. In 1992 it failed again, 258 to 135, with 41 not voting. Tragically, in 1992, on the very day we were debating this issue, the Chinese government sentenced Bao Tong, a prominent reformer, to seven years in prison after a secret trial. His crime? Counterrevolutionary incitement — that is, warning pro-democracy demonstrators at Tiananmen Square how the government planned to handle them.

Just after his 1992 election, Bill Clinton opposed the MFN trading status giving the Chinese preferential trading agreements. He had been very critical of George H. W. Bush for his trading with China and being too close to the Chinese. In his first State of the Union address, Clinton got up and said this. There's a picture of me standing up and applauding Clinton — the only Republican member in the audience who did so. But then Clinton reversed himself and became very, very close to the Chinese.

When the Clinton administration finally sent people to China to investigate forced prison labor, the Chinese — knowing they were coming — managed to shut down Beijing Prison Number One's hosiery factory before they arrived. And I wonder what those Tiananmen Square prisoners thought when President Clinton invited General Chi Haotian, the operational commander of the Tiananmen Square massacre, whose nickname is the Butcher of Beijing, to the White House and to several of our military bases. This man — who denied during his visit that anyone was killed at Tiananmen Square — should have been on trial for war crimes against humanity, and there was Clinton giving him a nineteen-gun salute.

Withdrawing MFN status from Romania had had far-reaching repercussions, which ultimately led to freedom for the Romanian people. Who knows what might have happened if we had taken MFN status away from the Chinese? We will never know.

We had a somewhat better foreign policy under President George W. Bush. At least he spoke out on religious freedom, and he denied funding to the United Nations Population Fund because of their complicity on forced abortion and sterilization. But he had a great opportunity to speak out when Chinese president Hu Jintao visited the White House, and a reporter (and Falun Gong practitioner) named Wang Wenyi shouted a protest during a welcome ceremony on the South Lawn.

Instead the president apologized for the disruption. In his speech, however, he did urge Hu to allow the people of China the freedom to assemble, to speak freely, and to worship.

· · ·

Every now and then I become frustrated with the lack of progress on human rights issues — including, tragically, slavery and the trafficking of women and children in various countries (including our own), and I start thinking about getting out of this business. But then I recall how long it took William Wilberforce to abolish the slave trade, and then slavery itself, in the British Empire: forty-six years.

Then I get back to work.

More than two hundred years ago, when Wilberforce was fighting British slave traders, many antislavery Brits gave up sugar in their tea — sugar harvested by slaves in the Caribbean. Are Americans willing to give up artificial flowers and toys and many other goods made by modern-day slaves?

The world spoke out when the Nike company was found to be using children to make soccer balls in countries such as Vietnam, Cambodia, and Pakistan — children who labored up to sixteen hours a day in sweatshops. Are we willing to speak out so loudly that companies making huge profits off the backs of Chinese slaves will be shamed into changing their ways?

America needs to do more to prevent these products from being imported into the United States and prosecute importers who violate our laws. Fortunately, history proves that even when our government is slow to act, when Americans learn about human rights violations, they do something about it. Not only because forced-labor products hurt American competitors who cannot compete but also because we genuinely care about how companies treat workers in the developing world.

The Chinese are a gentle, industrious, and good people. At some point, we Americans are going to have to decide if we are going to allow our business community to dictate our human rights positions or let our national conscience determine them. We have to decide which is more important: importing cheap products from China or doing our best to keep human rights advocates and people of faith out of Chinese prisons, where they are undoubtedly making some of those toys we put under the Christmas tree for our own kids.

Even when Chinese products are not made by prisoners, there's reason to be concerned about working conditions in Chinese factories. On June 1, 2010, *Slate* ran an article about the high suicide rate among workers at China's Foxconn, where workers endure "a physically and psychologically brutal job of putting together products for Apple, Dell, HP, Microsoft, Nintendo, and other electronics companies," working twelve hours a day for three hundred dollars a month, wrote Farhad Manjoo.

"In other words if you've got an iPod, iPhone, iPad, Mac Mini, Xbox, Wii, or one of a number of generic PCs, it's likely your gadget was made at Foxconn," Manjoo noted. That makes American consumers complicit in what's going on at Foxconn, Manjoo added, which means it's our job to help stop it. "Would the globe's electronic giants be making their products at Foxconn if customers expressed moral misgivings about how our gadgets are made?"[9]

I doubt it. But *are* we going to speak out? After all, we love our electronics — and their cheap price.

. . .

In 1998 I attempted to get the House to pass the International Religious Freedom Act, which would allow for independent monitoring of the status of freedom of thought, conscience, and religion abroad. Independent commissioners would then give policy recommendations to the president, the secretary of state, and the Congress.

The business community strongly opposed me on this. So did the Clinton administration. secretary of State Madeleine Albright gave a major speech against it.

We fought them off and managed to get it passed in the House. I have always been grateful for how Senators Dan Coats of Indiana and Don Nickels of Oklahoma led the charge in getting it through the Senate. At every step, business leaders and members of the Clinton administration were complaining about how this law would damage our relationship with China.

We got the bill passed into law on the last day of the session — one small step for those who languish in faraway prisons for the crime of speaking their minds.

. . .

On November 10, 2009, I was in a congressional hearing room, listening to some of the most horrific testimony I'd ever heard. A Chinese woman testifying under the name of Wujian was telling us how she'd been forced to abort her baby after becoming illegally pregnant.

"The room was full of moms who had just gone through a forced abortion," Wujian testified. "Some moms were crying, some moms were mourning, some moms were screaming, and one mom was rolling on the floor with unbearable pain."

Finally, it was Wujian's turn. The doctor "put the big, long needle into the head of my baby in my womb." The procedure failed, so the doctor switched to a surgical abortion, using scissors and a vacuum pump. "I could hear the sound of the scissors cutting the body of my baby in my womb.…

"Eventually the journey in hell, the surgery, was finished, and one nurse showed me part of a bloody foot with her tweezers. Through my tears, the picture of the bloody foot was engraved into my eyes and into my heart, and so clearly I could see the five small bloody toes. Immediately the baby was thrown into a trash can."[10]

As co-chair of the Tom Lantos Human Rights Commission (named after the late Rep. Tom Lantos, a Holocaust survivor with a passionate concern for human rights), I'd heard some pretty bad stuff. But this description of China's one-child policy, as recalled by someone who'd endured it, sickened me.

Wujian, who'd found herself pregnant without a birth permit, ran away and hid in a shack in a remote area for months to avoid China's pregnancy police. As is typical when women do this, the authorities went after family members. They arrested her father and beat him, trying to force him to reveal his daughter's whereabouts. In the end, they broke into the shack where Wujian was hiding and dragged her off to a hospital.

The Chinese government denies that forced abortions occur in China, but Wujian's doctor told her that in her own county alone, more than ten thousand women had undergone them that year. Reggie Littlejohn, an attorney and founder of Women's Rights Without Frontiers,[11] has studied forced abortion in China. She documents the fact that China's one-child policy has led directly to at least ten other human rights violations.

For instance, it has led directly to "gendercide," the killing of female fetuses — and even babies — because of China's cultural preference for boys. There are now some thirty-five million more men than women in China, and the shortage of women "is a powerful, driving force behind trafficking in women and sexual slavery" across Asia, Littlejohn notes.[12] Forced abortion traumatizes women and is a major contributor to the fact that some five hundred Chinese women commit suicide every day, Littlejohn says.

The policy has also created a huge market in stolen children — seventy thousand a year — as parents who gave birth to a daughter but desire a son steal little boys. It's led to cases of "illegal children," as China calls them, in which parents give birth to a child without a birth permit. China's government punishes these children by refusing to provide them with an education or health care.

The one-child policy has also aided and abetted ethnic cleansing. According to the Uyghur Human Rights Project, China has employed "deception, pressure, and threats" to transfer hundreds of thousands of young Uyghur women out of East Turkistan into other provinces, where they are either forced to become brides to Chinese men or forced into prostitution or other forms of slave labor. Without women to marry, Uyghur men are unable to form families of their own.[13]

"No government policy anywhere in the world has caused more suffering to women and girls than China's One-Child Policy," Littlejohn maintains.[14]

The United States needs to pressure the Chinese government to end this destructive and unnecessary policy. And we must make certain, year after year, that none of the money we appropriate to the United Nations Population Fund is used for abortions in China.

The Chinese people, who suffer so much under their Communist leaders, are in my thoughts and in my heart almost every day. I think about that day I stood in Beijing Prison Number One, holding the socks made by Tiananmen Square inmates, and I wonder if America's golfers think about where their socks came from, and who made them, when they're enjoying a Saturday afternoon on the links.

America — and especially our churches — is failing the oppressed peoples of the world. So many passages in Scripture tell us to advocate on behalf of the oppressed and for those being persecuted. And yet our churches seldom advocate for individual freedom or for fellow Christians languishing in prison.

Political prisoners will tell you their life gets better when somebody advocates for them. The warden will give them more food because all these letters are coming in about Mr. X or Mr. Y. They don't quite understand why all of these letters are coming in from Congress or concerned citizens in the West, but it can sometimes put an umbrella of protection around them.

Jesus told us to visit those in prison and to pray for them. But how many American Christians do this? When the stories came out about Catholic and Protestant pastors being arrested and thrown in prison, why didn't President Clinton speak out? Why didn't President Bush speak out? And why doesn't President Obama speak out? They may have raised the issue privately, but it would have heartened prisoners of conscience if they had done so publically, as well.

. . .

In 2001 I learned of yet another atrocity perpetrated upon the Chinese people by their government — something so horrific, one is at first tempted to think it has to be one of those Internet myths that get spread around: China's practice of killing political and other prisoners in order to sell their organs to the wealthy and well-connected.

Here's how it works. Say you need a new kidney, and happen to have thirty thousand dollars in cash. You fly to China, and they put you up in a first-class hotel. They do a medical workup on you and determine your blood type. Then they go into the prisons and search for a healthy young man (or woman) who shares your blood type. They lead him into a field, force him to his knees, and shoot him in the back of the head. After throwing his body into an unmarked surgical van, they race to the local military hospital, where you're being prepped for transplant surgery. During the drive, doctors are cutting open the prisoner's body and taking out his kidneys because the sooner you transplant a kidney from a corpse, the greater the likelihood that it will take.

Not surprisingly, the number of prisoners who are executed

has gone up dramatically as the wealthy from around the globe — thousands every year — learn about this new source of healthy organs and purchase a ticket to Beijing.[15] According to human rights groups, the number of people being sentenced to death in China is higher than at any time since the 1950s; even the Chinese government acknowledges that executed prisoners supply the vast majority of organs for transplant.[16] The profits — which support China's military — are enormous.

Some of the organ donors are young people who leave home, find they cannot support themselves, and turn to petty crime, running afoul of one of the sixty-six crimes that result in the death penalty, including tax fraud.

The Chinese don't just sell kidneys. If you need a cornea, they'll sell you one of those, too. The only difference is, they shoot the prisoner in the heart instead of the head so as not to damage his eyes.

I've seen videotapes of the execution of prisoners for their organs, and they're pretty brutal. If you have the stomach for it, you can visit the website of the Laogai Research Foundation and see for yourself pictures of a young, female "organ donor" being executed.[17]

The Chinese government claims that taking organs from prisoners happens rarely and that its organ transplant program is a means of enabling condemned men to pay their final debt to society. They also claim that the organs are donated only with the consent of the person being executed or his family — something that in reality rarely happens, because the Chinese government doesn't ask the families for permission. Even in the case of natural death, there are strong cultural feelings against removing organs from the body.

Harry Wu exposed the transplant tourism trade in his book *Troublemaker*.[18] Traveling undercover to China with a journalist during the 1990s, Harry met with a doctor at First University Hospital at West China University of Medical Sciences in Chengdu, pretending he had an uncle who needed an immediate kidney transplant. No problem, the doctor said as the journalist secretly videotaped him; a kidney would be available within two or three weeks. Where did the organs come from? Brain-dead people. And who were these brain-dead people? The doctor claimed not to know and said he was not allowed to talk about it.

The BBC aired the resulting program later that year, but it has never been seen in its entirety by American viewers.

On July 10, 2001, I testified about China's organ harvesting before the Subcommittee on Trade of the House Ways and Means Hearing on Renewal of Normal Trade Relations with China. I told my colleagues that I had recently read the graphic testimony of Dr. Wang Guoqi, a Chinese skin and burn specialist who participated in the removal of organs and skin from executed prisoners in China.[19]

"Dr. Wang writes that his work 'required me to remove skin and corneas from the corpses of over one hundred executed prisoners, and, on a couple of occasion, victims of intentionally botched executions.' What kind of government skins alive and sells the organs of its own citizens?" I asked.

It's a question we should be pressing, hard, in the diplomatic and trade arenas.

* * *

The Chinese government keeps a wary eye on what I do, from a distance of seven thousand miles away. But when I arrived at my office one day in 2006, it became clear that their attentions had become dangerously up close and personal. My chief of staff, Dan Scandling, and my legislative director, Janet Shaffron, told me someone had hacked into four of my office computers. The names and addresses of every human rights activist, every political dissident, emails, casework — *everything* was wiped away. Even worse, whoever had done this — and I strongly suspected the Chinese government — now knew about every human rights case I ever worked on, a dangerous situation for every dissident who has ever come to me for help — or told me secrets.

I contacted the FBI to have them look into this, and they verified that the Chinese had indeed been behind the cyber attack. I subsequently learned that computers in the offices of sixteen other members, including Chris Smith, were similarly compromised. The cyber attacks permitted China to probe our computers to evaluate our system's defenses, and also to view and copy sensitive information about U.S. foreign policy and the work of Congress. When I began to voice objections to this cyber attack, officials of the House told me to keep quiet about it; nobody wanted to acknowledge it publicly. But after two years went by without any evidence that something was being done, I got fed up. I got up on the House floor and offered a privileged resolution in an effort to force Congress to deal with this matter.

"Madam Speaker," I said, "in August 2006, four of the computers in my personal office were compromised by an outside source.... On these computers was information about all of the casework I have done on behalf of political dissidents and human rights activists around the world.

"I am aware that computers in the offices of several other members were similarly compromised, as well as a major committee in the House — the Foreign Affairs Committee. It is logical to assume that critical and sensitive information about U.S. foreign policy and the work of Congress to help people who are suffering around the world was also open to view from these official computers.

"In a subsequent meeting with House Information Resources and FBI officials, it was revealed that the outside sources responsible for this attack came from within the People's Republic of China. These cyber attacks permitted the source to probe our computers to evaluate our system's defenses, and to view and copy information. My suspicion is that I was targeted by Chinese sources because of my long history of speaking out about China's abysmal human rights record.

"I have also learned that this threat exists not only here in the Capitol complex but also when members travel overseas. I have been told that, particularly in countries in which access to information is tightly controlled by the government, members are at risk of having their conversations and information recorded or stolen from their cell phones and BlackBerry devices.

"I am speaking out about the threat of cyber attacks from China and other countries on the entire U.S. government, including our military, because of my deep concern about maintaining the security and integrity of our government.

"The apparent complacency in both the private and public sectors toward this threat is astonishing. The potential for massive and coordinated cyber attacks against the United States is no longer a futuristic problem," I warned. "The oceans that surround us are no protection from sophisticated hackers, working at the speed of light on behalf of nation-states and mafias. We must prepare ourselves now and develop procedures for responding to this threat."

I wasn't exaggerating the danger. Computer systems control all critical infrastructures, and nearly all of these systems are linked together through the internet. This means that nearly all infrastructures in the United States are vulnerable to being attacked, hijacked, or destroyed by cyber means. Many analysts are skeptical that if a major cyber attack or incident were to occur, the U.S. government could adequately recover and reconstitute the internet.

According to a report from the Congressional Research Service, U.S. counterintelligence officials reportedly have stated that about 140 different foreign intelligence organizations regularly attempt to hack into the computer systems of U.S. government agencies and U.S. companies.[20]

A *Business Week* article states that U.S. government agencies reported almost thirteen thousand cyber security incidents in fiscal year 2007 — triple the number from just two years earlier.[21] Lieutenant General E. Croom, head of the Pentagon's Joint Task

Force for Global Network Operations, said that incursions on the military's networks in 2007 were up 55 percent from the previous year. On two occasions in 2004, it was reported that viruses were found in top-secret computer systems at the Army Space and Missile Defense Command.[22]

The May 31, 2008, cover story in the *National Journal*, titled "China's Cyber-Militia," reported that "electronic devices used by U.S. Commerce Secretary Carlos Gutierrez and his party during a December 2007 visit to China were invaded using spyware that could steal information."[23]

"Gutierrez was in China with a high-level delegation to discuss trade-related issues such as intellectual property rights, consumer product safety, and market access," I told my colleagues. "The Associated Press also reported on this breach.[24] Why did we learn about this in the press instead of from our own government officials? Did our government do anything about this attack?"

China — which denied the attacks and told us to stop being paranoid — in particular is actively engaged in espionage against the United States.[25] I read the U.S.-China Economic and Security Review Commission's 2007 Classified Report to the Congress and found the report's conclusions to be very alarming. It addresses Chinese activities in the areas of espionage, cyber warfare, and arms proliferation. I strongly urged my colleagues to read the report.

The Government Accountability Office reported in 2007 that no comprehensive strategy exists yet to coordinate improvements of computer security across the federal government and the private sector.[26] The apparent lack of a sense of national urgency to address this problem only gives those who would wish us harm an extra advantage.

Despite everything we read in the press, our intelligence, law enforcement, national security, and diplomatic corps remain hesitant to speak out about this problem. Perhaps they are afraid that talking about this problem will reveal our vulnerability, but our adversaries already know we are vulnerable. As a nation, we

A winning 1980 team. Ronald Reagan, George H. W. Bush, and me. I grabbed presidential candidate Ronald Reagan's coattails, held on tight, and he pulled me across the finish line.

Photo by National Republican Congressional Committee

My 1984 trip to Ethiopia opened my eyes to the suffering of hungry and oppressed people in the world. I am with refugees in the feeding camp at Alamata, Ethiopia.

Photo by World Vision, Bob Latta

The starving children I met broke my heart. Alamata feeding camp, Ethiopia.

I am on the left with (from left to right) a representative of Christian Solidarity International, Father Calciu, and Congressman Tony Hall and Congressman Chris Smith. We met with Father Calciu after his release from prison in Romania.

President Ronald Reagan (on right, back to the camera) with (clockwise) Senator Bill Armstrong, Senator Jesse Helms, National Security Advisor Colin Powell, a White House aide, and me. I met with President Reagan at the White House in 1987 to urge the administration to deny "Most Favored Nation" trade status for Ceaucescu's Romania.

Press conference at Washington's Dulles Airport when I brought Dana Pacepa to the U.S. from Romania to be reunited with her father. Dana is in the center with an interpreter on the right.

Photo by Charles White, staff of Congressman Frank Wol.

Congressman Chris Smith (background) and I met with many of the political prisoners held in Perm 35, a Soviet gulag in the Ural Mountains. Here we are meeting with Mikhail Kazachkov.

Photo by Richard Stephenson, files of Congressman Frank Wol.

As we drove up to the Perm prison camp we saw these prisoners in the yard outside their barracks.

Photo by Richard Stephenson, files of Congressman Frank Wol

With Congressman Chris Smith, representatives of Christian Solidarity International, and prison officials outside Beijing Prison Number 1, where we saw socks being made in the prison factory. Some of the prisoners had been student demonstrators at Tiananmen Square in 1989 and were still imprisoned two years later when we visited.

Congressman Chris Smith and I, along with other officials, met with Premier Li Peng in 1991, when I presented him with a list of political and religious prisoners. He ignored the list.

Photographer unknown, files of Congressman Frank Wol

At President Clinton's 1994 State of the Union Address, I stood to applaud when the president stated that he would oppose granting "Most Favored Nation" trading status to China, a position he later abandoned.

U.S. House of Representatives photograph

At a Tibetan monastery outside of Lhasa.

Photo by Charles White, staff of Congressman Frank Wolf

Meeting with His Holiness the Dalai Lama during his visit to the U.S. Capitol.

U.S. House of Representatives photograph

Crossing the stream to meet with John Garang at his camp in the bush in Southern Sudan.

Photo by Edward Newberry, staff of Congressman Frank Wolf

Meeting with John Garang in Southern Sudan.

Photo by Edward Newberry, staff of Congressman Frank Wolf

Meeting in Khartoum, Sudan, with Sadiq al-Mahdi, leader of the government of Sudan
at the time.

Photo by Edward Newberry, staff of Congressman Frank Wol

With a soldier of the Sudan People's Liberation Army in Southern Sudan, 2001.

Photo by Daniel Scandling, staff of Congressman Frank Wol

With children at a feeding camp in Southern Sudan.

Photo by Charles White, staff of Congressman Frank Wolf

President George W. Bush's signing ceremony for the Prison Rape Bill that I worked on with Senator Ted Kennedy and others. Left to right: Michael Horowitz (the Hudson Institute), John Kaneb (chairman of the Prison Rape Commission), Senator Orrin Hatch, Senator Ted Kennedy, Pat Nolan (Prison Fellowship), me, Congressman Bobby Scott, Senator Jeff Sessions, and former Attorney General John Ashcroft.

White House photograph

With some of our brave military personnel in Iraq.

Photo by Daniel Scandling, staff of Congressman Frank Wolf

A wedding celebration I attended in Al Kut, Iraq.

Photo by Daniel Scandling, staff of Congressman Frank Wolf

At the ziggurat built around 2100 BC at Ur, present day Nasiriyah, Iraq.

Photo by Daniel Scandling, staff of Congressman Frank Wolf

Congressman Chris Shays and me, meeting with sheiks in Iraq.

Photo by Daniel Scandling, staff of Congressman Frank Wol

Another photo of Congressman Chris Shays and me, meeting with sheiks in Iraq.

Visiting a boys' orphanage in Afghanistan.

Photo by Daniel Scandling, staff of Congressman Frank Wolf

Congressman Tony Hall, Congressman Joe Pitts, and me, meeting with Afghani
President Hamid Karzai.

Congressman Joe Pitts and me, meeting with President Pervez Musharraf of Pakistan

Photo by Daniel Scandling, staff of Congressman Frank Wolf

A burned-out village in Darfur, Sudan.

Photo by Daniel Scandling, staff of Congressman Frank Wolf

Janjaweed on camels on the outskirts of the Mornin refugee camp in Darfur, Sudan.

Photo by Daniel Scandling, staff of Congressman Frank Wolf

With refugee children at a camp in Darfur, Sudan.

Photo by Daniel Scandling, staff of Congressman Frank Wolf

must decide when we are going to start considering a threat to our national security a threat that we must confront and from which we must protect ourselves.

My resolution helped to spark national attention regarding the protection of our government, business, and infrastructure networks from foreign cyber attacks. The House finally began to deal with this problem with briefings for members and staff and by requiring password protection for BlackBerries. I made sure the computers in my own office were cleaned, and I have since implemented a strict computer security policy to protect my work and my constituents.

During the 110th Congress, I and several colleagues introduced the American Cybersecurity Commission Act to establish a bipartisan commission to study weaknesses in our nonclassified government, business, and national infrastructure computer networks. The commission would make recommendations to Congress on how to best protect these important networks.

The act died in the Oversight and Government Reform Committee, as I'm sure the Chinese were delighted to learn.

·   ·   ·

China's cyber attacks blew into the news again in early 2010, when journalists reported that the giant search engine company Google was threatening to pull out of China because the Chinese government had attacked Google's computer network, targeting its email service and corporate infrastructure. Google believed that "a primary goal of the attackers was accessing the Gmail accounts of Chinese human rights activists."[27]

According to the *Washington Post*, up to thirty-four other finance, media, and chemical companies were also targeted.[28] More ominously, the Chinese appeared to be seeking information on weapons systems from defense firms and "seeking companies' 'source code,' the most valuable form of intellectual property because it underlies the firms' computer applications."[29]

Google responded by announcing that it would no longer cooperate with China's demand that Google censor certain sites.[30] In March it began rerouting search queries to Google.com.hk in Hong Kong, which is not subject to Chinese laws. This act allowed Google to bypass Chinese regulators, which means mainland Chinese internet users could visit any site they wanted without being subject to censorship by Chinese authorities.

While I wish Google had never agreed to censor searches in the first place in exchange for getting its mitts on China's three hundred million web users, I was so pleased to see the company taking a stand now that I praised Google's actions on the floor of the House. "This principled stand on the part of Google will surely give hope to the millions of Chinese people who yearn for freedom and cry out for basic human rights," I noted.

In fact, Google was taking a stand reminiscent of that of the companies that pulled out of apartheid South Africa and fascist Germany.

In July of 2010, China renewed Google's license to operate for another year after Google agreed to stop automatically rerouting users to its Hong Kong site. Mainland Chinese Google users will now have to click twice in order to get to the Hong Kong site, something the Associated Press called a "small concession by Google ... as the company tries to uphold its anti-censorship principles while protecting its economic interests."[31]

Many people continue to assert that human rights in China will improve if we encourage trade with the Chinese. But contrary to what America's business community claims, China is not progressing; it is regressing. It is more violent, more repressive, and more resistant to democratic values than it was before we opened our ports to freely accept Chinese-made products.

In order for our soaring words about freedom, liberty, and democracy to ring true to the ears of countless dissidents languishing in prisons the world over, they cannot be applied only to pariah states like Burma and North Korea. They must also be applied consistently to places like China, Egypt, Vietnam, and Saudi Arabia, where these virtues are daily under assault. Yes, our national interests are complex. But it always befits a great nation to boldly stand with the forgotten, the oppressed, the silenced, and the imprisoned.

More than twenty years have passed since the crackdown at Tiananmen Square, and the Chinese government continues to ignore the peaceful protests of its own citizens for democratic reform. Many Tiananmen Square demonstrators, I am told, still languish in prison. China's leaders have made painstaking efforts to erase from history the events that took place on the Square on that June day in 1989. All references to the Tiananmen uprising are missing from student textbooks, and the topic is off-limits for the state-run media.

Nevertheless, the Chinese people continue to long for freedom from the oppressive rule of the Communist Party. In the winter of 2008, a group of Chinese democracy activists published Charter '08, a document modeled after Charter '77 issued by dissidents in Czechoslovakia. It calls on the Chinese government to implement democratic reforms and respect the dignity and fundamental human rights of all Chinese citizens. The Chinese government responded by systematically incarcerating and harassing the brave group of individuals who signed the charter.

China's chronically outraged leaders were upset again in October of 2010, when the Nobel Committee awarded the Peace Prize to one of the authors of Charter '08: Dr. Liu Xiaobo. Liu took an active role in the Tiananmen Square protests and was given an eleven-year sentence in 2009 for "incitement to the overthrow of the state power and socialist system and the people's democratic dictatorship."[32] In other words, he exercised his free speech rights, which China's constitution claims to protect.

As Nobel Committee chairman Thorbjorn Jagland noted in his award ceremony speech, "We regret that the Laureate is not present here today. He is in isolation in a prison in north-east China.

Nor can the Laureate's wife Lui Xia or his closest relatives be here with us. No medal or diploma will therefore be presented here today. This fact alone shows that the award was necessary and appropriate."[33]

On Constitution Day, 1987, President Ronald Reagan described the United States Constitution as "a covenant we have made not only with ourselves, but with all of mankind."[34] We have an obligation to keep that covenant.

I strongly believe that in my lifetime, we will see the collapse of the Chinese Communist Party, just as we witnessed the collapse of Soviet Communism. Christian leaders played a prominent role in the fall of the Soviet Empire, and it will be interesting to see what role China's growing Christian population will play in China's future. According to David Aikman, author of *Jesus in Beijing: How Christianity Is Transforming China and Changing the Global Balance of Power*, many of China's elites are embracing Christianity, including party members. Aikman predicts that one day, perhaps 20 percent to 30 percent of China's vast population will be following Christ.[35]

Just after the fall of the Soviet Union, I spoke at a meeting at a restaurant in my hometown. I was praising the actions of the Reagan administration, the B-1 bomber, and our cruise missiles as the reasons for the Communist fall. A woman in the back of the room raised her hand.

"No, Congressman," she said. "Those things may have helped. But the real reason for the fall is the fact that many people have prayed for years for this to happen."

As I recalled the many years, even from my youth, that I myself had prayed for Communism to be defeated in the Soviet Union, I knew that she was right.

CHAPTER SIX

SNEAKING INTO TIBET

Again I looked and saw all the oppression that was taking place under the sun: I saw the tears of the oppressed—and they have no comforter; power was on the side of their oppressors—and they have no comforter.

Ecclesiastes 4:1

TIBET IS A MYSTICAL COUNTRY on the roof of the world — one with a fascinating culture and gentle people. At night, when the skies are clear, more stars beam down than one can possibly imagine. Beneath this roof, nestled in the hills above Lhasa, is the Potala Palace, once the home of the Dalai Lama.

Tragically, the Dalai Lama — now living in exile in India — would scarcely recognize Tibet today. For more than five decades, China has relentlessly attempted to squeeze the life and soul out of his country, his culture, and his peace-loving followers. It's been estimated that in recent decades the Chinese have killed, starved, or tortured approximately one million Tibetans. At the same time, China has sent huge numbers of Chinese people to live in Tibet, which means the Chinese now outnumber Tibetans in their capital city of Lhasa.

For some time I had been hearing disturbing stories, from the International Campaign for Tibet, about China's brutal treatment of the Tibetan people: torture of Buddhist monks and nuns, and citizens being thrown in prison for the "crime" of possessing a picture of Tibet's beloved spiritual leader. Tibet is one of the most closed societies in the world; few outsiders venture there, and when they do, ever-present government agents and spy cameras guard against personal contact with the Tibetan people. I was told that Tibetans who dared to speak frankly to outsiders were dealt with swiftly and brutally.

In 1996 the House passed three measures concerning human rights — one specifically relating to Tibet. The following year I introduced the International Religious Freedom Act, which contains specific provisions relating to Tibetan Buddhism. The bill had over one hundred cosponsors, and the House passed it 375 to 41. The Senate later passed it by a unanimous vote, and President Clinton signed it into law in 1998. Clearly, many Americans cared deeply about the fate of the Tibetan people.

As valuable as this legislation was, I wanted to do more to help the Tibetan people. I wanted to see for myself what was going on in Tibet and do everything I could to help stop religious persecution and protect human rights there. But the Chinese had allowed few members of Congress to travel there since invading the country in 1958 and beginning their long and brutal occupation. Those who had been allowed to visit Tibet were closely shepherded at all times by a phalanx of Chinese police and the Chinese ambassador, who prevented their seeing anything the Chinese didn't want them to see or talking to anyone the Chinese didn't want them talking to.

I knew that the chances of Chinese leaders allowing me, in particular, to visit Tibet were almost nonexistent. The Chinese didn't like me, to put it mildly. I'd made too many speeches about their cruel repression of their own citizens. They had denied my last visa application to visit China itself, and, given my criticism of Chinese leaders over the years, I was probably the last congressman they would ever allow to set foot in Tibet. Their answer would be *"Bu shi zhe yang"* — which, loosely translated, means "Not on your life, Congressman Wolf."

I decided to go to Tibet anyway.

I knew I'd have to strategize carefully in order to fly into Tibet under China's radar screen, so to speak. In the spring of 1997 I obtained a "clean" passport — one that was marked "tourist" instead of "diplomat," so the Chinese wouldn't realize I was a congressman. The new passport also prevented them from knowing I'd once traveled to China.

Next, working with the International Campaign for Tibet, I applied again for a visa, this time through the Chinese consulate in Chicago. And this time I identified myself simply as an attorney (which I am) who was planning to travel through Tibet as a member of a trekking group.

The ruse worked. I got my visa.

Third, to enable me to speak with ordinary Tibetans, the International Campaign for Tibet put me in touch with Daja Meston,[1] a young man who spoke both English and Tibetan. Daja was the son of American "flower child" parents who had traveled to Nepal and India in the sixties in search of spiritual enlightenment when Daja was a toddler. His mother — who decided to become a Buddhist nun — left Daja in the care of a Tibetan family. With his mother's consent, this family turned him over to a Buddhist monastery, when he was six years old, to be ordained as a monk. Unhappy with his life there, Daja went to live in California when he was seventeen, and later attended Brandeis University. At the time of our trip, Daja was in his late twenties, was married to a lovely Tibetan woman named Phuni, and was active in the fight for Tibetan freedom. He agreed to be our guide and interpreter — a decision that the Chinese would later punish him for.[2]

On August 9, 1997, my chief of staff, Charlie White, and I flew to Bangkok, where we linked up with Daja. We flew on to Kathmandu, Nepal's capital city, spent a day or two there, and then headed for Lhasa. On the final leg of our flight, as we broke through the clouds and the snowcapped Himalayans came into view, I simultaneously mused on how incredibly beautiful the mountains were and on how much trouble I'd be in if the Chinese authorities found out I was coming. "If they learn what we're up to,"

I thought as we landed at Gongkar Airport, "we'll all be in deep yak *ri-ma*." I didn't have diplomatic immunity, and I had no idea what they'd do to me.

As I climbed down the stairs to the tarmac, carrying the duffel bag the trekking group had given me in order to maintain the facade, I immediately noticed three things: the thinness of the air, the brightness of the sun, and the ever-present, unsmiling Chinese security apparatus. We weren't allowed to leave the airport until they had interrogated us at length about the purpose of our trip and carefully checked our papers. If they didn't like your looks, Daja had warned me, they wouldn't hesitate to put you right back on the plane. Worse, they might take us away for more intense questioning.

After the three of us managed to get through security without anyone discovering who we really were, we took a bus into Lhasa, where we spent the night in a kind of family-run guesthouse. I was put into a room by myself, and Charlie and Daja were together in the room next door.

The next morning dawned bright, cool, and windy. After breakfasting on pita-like bread and butter tea, Charlie, Daja, and I managed to break away from the trekking group and set out for downtown Lhasa, cameras slung around our necks to make us look like ordinary tourists. Since Daja was Caucasian, with light brown hair and hazel eyes, the Chinese police, who loitered on every corner, paid little attention to him. They had no idea he could speak fluent Tibetan.

We wandered into the busy marketplace, filled with vendors in open-air stalls selling everything from butter and cheese to religious beads and statues to copper pots and dress fabrics. The streets were crowded with red-robed monks, brightly dressed Tibetan children, and Chinese men and women in dull Mao jackets. Prayer flags fluttered in the breeze from various walls, and we saw Tibetans waving prayer wheels in an effort to obtain better karma.

Because Daja had lived in Nepal among exiled Tibetans for most of his youth, he knew how to approach Tibetan strangers and strike up a conversation. I had been told before I left the States that when Tibetans realized we were Westerners, they would seek us out and tell us their stories. This would, I knew, be extremely dangerous for them. Informers were everywhere — disguised as shoppers, tourists, or even monks — and being caught talking to a Westerner could result in a prison sentence, or worse. Frankly, I was skeptical that anyone would approach us.

I was wrong. After starting a conversation with a passerby, Daja would whisper that we were from the United States. The passerby would pull Daja aside and tell him about a member of his or her family who had been sent to prison or tortured. Many, many Tibetans took advantage of an opportunity for a guarded word or two. Daja had to constantly translate for me, since I didn't know a word of Tibetan.

One young woman wept openly and — not knowing I was a congressman — said, "Please tell President Clinton to help us. When the United States speaks out and puts pressure on the Chinese government, things get better. Prisoners get released. But when the United States is silent, as it is now, things get worse." She told us that the Tibetan people listen to Radio Free Asia and Voice of America, so they know what's going on in the U.S. and how committed its leaders are to helping the Tibetan people. (Or not committed, as in the case of the Clinton administration, which decided to split trade and human rights, a fundamentally immoral policy, in my view — and, I suspect, in the view of six million Tibetans. The Obama administration followed this approach for its first two years; I was glad to hear Obama speak out at last on the rights of Tibetans during the visit of China's president Hu Jintao in January of 2011.[3] Better late than never.)

Our most significant encounter was with a young Tibetan taxi driver whom we flagged down. When he realized we were Americans — and that one of us was fluent in Tibetan — he could not contain himself. "Many are in jail, most for political reasons," he told us.

This man drove us to see the Sangyip prison complex — a squat, ugly series of buildings — and then the Gusta prison. Both were home to hundreds of political prisoners. The driver also took us to the Drapchi prison, which is off the beaten path in a slum area. Guards were everywhere. Seeing them, we warned our driver not to take any more chances.

"I don't care," he responded. "It's too important for you to see these places."

We continued on what had become a nightmarish tour. We passed the main security bureau, the intelligence headquarters, and then the prison bureau, each heavily guarded. All the while our driver was telling us about the monks and nuns and ordinary citizens who were regularly dragged away to prison and tortured.

Daja again warned our driver about the police watching us from a short distance away. "Don't worry about me," the driver said, and he continued to describe the torture to which political prisoners were subjected — torture that he might soon be enduring himself if he was caught talking to us. While Charlie discreetly took pictures, I listened in growing horror as Daja translated his words.

"Prisoners are routinely beaten and kicked and poked with electric sticks," he told us, referring to cattle prods with a huge electric charge. "Political prisoners are isolated from the general population and kept in unlighted and unheated areas with no sanitary or medical facilities and almost no food or water."

The Tibetan people have no rights, he added. "We must have permission from the Chinese to do everything. We can do nothing on our own."

Even though Tibetans view the Dalai Lama as both their spiritual and political leader, they are forbidden to demonstrate their love for him. Possessing a picture of His Holiness (as Tibetans call him) is an offense that could draw harsh punishment and imprisonment.

"The Chinese say we have freedom of religion, but that's a lie," the young Tibetan told us, anger spreading over his face. "We have no freedoms — not one. Everything is controlled by the Chinese, and we are repressed. We hear on Voice of America that the West supports Tibet. And yet you continue doing business with China. That doesn't help. Tibet feels left out and ignored.

"The Dalai Lama has asked America and Taiwan for help," he continued. "Please help the Dalai Lama because we are being ruined. The Chinese send Tibetan children to China for education and teach them Chinese ways. Tibet is disappearing little by little. The Tibetan language is being increasingly deemphasized in schools, and our culture is being wiped out."

All this from one man, spilling out a lifetime of agony, and the agony of his people. And yet despite everything, he had hope for the future. "I am not afraid. Someday the sun will again shine in Tibet," he said confidently.

That evening, as we dined on yak burgers at a Holiday Inn, I wanted nothing more than to discuss the desperate plight of the Tibetan people and how I hoped to relieve it when I returned home. But I didn't dare. Chinese spies might have been seated at nearby tables, listening to every word.

The next morning, we set out to visit the beautiful Jokhang Temple, the most sacred pilgrimage site in Tibet. As the smell of juniper incense floated out of the temple, Tibetans young and old prostrated themselves. We went up to the third floor, where, Daja told me, during demonstrations in 1987 the Chinese had thrown monks out the windows. Now, he said, the Chinese wanted to turn this sacred site into a museum, suggesting that Buddhism was a thing of the past.

As we were leaving the temple, Daja pointed to a humiliating sight: a monk was being forced by a Chinese official to have his picture taken with a giddy female tourist, as though he were an exhibit at the zoo.

We spent the third and fourth days of our tour visiting

numerous monasteries in Lhasa and out in the countryside. Daja arranged these visits, during which we could talk secretly with the monks in the bowels of the monasteries, where yak butter candles burned as we conversed.

Every monastery was tightly controlled by a small cadre of resident Chinese public security police. Imagine having your own local church or synagogue or mosque run by military police or the FBI. It's appalling.

Despite the ominous presence of the Chinese police, monks and nuns sought us out at every monastery. They told us the Chinese had cut deeply into the number of monks allowed at each monastery, despite Chinese claims to the contrary. Young monks under fifteen years of age were being turned out. Since the Cultural Revolution, many monasteries had been largely destroyed, and rebuilding had been painfully slow. The slightest resistance to Chinese interference was met by harsh punishment. We were told of nuns being tortured and of monks being imprisoned or subjected to "reeducation," which involves turning one's back on the Dalai Lama.

Imprisonment means years of brutal beatings and isolation from outside visitors. When monks are finally released from prison, the Chinese authorities expel them from their monastery and exile them to their home village. Many try to escape to India or Nepal, and some do not survive the attempt. They die of starvation or exposure on the mountains, or they are shot by the Chinese.

"All monks are afraid," one monk told us. "We are not allowed to practice our religion, and the people are suffering greatly."

Their greatest hope is to be free from China. "Please help us. Please help the Dalai Lama," another monk implored us.

The squalor was not limited to what the Chinese were inflicting on the Tibetan people. As I looked around me, I could see Tibetan culture disappearing almost before my eyes. Stores, hotels, bazaars, businesses, and tradesmen are largely Chinese. Storefront signs bear large Chinese writing beneath much smaller Tibetan inscriptions. Chinese karaoke bars and prostitutes line the streets of Lhasa. Young Tibetan men, denied a meaningful role in society, are idle and increasingly alcoholic.

Driving out from Lhasa, one encounters as many Chinese villagers, shepherds, farmers, construction workers, and travelers as Tibetan. I did not see a single newspaper or magazine available to the people. Television is extremely limited and tightly controlled by the Chinese. Outside press is forbidden.

The tragic truth is that the Chinese have dominated Tibet for so long that Lhasa is no longer truly a Tibetan city; it's a Chinese city. At the time of my visit, it was estimated that there were about 160,000 Chinese in Lhasa to 100,000 Tibetans, who have become second-class citizens in their own homeland.

Many Tibetan buildings have been demolished. In front of the Potala Palace, the Chinese had bulldozed every Tibetan structure and turned the property into a miniature Tiananmen Square with a Chinese fighter jet in the middle. It just enraged me.

I also saw severe environmental degradation. Tibet is rich in resources, including agriculture, timber, and minerals, but the Chinese are stripping huge areas and removing Tibet's natural treasures for use in China.

Everything I witnessed during my four days in Tibet both saddened me and made me determined to do everything I could to help the Tibetan people. One thing I want to see happen is groups such as Amnesty International, Human Rights Watch, and the International Red Cross being permitted to visit prisoners of conscience in Tibet. These groups could then tell the world about the terrible conditions political prisoners are forced to live under.

I also hope more Americans will take up the cause of Tibetan freedom. The problem is, Tibet is so far away. It's difficult to get into the country and too easy for people to simply say, "There's nothing I can do" — beyond, perhaps, slapping a Free Tibet bumper sticker on the back of their car.

·   ·   ·

On our final day in Tibet, we visited the Potala Palace, where the Dalai Lama once lived. Tibetans revere this palace, and many Americans, who have seen the film *Seven Years in Tibet*, know something of its history and of how the Dalai Lama, as a child, studied with Austrian mountaineer Heinrich Harrer in the 1940s before fleeing with his followers to Dharamsala, India, in 1959. We knew that some of the Chinese "tourists" at the Potala Palace were, in reality, members of the secret police, keeping an eye on tourists. The palace was beautiful and is one of the few Tibetan structures being maintained.

The next morning, Charlie and I packed our bags, said goodbye to our guesthouse hosts, and returned to the airport. We thanked Daja and said goodbye to him, as he was planning to stay another two weeks in Tibet. And then we ran up the steps onto the Chinese airplane with other tourists.

That's when things got interesting. After the flight to Kathmandu, we broke through the clouds, approached the airport — and then the plane just zoomed out of there. Nobody told us what was going on (this was Air China, not United Airlines). Presumably, the pilot didn't feel confident attempting to make the runway — it's a steep, dangerous descent, and there are many accidents at this airport. Or maybe the weather was too bad to attempt a landing. Or just possibly, I thought uneasily, they had somehow discovered that they had a U.S. congressman on board who'd been snooping around Tibet, asking nosy questions.

We flew back to Lhasa and landed. After being taken off the plane, we were put on a bus and driven to a hotel. The parents of a former staffer of mine were waiting to pick us up in Kathmandu, and of course they had no way of knowing we'd been taken back to Lhasa. So Charlie and I left the hotel and walked several miles back to the airport in search of a telephone. We wanted to let our friends know what had happened and where we were, but the airport was completely deserted and no telephone was available, so we walked back to the hotel. We were startled when we heard our hosts locking us into the hotel for the night. Fortunately, the facilities were in the rooms.

For twenty-four hours, nobody knew where we were. I hadn't told anybody in our government where I was going.

There was worse to come. At that altitude, if you overexert yourself, as I had done, hiking back and forth between the airport and the hotel, and don't drink enough water, you get sick. I'd run out of bottled water earlier in the day, and that night I learned the meaning of altitude sickness. Boy, was I sick. I'd been put into a room with a strange Chinese man, and the poor guy had to spend the whole night listening to me retching. I thought I was going to die.

At about 2:00 a.m., badly dehydrated, I got up and went down to the lobby. Charlie was sitting in the lobby, and he took pity on me, giving me some of his own precious bottled water.

Later that morning, they put us back on the bus and took us over to the airport. We all lined up to get back on the plane. For five days I'd managed to keep the Chinese from finding out who I really was, but now I began to wonder if my luck had run out. They checked my passport, looked at me suspiciously, and again checked my passport against their lists. Then they went into a back room and talked. They came out and stared hard at me and Charlie again. "Maybe," I thought, "we're not going to get out of this place."

Once more the security people opened my passport and checked it against their lists. I tried not to appear too interested in what they were doing; I was just another tourist who wanted to go home.

Finally, to my great relief, they let me back on the plane. We flew past Mount Everest, an amazing sight, and landed in Kathmandu. I flew on to India to visit my son, Bud, who worked there at the time, and then caught a flight back to the United States.

On the long journey home, I thought about all I had seen in a remote and beautiful country few Westerners will ever visit. Two pictures, both taken by Charlie, symbolize Tibet's past — and possibly its future. In the first picture, a little Tibetan boy in Western clothing (probably Chinese-made) is standing in the ruins of a colorful monastery, staring curiously out at us. Someone, at some time, had deliberately damaged the beautiful frescos on the outer walls.

The second picture shows a young man in a bright gold sweater. Daja had gone up to him and whispered a few words. The young man's face immediately lit up. He pulled out a picture of the Dalai Lama and proudly held it in front of him. Charlie shot the picture so that most of the young man's face didn't show, because you can go to prison for owning a picture of the Dalai Lama. But you can see his joyful smile.

When we arrived back in Washington, I held a press conference at the National Press Club, which was attended by dozens of print and television journalists. What I had to say blew the lid off the story of what was really going on in Tibet, minus the Chinese spin. The story instantly went global, partly because I was the first member of Congress (and probably the only political figure from any Western country) to visit Tibet without having Chinese handlers along to keep an eye on me, and partly because I exposed the oppression, the torture, and the sheer, everyday misery of life under the Chinese.

As flashbulbs went off and dozens of video cameras recorded every word, I repeated what a Buddhist monk had whispered to me at a decaying monastery: that the Chinese government was committing cultural genocide against the people of Tibet, systematically destroying the very fabric of Tibetan society.

Not surprisingly, the Chinese were incandescent with rage over the fact that I had "sneaked" into Tibet. Nor did they appreciate my comments about their vicious misrule there. They denounced me in at least eight different press releases, calling me a "slanderer" and dismissing my "sensational lies" about human rights abuses as a "malicious attack" and "claptrap." One somewhat ungrammatical press release began, "Republican representative Frank Wolf, who recently sneaked into Tibet in the disguise of a tourist, sensationally announced that during his four day tour of Tibet he saw that the region was being 'swallowed' by China through mass arrests and brutal repression and Tibetan language and culture were being destroyed."

In the aftermath of my trip, I learned that the Chinese had figured out where Charlie, Daja, and I had stayed in Lhasa and temporarily closed down the guesthouse (kicking out the unfortunate tourists who happened to take rooms there after we left) and that travel restrictions had been imposed on American visitors. Tourists returning from Tibet reported that armed troops in riot gear were now patrolling the streets of Lhasa and that security measures had been stepped up. According to Nepali travel agents, all American tourists had been ordered to leave Tibet by September 30.

One outcome was China's acknowledgement, for the first time, that it had built three prisons in Tibet, which held nearly two thousand prisoners, many of them prisoners of conscience, although that's not what the Chinese called them, of course. Unfortunately, prisons are a growth industry in Tibet.

· · ·

Since my trip to the roof of the world in 1997, there have been many changes in Tibet. I am told by those who work tirelessly on behalf of the Tibetan people that my trip contributed to the general awareness of their plight and to how Tibet figures in U.S.-China policy.

In 2002 the U.S. Congress adopted the Tibetan Policy Act, which puts into law some important policies and programs for which I have long advocated for Tibetans, including safeguarding their distinct identity and making it the policy of the United States to "support economic development, cultural preservation, health care, and education and environmental sustainability for Tibetans inside Tibet."

In 2007 the Congress — to the outrage of the Chinese — awarded the Dalai Lama the Congressional Gold Medal, which was presented by President George W. Bush. The Congress has also instituted a new program for sustainable economic development for Tibetans inside Tibet — a small but important step because it allows the U.S. to reach inside Tibet to provide assistance.

In the State Department there is now a special coordinator for the Tibetan issue, supported by a staff, who provides oversight to U.S. programming and has policy input on U.S.-Tibet policy. World leaders and heads of governments have in recent years given greater voice in support of Tibet. Since 1997, there have been eight rounds of face-to-face dialogue between Chinese government officials and envoys of the Dalai Lama.

Despite these hopeful signs, Tibet today remains inaccessible to those who go seeking information. In 2009 House Speaker Nancy Pelosi took a congressional delegation to Dharamsala, India, the seat of the exiled Tibetan government, to meet with the Dalai Lama. The delegation asked for, and was refused, permission to enter Tibet.

Chinese atrocities against the Tibetan people continue. Every year, between 2,500 and 3,500 Tibetans attempt the dangerous trip over the Himalayas to Nepal to escape brutal Chinese misrule. On September 30, 2006, Chinese border police shot at a group of some seventy Tibetans attempting to cross the Nangpa Pass into Nepal. Chinese soldiers fired repeatedly at the defenseless group, which included many children. At least one Buddhist nun was killed, and many others were injured and unable to continue the trip. Only forty-three members of the group arrived safely in Nepal. British climber Steve Lawes, who witnessed the shootings, said the Chinese later captured many of the Tibetan children.[4]

Many Tibetans continue to be arrested and imprisoned for expressing loyalty to the Dalai Lama. In the spring of 2008, a wave of demonstrations broke out, spreading across the Tibetan plateau. The demonstrations resulted in intense security crackdowns by the Chinese security apparatus. Some two hundred Tibetans were killed and, according to human rights groups, twelve hundred Tibetans remain unaccounted for.

The dialogue between the Chinese and Tibetan leaders is now at an impasse. In the wake of the demonstrations, the Chinese have adopted a hard-line anti – Dalai Lama campaign.

Every year, the U.S. State Department puts out a Country Report on human rights violations. The report contains a special section on China's continued brutal treatment of the Tibetan people in their own country. According to Students for a Free Tibet, there are some eight hundred known prisoners of conscience in Tibet today.

Will the Tibetan people ever again live in freedom? Will the Dalai Lama, whom I have met and greatly respect, ever be allowed to return to the country of his birth?

I believe these things will one day happen. If this sounds like a pipe dream, given China's long history of oppression, remember this: In 1985, if you had asked people, "Will the Berlin Wall ever come down?" or, "Will the Soviet Union ever collapse?" most of them would likely have said, "Maybe someday, but I probably won't live to see it happen." And yet the wall did come down just four years later in 1989. And the Soviet Union disintegrated just two years after that. I believe that with enough pressure from the West, the gentle people of Tibet will one day gain their independence.

But it will not happen without our help. Are we Americans willing to apply that pressure — risking, perhaps, billions of dollars in business profits if we anger China's leaders enough? In 1996 the Disney company faced this sort of dilemma when China threatened Disney's future access to China's huge markets unless it pulled out of distribution of *Kundun*, a beautifully shot film about the life of the Dalai Lama. Chinese officials claimed that the film "glorified" Tibet's spiritual leader and was thus "an interference in China's internal affairs."

To its everlasting credit, Disney did the right thing: it refused to sacrifice its own free speech rights in the face of China's bullying; the film was completed and distributed around the world. (According to *Time* magazine, Universal Pictures, which had earlier been offered the chance to distribute *Kundun*, turned it down "for fear of upsetting the Chinese.") China's threat to Disney turned out to be of the paper tiger variety: Disney still does plenty of business with China today.

How many other companies would be willing to act as the Disney company acted? And how many Americans would be willing to pay more for the clothes and toys and electronics we now import from China — consumer goods that would cost more if, as a result of intense diplomatic pressure on the Chinese over Tibet, we had to import them from another country?

It bothers me that Republicans and conservatives don't concern themselves very much with these issues. Ronald Reagan frequently articulated the values of human rights and religious freedom for all. As I mentioned earlier, he talked about our Constitution being a covenant with the entire world, and he backed up his talk with action: he stood firmly with Soviet dissidents and with the Jewish community in the Soviet Union. But when I attend freedom-for-Tibet events, most of the other participants are Democrats.

If we are tempted to dismiss from our minds the fate of the Tibetan people, we should remember how much God cares for those who suffer — and how much anger he expresses toward those responsible for the suffering. In the biblical book of Micah, we read, "Woe to those who plan iniquity, to those who plot evil on their beds!... They covet fields and seize them, and houses, and take them. They defraud people of their homes, they rob them of their inheritance" (Mic. 2:1 – 2).

In Tibet, China has stolen the inheritance of an entire people. We must do all we can to help them retrieve it,[5] remembering the words of our own Declaration of Independence: "We hold these truths to be self-evident, that all men are created equal ... [and] are endowed by their Creator with certain unalienable Rights." These words were not written just for the American people; they were intended to be a witness to the world regarding how people should organize their lives together.

These very words were spoken aloud in Tiananmen Square in 1989. They are remembered by freedom-seeking people around the globe — including the gentle people of Tibet.

CHAPTER SEVEN

THE ECUADORIAN JUNGLE

He is no fool who gives what he cannot keep to gain
what he cannot lose.

Jim Elliot

Snakes ... Why did it have to be snakes?

Indiana Jones in Raiders of the Lost Ark

IN 1956 THE WORLD WAS STUNNED when the bodies of five young missionaries — Jim Elliot, Pete Fleming, Ed McCully, Nate Saint, and Roger Youderian — were discovered floating in the Curaray River of southeastern Ecuador. In their effort to make meaningful contact with members of the Auca tribe (now called the Waodani), the young men had been speared to death. The missionaries had known the risk: the Waodani tribe was considered the most violent culture in the world, with a long history of killing all outsiders, as well as each other.

When the missionaries went missing, believers the world over prayed for their safety. And when their fate became known, the response was immediate and broad as other young men and women followed in their steps, led by Elisabeth Elliot, widow of Jim Elliot, and Rachel Saint, sister of Nate Saint. The result was that many of the Waodani decided to "follow God's trail." Within two years of the attack on the missionaries (and months after Elisabeth Elliot and Rachel Saint came to live among them), most of the tribal members had stopped their killing, and for the most part they have lived peacefully ever since.

I first heard about the five martyred missionaries from my daughter Virginia, who heard Elisabeth Elliot speak at Wheaton College. I later heard Elisabeth Elliot interviewed on the radio. Little did I know then that one day I would travel to the vast Amazon jungle with the son of missionary Nate Saint to visit the very spot where his father and his friends had died attempting to bring the good news of the gospel to a Stone Age tribe.

Steve Saint arrived at my office unannounced one day in October of 1998. With him were two Waodani warriors, including a man he now considered a beloved family member: "Grandfather Mincaye," the tribesman who had speared his father to death. I was out that day, and Jennifer, a member of my staff, was warily trying to figure out who these strangers were — especially the one with huge holes in his ears who wore a feather headdress and a wild pig tooth necklace over his Western clothing. Steve was doing his best to explain when suddenly Jennifer's face lit up.

"Oh, I know who you are!" she exclaimed. Jennifer told them she had read Elisabeth Elliot's book *Through Gates of Splendor*,[1] which describes the events before and after the missionary killings.

The warriors could not understand Jennifer, but they could see from the expression on her face and the tone of her voice that her attitude toward them had changed. Pleased, Mincaye invited Jennifer, through Steve, to visit him in his village.

Steve had heard of my commitment to human rights from Congressman Tom Lantos and had brought his tribal friends to me to help with some of the problems the Waodani God-followers were experiencing as they attempted to interact with the outside world — a world that was endangering the survival of both their culture and their church.

The tribe was having difficulties with the Ecuadorian government, which claimed authority over them but was neglecting (or was unable) to offer the same services it offered to other Ecuadorians. The Waodani God-followers wanted my help with obtaining formal recognition as a legal entity with the government. Steve also wanted the Ecuadorian government to release his organization, the Indigenous People's Technology and Education Center (I-TEC) to provide services for the Waodani that the government was neglecting to provide.[2]

The Ecuadorian government was not the tribe's only problem. Oil companies were pressuring the Waodani way of life in their efforts to produce oil in large tracts of Waodani land. Finally, there was tension between the Waodani and nearby tribes, and stress related to the fact that some of the younger Waodani wanted to live like outsiders. Tragically, some of these young people had succumbed to alcoholism and other "outsider" vices.

Steve had spent most of his childhood in Ecuador before returning to the United States to attend college and become a businessman. In 1994 he traveled to Ecuador for the funeral of his aunt Rachel, who had spent some forty years bringing, and living out, the gospel to the Waodani people. Had it not been for her work, and that of other missionaries, the Waodani might very well no longer be an identifiable tribe. In the 1950s, before the missionaries' arrival, six of every ten Waodani were speared to death or killed with a machete wielded by a fellow tribesman.

When Steve was attending his aunt's funeral, the Waodani elders asked him to come live with them to help protect their interests from outsiders, to teach them how to help themselves, and to assist them in obtaining medical care. Steve, his wife, and their four children agreed that this was where God was leading the family, and they subsequently spent eighteen months living and working among the Waodani, trying to help them become more independent of outsiders. Building the things they needed, such as an airstrip and their own church building, gave the Waodani a sense of ownership they did not enjoy when outsiders — however well-meaning — built these things on their behalf.

After conferring with Steve, I decided to travel to Ecuador to see the problems close-up and see what we could do to help. I invited my good friend Dick Foth to come along with me.[3] As usual with my overseas trips, I packed my granola bars and juice boxes to avoid becoming sick.

We flew to Quito, Ecuador's capital, on January 9, 1999, past snowcapped volcanoes, the glacier-covered peaks of the Andes mountain range, and the immense Amazon rain forest, which covers more than two million square miles.

We were met by Peter Harding, a political officer at our embassy there, and Alicia Duran-Ballen, the daughter of a former president of Ecuador, who acted as our hostess and interpreter in Quito. We spent the night at Alicia's, and the next morning she took us back to the airport, where a pilot with Missionary Aviation Fellowship flew us in a tiny plane to the miniscule airstrip at Nemompade, a Waodani village in the Amazon Basin 160 miles southeast of Quito. To have hiked into this area, or traveled by boat, would have taken many days. The village consisted of a few huts and was located just a few miles from "Palm Beach," the site on the Curaray River where Steve Saint's father and his friends were killed.

Steve, who had flown back earlier, met us there. With him were about a dozen students from Wheaton Academy in Chicago, whose legs, I noticed, were covered with chigger bites. As we began talking, we could see Waodani beginning to come out of the jungle. They were wearing T-shirts and shorts, and one guy was wearing a Philadelphia Phillies baseball cap. Steve showed us where his aunt Rachel was buried in Tonampade, less than a mile from where her beloved brother had been killed.

Steve wanted us to see the little traditional village the Waodani people had built for visitors who wanted to learn how the tribe lived, without intruding on their lives. We trekked about a mile through the jungle with Steve and the Waodani, but it took about an hour because it was so dark and you spend so much time climbing over things and watching out for snakes — especially the anaconda, which are up to twenty-six feet in length, have up to one hundred extremely sharp teeth, and can weigh over two hundred pounds. I had no desire to meet one.

With every step I took, I wondered if I was going to come across a snake. Twice we saw thousands of large ants crawling in a line over a tree stump into a hole. It was a very long, very hot, very wet hike.

That evening, sitting around a campfire, we were served roasted wild pig, papaya, and manioc root, a tuberlike sweet potato that grows rapidly there in the jungle because of the humidity. I ate my usual granola bars, which stirred the curiosity of the Waodani, who couldn't believe I was turning down roasted pig. "So this man — he doesn't eat this?" they asked, puzzled. After that I reluctantly tried what everyone else was eating and drinking, remembering previous illnesses I'd endured while traveling in Africa and Central America. I just didn't have an appetite for some of the other things they were eating, such as roasted monkey meat.

The sun goes down quickly on the equator, and after the darkness arrived, the Waodani lit a single candle and placed it in a mound of dirt. Then we all sat around the fire together: Waodani Indians, a bunch of American high school students, Steve Saint, a businessman, and a U.S. congressman.

Steve suggested to one of the Waodani elders that he give a little teaching, so one of the warriors stood up and taught something out of the gospel of John. And then we prayed together.

The first Waodani prayer was that the snakes would not bite us and that we would not get mosquito fever (malaria). *That* really caught my attention. I learned that they pray regularly for protection against snakes, for almost everybody who has grown up in the tribe has been bitten by a poisonous snake. Women are usually bitten on the hand because they are working down low with machetes, harvesting crops, when they startle the snakes. Men usually get bitten in the lower leg when they're hunting, because they're looking up at the trees.

Almost all venomous snakes in the Amazon are what they call bleeders — their venom prevents your blood from clotting, so you begin to bleed from your gums and your eyes. The poison also breaks down muscles and tendons, which means a snake bite can cripple someone for the rest of his life. We encountered one man who'd been bitten and had to walk on the side of his foot. Steve got him boots that laced up to hold his ankle in place so he could walk normally.

After the prayers, Steve whispered to Dick, "Why don't we have Communion?" Dick asked him what the elements were, and they came up with a muffin they'd baked over the open fire, and some orange Tang in a tin cup. So we passed that around for everyone, and we had Communion.

And then Steve said, "Why don't we sing a song?" Dick asked if they knew "Amazing Grace," and we all stood and held hands on the bank of the Curaray River, just a short distance from where Steve's father and his friends had died, and sang that old hymn. Wouldn't John Newton have been surprised at this scene in a country he never knew and people he could never imagine, singing his hymn in the Amazon jungle? We then sang, "I Have Decided to Follow Jesus" in English, Spanish, and two tribal languages — Wao-Tededo and Shuar.

After we sang, we all hugged one another and then went to sleep in woven hammocks, covered with wool blankets because it gets pretty cold at night. Waking up to go to the bathroom in the pitch-black darkness meant walking down a path in the jungle with only a small flashlight. My thoughts were constantly on snakes.

The next morning, we spent more time with the Waodani, observing their culture and how they lived, learning how they prepared meals, and talking with them about their concerns for the future. Steve also took us to the nearby village where he and his wife, Ginny, had lived for eighteen months and where the Waodani had built a small medical and dental clinic, which they ran themselves. Then we traveled by dugout canoe to see where the women planted manioc roots. They let us try to help them harvest the crop, hacking away with machetes. We weren't very good at it.

To cool off, we went bathing in the same river where the bodies of the missionaries had been found. The river contained flesh-eating piranha fish, which, I was happy to learn, don't attack you unless you're bleeding.

The Waodani hunt with nine-foot-long blowguns, so later they showed us how they made poison for their darts by distilling poison from a vine and then dipping the tip of the darts into it. Then they invited us to go hunting with them.

I didn't want to go. Despite all the plunging through the bush we'd already done, we'd managed to keep from being bitten. There weren't really that many poisonous snakes, but we imagined them everywhere. But the Waodani kept saying, "Come with us." So off we went: Dick, me, a Waodani named Monga, and one or two other Indians.

The lead guy had a machete, and he would hack away the brush, and the guy behind him had a blowgun. I think they got a couple of birds. The poison doesn't kill them; it paralyzes them, and then they fall out of the tree.

Dick and I practiced shooting the blowguns with our own mouths, which is a bit tricky. As we hiked through the jungle, the Indians would be looking up for birds and monkeys. When they saw something in a tree, they blew on the gun — *pfft*! Down came a little bird the size of a sparrow, which they gave to me. I held it, then tossed it away, which upset the Indians because they'd planned to eat it.

In the back of my mind, of course, always were the snakes. We were hiking through low brush and growth, and we could hardly see the sun, never mind snakes. And then Dick, who has a somewhat twisted sense of humor, crept up behind me and ran a stick along the back of my neck. I almost jumped out of my skin, took off running, tripped over a vine, and fell face-first into the mud. The Waodani doubled over with laughter.

· · ·

Our trip to Ecuador taught us that the challenges facing the Waodani people have to do with learning to live interactively with an encroaching high-tech civilization while maintaining their own unique identity. Historically, the Waodani have been a highly egalitarian tribe, without much vertical social order. That reality has been moderated somewhat in the last fifty years to include community elders who help guide life in the tribe. The Waodani have also become less nomadic in recent years.

Steve Saint's approach has been to understand that the people in this region will continue to interact more and more with interests outside their local environment. The question is not when will this process happen but with whom, and can they survive it as a tribal group? The Waodani believe they need to learn to be both independent and interdependent within the national culture, avoiding the pitfalls of becoming welfare recipients. To assist them in that journey, Steve invites small groups — such as the Wheaton Academy students — to visit for a few days in the rain forest and interact with the Waodani people at the little simulated traditional village the Waodani had built. Each visitor pays a fee, and the profits are put into a bank account in the nearest large town, in the names of the village elders. In that way, the Indians are creating a productive economy that they can control.

The medical and dental clinics help the Waodani improve their health without the need to travel outside their territory. A simple but ingenious form of dentistry, involving a foot pump, has been taught to members of the tribe, allowing them to fill teeth decayed from eating large amounts of manioc root, a starch that readily converts to sugar. A tribal member has been taught to pilot a small aircraft so that they do not have to wait for outsiders to respond in an emergency. Every effort is being made to help the Waodani become self-sufficient on their own terms and with their own resources, which is important for both cultural and religious reasons.

As Steve notes, "One of the great barriers that has prevented indigenous churches from growing to maturity is their continuing dependence on the welfare of outsiders. A native church that relies on the leadership, technology, and financial support of foreign missionaries rarely can stand on its own when that support is withdrawn. We are convinced from the Scriptures, however, that the goal of the Great Commission is to establish churches that are self-supporting, self-governing, and self-propagating."

. . .

This is why Steve founded I-TEC: to train and equip indigenous Christians to meet their people's physical and spiritual needs. For instance, I-TEC sent portable, solar-powered radio transmitters to Amazon tribes, which allows these God-followers to share the gospel with neighboring villages. They've also taught indigenous church leaders to use a computer so they can draft their own governing documents for their church.

Sending money and other forms of aid to the global poor may make Americans feel good. But recent research has confirmed that helping people help themselves — not just sending aid — is the best approach. In her book *Dead Aid*,[4] economist Dambisa Moyo says the tsunami of foreign aid money sent to Africa over the decades has done more harm than good. Aid money unattached to demands for positive change fosters corruption; much of the money ends up in the Swiss bank accounts of the despots who run African nations. No matter which country aid money is sent to, it promotes dependence and harms efforts of the poor to work their way out of poverty. For example, when the West sends mosquito nets to Africa, it destroys the market for Africans who are attempting to support themselves by making and selling nets. The real answer, Moyo writes, is investment — something that has already helped grow the economies of countries such as Brazil and Argentina.[5] Economist Muhammad Yunnus, who originated the microloan concept, agrees with this approach.[6]

Contact with outsiders has changed the Waodani people's understanding of themselves. While they typically have plenty of food and adequate shelter, seeing the many "things" outsiders own has given them a perception that they are poor, Steve notes.

* * *

On our last day, as we began the flight out of the jungle, Steve said, "Why don't I fly you over Palm Beach?" This was the name the five missionaries had given the area of the beach where they set up camp in the expectation of interacting with the nearby Waodani in the mid-1950s. Steve brought us about one hundred feet above the beach, pulled back on the motor, and banked the plane so we could look down at the site. He pointed out the spit where the five missionaries had built their tree house — their sleeping quarters for the brief time they lived there — in an old ironwood tree. The tribesmen had cut the tree down in 1956 in order to obtain any nails that had been used in the tree house's construction. What was left of the tree now lay partially in the river, marking the spot of the martyrdom of five faithful servants of Christ. It was forty-three years, almost to the day, since their deaths, and a very moving moment. Then Steve gunned the plane's motor and pulled up into the clouds.

* * *

We flew to Shell Mera, the main jumping-off place, where Shell Oil had once had their headquarters. We caught a bus back to Quito, where we were scheduled to meet with the president of Ecuador, Jamil Mahuad, who was joined by U.S. ambassador Leslie Alexander. The juxtaposition of sharing roast pig with a Stone Age tribe one day and sipping coffee with the president of Ecuador the next was jarring.

"What are you doing in Ecuador?" the president asked us. He was surprised when I said we were meeting with the Waodani. He told us that 99 percent of Ecuador's own citizens had never glimpsed this tribe. We had a pleasant conversation, and at one point, knowing he was a faithful Catholic, I asked him, "Mr. President, who do you have praying for you?"

"My mother goes to Mass, and she prays for me," he replied.

"But who in the government upholds you with all this responsibility?" I asked. "At home in Congress, we have a group of people from different parties and backgrounds that meets together to study the Bible and pray for one another. Without them, I couldn't do my job."

I invited President Mahuad to come to the U.S. to attend the National Prayer Breakfast, which was to take place in about three weeks.

"I can't," he said. "I'm going to be in Washington meeting with the president of Peru." For reasons of protocol, if the Peruvian president wasn't invited to the breakfast, he said, he couldn't attend, either. So I arranged for both of them to get an invitation, and they both came. The presence of these two leaders, whose countries had engaged in numerous border disputes over the years, did not go unnoticed. In his Prayer Breakfast speech, President Clinton spoke about how much easier it is to talk about peace than to actually make peace, and he asked for prayer "for the agreement made by the leaders of Ecuador and Peru."[7]

Did my trip make any difference? I did intervene with the Ecuadorian government on behalf of the Waodani God-followers for formal recognition as a legal entity. A delegation of Waodani also traveled to Quito to lobby their government, and I'm happy to say that between us, we were able to convince Ecuador to give the recognition the Waodani desired.

My trip made a difference in other ways, as well — some I did not anticipate. Steve Saint puts it this way: "The biggest thing Congressman Wolf did for us is that he showed respect for the Waodani people by coming to visit them. Whenever anyone wanted him to take part in something, he'd say, 'No, I'm a guest of the Waodani — you need to talk with Steve Saint.' That gave us standing in the missionary community, with the Ecuadorian government, and the U.S. Embassy. Before he came, I had tried for three months to open a bank account in the name of the Waodani church, but the bank would just not open an account for Indians. But when a United States congressman showed respect for these people, boom, the bank opened an account right then and there.

"Congressman Wolf also told us that the United Nations puts limitations on what countries can and cannot do. Countries cannot practice genocide, and they cannot keep outside groups from offering needed services. If they claim authority over a people, they cannot then refuse to give them services they give to other citizens.

"There have been times when I have called his office to help get a visa for someone from the tribe to come to the U.S. for meetings, or who were doing publicity for the movie [*End of the Spear*, about the killings of the five missionaries and the aftermath].[8] His office has always been responsive. We don't have to worry if they will remember who we are. We feel like we're family. When you've been an invisible person, you can't imagine what it's like for someone to make you visible. Congressman Wolf made the Waodani people visible to people to whom they just didn't exist."

I brought a machete back from Ecuador, a gift from Steve. It reminds me of my visit with a once-deadly tribe, some of whom, thanks to the willing sacrifice of a handful of missionaries, have become faithful God-followers.

I often think of the Waodani. But I don't miss the snakes.

CHAPTER EIGHT

SUDAN: EVIL UNDER THE SUN

I have seen another evil under the sun, and it weighs heavily on mankind.

Ecclesiastes 6:1

THE MARKETPLACE WAS PACKED the day the bombs rained down; the townspeople had no place to hide. Knowing they were the targets, they scooped up their children and began to run.

Within minutes nineteen lay dead, and fifty-two were wounded.

Three months later I was standing in that very spot, in the Southern Sudan town of Yei, viewing the aftermath of that terror. Before me a slender young boy described how his left arm had been blown off when Sudanese pilots from Northern Sudan rolled fourteen bombs out the back of a Soviet-made Antonov bomber in the middle of a quiet afternoon. My eyes slid down to his legs, badly scarred by shrapnel injuries.

Looking beyond the boy, I saw the crude bomb shelter where several young children had suffocated that terrible November day in 2000. Norwegian People's Aid had filmed the scene just minutes after the attack. It showed women and children lying in their own blood, their limbs blown off. Others were screaming amid the carnage, running for shelter that did not exist.

I had seen much to shock me in my travels around the world, but little could match what had happened here, where innocents

153

far from the front lines had been deliberately slaughtered. Truly, this was "evil under the sun," as the author of Ecclesiastes put it.

Few Americans knew in 1983 that Sudan's Khartoum (Islamic) government was waging a savage war against the Christian and animist people of the South—people who were fighting for self-determination and religious freedom. This war, as well as the famine and disease that accompanied it, had killed more than two million people, mostly civilians—women and children. Millions more had been displaced.

Tragically, more people have been killed in Sudan during the last three decades than in Kosovo, Bosnia, Somalia, and Rwanda—yes, Rwanda—combined. Death, famine, and disease continually stalked them—and still stalk them today.

Sudan achieved independence from the British in 1956, and since then the country has been at war with itself about 80 percent of the time. The northern part of the country is Arab and Islamic in orientation, and the southern part is African and made up of Christians, adherents of traditional religions, and some Muslims.

I first visited Sudan in January of 1989. I had heard alarming reports about the growing conflict between the Muslim North and the Christian/animist South and wanted to see for myself what was going on and meet with people from both sides.

I flew to Khartoum with Ed Newberry, who was then my press secretary. We spent a couple of days there meeting with government leaders, including Prime Minister Sadiq Al-Madhi, who was deposed a few months later by Hassan Al-Turabi, then the powerful head of the National Islamic Front. Al-Madhi was from a powerful family and was a descendant of the Mahdi who had killed England's famed General Charles Gordon, who led military campaigns in North Africa. He was a tall man in flowing white robes, with a white turban around his head. He was very friendly and talked about the conditions in both the North and South while the U.S. ambassador to Sudan and I listened.

I also met with Al-Turabi, an intelligent, well-educated man, also clad in flowing white robes and a turban, who personally invited Osama Bin Laden to live in Sudan. Bin Laden accepted the invitation and based his al-Qaeda operations there for five years in the early 1990s.

We then flew to Nairobi, Kenya, intending to go from there to South Sudan, which was at that time controlled by the Sudanese People's Liberation Army (SPLA) rebels. The U.S. Embassy in Kenya did not approve of our visit and refused to help us travel to Southern Sudan.

"No, don't go," they warned. "It's too dangerous."

Egil Hagen, a former Norwegian Special Forces guy who regularly flew into the South on a plane chartered by Norwegian People's Aid, heard I wanted to go there.

"You want a ride in our plane?" he asked. "Meet us at Wilson Field at four o'clock tomorrow morning. We'll get you in."

At four a.m. the next morning, we met at Wilson Field, which many will remember if they saw the film *Out of Africa*. I watched them load medical supplies onto the small plane, and then we took off and flew north for several hours, from Kenya into Southern Sudan. We had no visas, as the Khartoum government had lost control in the South, so we went in sort of illegally.

After we landed, a Land Rover took us to Kapoeta to meet with the rebel leaders, the NGOs working there, and a Catholic priest, who told us how bad things had been there during the civil war.

While we were there, we saw a gunfight over rustlers trying to steal somebody's cattle. It was like something out of America's Wild West. Cattle in South Sudan are a valuable property. In the end, in a blaze of bullets, the good guys scared the cattle thieves off.

By the time we returned home, having spoken to leaders on both sides, we had a pretty good idea what was going on. The Northern leaders wanted to quell the rebellion and subdue the South; the South desired freedom and perhaps independence, wanting Khartoum to stop trying to drive their families off the land and steal the oil that lay beneath.

Back in the early and mid-1980s, what was going on in Southern Sudan still wasn't on anybody's radar screen. There was no constituency in the U.S. working on this issue. Roger Winter, then-director of the U.S. Committee for Refugees, along with people working with Norwegian People's Aid, decided it was time to create one by inviting journalists and members of Congress to visit Sudan.

By the late 1980s I had something of a reputation as somebody who was concerned about human rights and might be interested in traveling to Sudan a second time in the spring of 1989 — just three months after my first visit — to look into the problems there in greater depth. Roger called me up. Was I interested in going?

I was. So was Senator Gordon Humphrey, a Republican from New Hampshire, Rep. Gary Ackerman from New York City, and Dr. Bob Arnot, the medical correspondent for CBS at that time. Bob is also a pilot and is fearless about making dangerous trips like the one we were about to embark on.

In April of 1989 we flew out of Westchester County, New York, to Nairobi in a private plane chartered by the NGO AmeriCares. We then caught another plane to Lokichogio in the northern part of Kenya, and then headed into South Sudan itself.

In those days, the whole of the South was a war zone, and visitors like us had to be escorted by an SPLA military unit. We were planning to meet with the leader of the rebels — Dr. John Garang, who had earned several degrees at American schools, including a PhD in economics from Iowa State University. Garang had spent many years in the Sudanese military but had pulled out in 1983 and joined the rebels to fight the Islamification of South Sudan and military rule — a rule that included the bombing of Southern villages, the raping of women, and children being taken away as slaves and soldiers.

We arrived in Kapoeta, where the land was bare, dotted with a few scrubby bushes. It was extremely hot and dry. We were expecting to meet Garang, but instead the SPLA told us to climb aboard a Jeep with broken seats and no springs or suspension system.

"What's going on?" I asked.

It turned out that Garang was no longer in the Kapoeta area; he was out in Torit, a drive of several hours, where the rebels had just taken the town. "You are going to have to get in this Jeep and drive," they said.

I didn't have very much food with me, but I had enough for the day, so I said okay, fine. We set out for Torit to find Garang.

In those days, the SPLA had few guns and little equipment. There were also no paved roads there, just track beds that everyone followed, made from the vehicles. It was a long, hot, bumpy trip. Khartoum soldiers had planted land mines along the track beds, and the drivers were constantly swerving to avoid places they thought mines could be. All along the way, we passed vehicles that had been blown up and abandoned.

Finally, we arrived at the place John Garang was supposed to be, but he wasn't there, either.

"Where did he go?" I asked. Having gone that far, we had little choice but to keep going.

At one point we came to a crossroads village called Lanya in the middle of nowhere. All of a sudden, people came running out with spears and AK-47s, hollering and shouting and dancing and shooting their guns in the air, celebrating the fact that they had just taken the village from Northern fighters. And then we discovered that the plan was for us to partake of some not-so-fast food.

The rebels got their hands on a cow and slit its throat in front of us with a huge knife. As it lay there bleeding into the dirt, custom dictated that everyone, including the guests, jump over the cow. It's an honor ceremony, and they were honoring us by doing that. We declined to jump, and I also declined to eat it after they had cut it up, roasted it, and served it to us, sans eating utensils — although Roger did and told me it was delicious.

I'd been so sick in some of the other places I'd traveled, eating the local food, I just didn't want to take a chance. I watched the preparations — everyone was ripping raw meat apart and throwing it on the fire — but after a while I excused myself, went back to a hut, and pulled out a granola bar.

At one point John Garang came out and stepped over the cow, so we finally got to see him. But almost immediately he disappeared, before we had a chance to talk with him.

Later, after we'd eaten, it was pleasant sitting around the fire, watching the sun set in this remote area, and listening to the men entertain themselves by telling stories.

When we began the day, we had thought our group was returning to Nairobi that night, and we'd brought no overnight supplies. Accommodations didn't exist; there was no War Zone Westin Inn in which to lay our weary heads — unless you counted sleeping in an abandoned hut on grubby pieces of old mattresses with blankets crusted over with filth, possibly dried blood. We got little sleep as it poured all night long on the tin roof. Guards were outside the hut, trying to sleep under tarps in the driving rain.

The next morning, first thing after I woke up, I had just one question on my mind: "Where is John Garang?" The whole point of the trip was to talk with him, and he kept disappearing on us. When I asked, the guides said, "He's not here. You have to go into the bush to see him, to Torit."

I was starting to get mad, frankly. "This is ridiculous," I complained to Roger. "I don't want to talk to the guy anymore. He was right here in the village last night, and now we have to go hunting for him. Let's go back to Nairobi."

But we couldn't go back. We were in the middle of nowhere, under the control of the SPLA. Besides, Roger didn't want to turn back. So we started driving through the mud toward Torit. We went as far as we could, and then we got out to walk the rest of the way. But when we came to the edge of a stream, I recalled something my doctor had told me before I left for Sudan: "Whatever you do," he warned, "don't touch the water." He didn't just mean don't drink it; he meant don't let it *touch* me, because of the microbes that can enter the body through the skin.

"I am not going to go through that stream," I announced — and I meant it. The rest of the crew was trying to figure out how they were going to get us together with Dr. Garang if I wouldn't budge. Roger noticed an old dugout canoe-like thing down the river, which we tried to snag, but it turned out to be waterlogged. Next they dragged some logs down to where we were standing and laid them side by side so that we could jump from log to log to log. I started to cross, but on about the third log I slipped off, fell into the water, and ended up having to wade across after all. I was really angry at John Garang at that point for putting me through all this.

After crossing the stream, we climbed a hill to where Garang was waiting for us, sitting in a chair under a thatch-covered hut with a big boom box beside him. He laughed when I told him about my struggle to cross the river.

Dr. John, as everyone called him, turned out to be a most personable guy. He was at that time almost forty, had a bit of a belly, and loved to laugh. He was a real straight shooter.

Dr. John spent the next hour or two giving us his perspective on the conflict and on the terrible conditions in which his people had to live. We left immediately afterward, heading back to Lokichogio and Nairobi. Roger Winter, who is still involved with several NGOs and travels frequently to Sudan, recalls of that trip, my second to Sudan: "Frank and Garang became fast friends. At the time of Frank's first visit, Dr. John had been in the bush for six years; Frank was the first significant American he had actually met. Whenever I saw Dr. John, he would ask me how Frank was, and I used to see Frank regularly because he became the point person for the issues of South Sudan in the House. That first trip was over twenty years ago, and Frank is still very involved in Sudan. He was the linchpin for creating a bipartisan constituency within the U.S. Congress. He developed a partnership with the African American chair of the House African Subcommittee, Donald Payne.

"There are many others who were ultimately brought into the Sudan Caucus of the House, but really the whole effort began with

Frank. Frank's trip wasn't a junket. He not only learned; he got converted, so to speak. He went back, he stayed up to date, and put in legislation and letters to the president, so he's really been recognized as a prime mover."

When I returned to Washington, my trip helped bring attention to what was happening in Sudan, and I urged the Bush administration to send food aid for tens of thousands of famine victims.

Some years after Dr. John and I first met, Roger passed along a message from him: a footbridge had been built across the stream I'd fallen into. He hoped I would come back, now that I didn't have to worry about the killer microbes.

Following the signing of the Sudan Peace Agreement in 2005, Garang became the first vice president of Sudan. Tragically, he died in a helicopter crash just a few months after taking office.

.   .   .

When I returned to the Horn of Africa in 1990 to see how conditions were, things had only gotten worse. Both Roger and Dr. John had been urging me to pay another visit in order to gather fresh information and plead their cause before the American people.

In 1993 I traveled to Sudan with my chief of staff, Charlie White. We flew into Southern Sudan in a small twin-engine plane carrying relief medical supplies for the Norwegian People's Aid organization. The plane that was originally scheduled to take us in had crashed, killing both pilots.

I arrived at the base camp of the Norwegian People's Aid, the only NGO with a permanent, round-the-clock presence in Sudan since four relief workers had been killed in a skirmish between factions of the SPLA. The Catholic Relief Service was also there, convoying food supplies to three refugee feeding camps in the Southern region — Aswa, Ame, and Atepe. These loosely defined camps — rows of white tents that stretched far into the distance — were located near the main road bisecting Sudan, on which hundreds of thousands of refugees were making their way south, driven by the relentless and unforgiving army of the Khartoum government. These refugees arrived without food, medicine, clothing, or hope.

I visited two of the three camps and witnessed the efforts that seemed, at best, only to fend off starvation and sickness for the moment rather than provide lasting sustenance. Twice each day, children holding their feeding bowls formed an endless line to receive meager rations of food, food that would prolong their existence until it was time to line up again and repeat the process.

One of the refugees, a Dinka woman named Rebekka, angrily told me she had lost her husband and three children. Then she told me three things that I heard over and over again throughout the region.

First, she said, "The world is silent to the suffering in my country because the victims are black." The reluctance to act, in her view and the view of others, was a matter of racial discrimination. Second, she said, "We are being persecuted because we are Christians" — starved, bombed, and killed for their faith. Third, the other humanitarian groups needed to come back to help — groups that had left the region after the killing of the relief workers. The aid workers were reluctant to return until some measure of security could be assured.

Unless significantly more relief became available in the form of food and medical care, people would continue starving to death every day. The people in Sudan had literally lost a generation and maybe more.

A few days later I visited hospitals, including one exclusively for victims of tuberculosis. Another structure, termed a hospital, was in reality a filthy, rat-infested building where the injured were huddled. I met a woman who'd been wounded in one of the high-altitude bombing raids the Khartoum government made over civilian areas, and the doctor showed me the shrapnel in her head. Whenever it seemed conditions were as bad as they could be, they got worse.

I met with representatives of the SPLA, the Sudan Relief and Rehabilitation Association, Catholic priests, local officials, and a number of "old hands" in Sudan. And once more I came back with recommendations that I hoped would lead to relief for the people of Southern Sudan. Among them: The U.S. *must* put pressure on the Khartoum government to stop the bombing and killing in the South. The Khartoum government and the SPLA must agree to buffer zones around pockets of refugees to keep soldiers out and allow relief groups in. Humanitarian relief organizations and medical teams must be encouraged to return.

I feared that an entire culture would be lost. Once more, too little was being done to mitigate the evil beneath the unforgiving African sun.

I traveled to Sudan again in 2001 with Dan Scandling, who had become my chief of staff in 2000 after Charlie White's death. This time, we went to the town of Yei, where I talked with the survivors of the bombing of their marketplace. Yei was not a military target, yet almost on a daily basis, a high-altitude bomber passed over the town.

Sometimes homemade bombs were rolled out of the planes, randomly falling to strike homes, churches, and hospitals. Some of the bombs were fifty-five-gallon oil drums packed with dynamite and nails. The planes flew remorselessly, morning, noon, and night.

An Antonov flew over the town the last morning I was in Yei, and immediately panic set in. When people heard the sounds of the bombers, which make a heavy, lumbering noise, they ran for whatever shelter they could find, even holes in the ground. Someone grabbed me and pushed me into a depression in the ground. In the end, no bombs were dropped. With many of these flights, Khartoum simply intended to terrify people. They were succeeding: I could see the fear in the residents' eyes and hear it in their voices.

The psychological warfare was clearly taking its toll. People were afraid to build houses, because they might be bombed the next day. Why try to raise a crop when it could be destroyed before the harvest? Marketplace peddlers dug foxholes under their tables, so that if a plane flew over, they could jump into the hole and pray the bombs hit somewhere else.

Bombs also hit relief agency compounds and civilian convoys. Getting food and supplies through Southern Sudan was difficult enough because of the deplorable conditions of the roads. It took us nearly four hours just to travel forty miles from the border of Uganda to Yei.

Bombing was not the only instrument of terror in Southern Sudan. Government-sponsored militias torched houses, looted property, raped, and murdered with impunity. They destroyed livestock. Political opponents to the Sudanese government were sent to "guesthouses" to be tortured, and slave traders from the North regularly swept down into villages and kidnapped women and children, who were then sold for use as domestic servants or concubines. International relief was obstructed. In 1998 this strategy exacerbated the famine in Southern Sudan that endangered millions and killed tens of thousands.

At the dawn of the twenty-first century, a new factor worsened the threat of genocide. In 1999 the Khartoum government began earning hundreds of millions of dollars from oil exports — money funding weapons for the war. Helicopter gunships were used in a vicious scorched-earth policy to wipe out ethnic groups such as the Dinka and Nuer from land under which the oil sits. The purchase of weapons like these caused increased suffering, allowing the Khartoum government to better target civilians, food and relief convoys, and outside relief organizations, as well as allowing the government to wreak havoc even farther into the South.

Where did they get the money for the gunships? They got it through the sale of oil to China. It's no accident the Chinese have the largest embassy in Khartoum, which I saw while I was there. China is also widely reported to be providing guns, ammunition, and parts for helicopter gunships and Antonov bombers, all used by government forces to maim and kill innocent Sudanese men, women, and children.

Another horror in this unending war is the problem of child soldiers. In Sudan (and elsewhere in Africa), children either are pressed into service or volunteer in hopes of getting a meal and a uniform. I met one young soldier who told me he was fourteen years old. He had joined the fighting at age eleven.

Throughout my trip, people told me over and over again that the U.S. just needed to show it cared. They didn't ask for troops to be deployed; they simply wanted America to send a signal that it would begin to focus on the plight of Africa before another generation is lost to civil war, famine, disease, and AIDS.

Just before I left Sudan, a minister came up to me. "Please, help bring peace to this region," he pleaded. He lived most of his life under war, he told me, and was afraid he was going to die before it was over.

I thought about that minister's words on the long flight back to the United States. Why, I couldn't help wondering, were we doing so little to help Sudan's suffering people? Why did we spend billions to keep peace in the Balkans (populated mostly by Caucasians) but turn a blind eye to the plight of black Sudanese? Had this been taking place in Southern Europe instead of Southern Sudan, I think the West would have responded much more aggressively, mainly because Europeans have the capacity to publicize tragedies and the Sudanese do not. If the international press were to shine a light on this struggle, as it did in the Balkans, the world would become galvanized in support of Southern Sudan.

When I arrived back in Washington, I recommended a number of actions I hoped would help bring a lasting peace to Sudan. I kept asking President George W. Bush and Secretary of State Colin Powell to appoint a high-profile envoy to Sudan who had a real interest in seeing the conflict resolved.

Bush, to his great credit, put his personal prestige on the line by announcing the appointment of former senator John Danforth as special envoy to Sudan at a formal Rose Garden ceremony. I attended the ceremony, which took place just four days before the September 11 terrorist attacks on us.

Eventually, Danforth's efforts led to the January 2005 Sudan Peace Agreement, signed in Nairobi, which resulted in a halt to most of the North-South fighting. I traveled to Nairobi to witness the signing, along with Colin Powell, Roger Winter, Congressman Donald Payne, and Andrew Natsios, who at the time was with the Agency for International Development. I felt guardedly optimistic.

I had a second reason for traveling to Kenya: I wanted to see our allies in the region pressured to become more engaged in Sudan. Egypt, for example, had a tremendous influence over the Khartoum regime. The U.S. has given more than forty-five billion dollars in foreign aid to Egypt since the Camp David Accords were signed in 1978. Why weren't we using that leverage?

The U.S. also needed to get serious with the Khartoum government and the international community about enslaving the people of South Sudan and about the incessant aerial bombing of civilians in the South. This suffering country is a litmus test for those who say they care about hunger, human rights, civil rights, and religious persecution. The ravages they continue to endure seem worse because they result not only from holocausts born of natural causes such as drought, disease, and plague but also from those that spring from man's inhumanity to man.

In October of 2002 Congress passed the Sudan Peace Act, and President Bush signed it into law. It condemned Sudan for genocide and authorized the spending of one hundred million dollars over the next few years to assist the South and make sure Khartoum was not interfering with relief efforts. It also required the president to gather information about possible war crimes, crimes against humanity, and other violations of international law.

In early 2003 a second conflict emerged in Sudan's western region of Darfur — and this time we were seeing Muslim-on-Muslim violence. Government-backed Arab militias, called the Janjaweed, began violently driving black African Muslims from their homes. Hundreds of thousands died, more than 2.5 million people were forced to flee their homes, and the refugee crisis on the border with Chad worsened. The violence was so horrific that the Committee on Conscience of the United States Holocaust Memorial Museum issued a genocide warning for Sudan.

I returned to Sudan in June of 2004 with Senator Sam Brownback and Dan Scandling to visit the western region of Darfur shortly after this violence began. As the first congressional delegation to visit this area, we flew to Khartoum and then boarded a smaller plane headed for Darfur. The Sudanese ambassador had flown from the U.S. back to Khartoum in order to come with us, but we didn't want him on the plane. We wanted to see everything and didn't want a handler interfering with us, telling us what we could and could not see. In the end, we managed to keep him off the plane.

Of all my trips to Sudan, this was the worst.

I was sitting on the ground in a refugee camp, listening to two young girls in colorful clothing describe what had befallen them just prior to our arrival at the camp. They had gone out to collect straw to feed the family's donkey, they told us, when the Janjaweed — which means "Wild Men on Horses with G-3 Guns" — attacked and raped them. "We will make light-skinned babies!" the men told the terrified girls.

One of the two assaulted girls was too shy to tell her story in front of men, but she was willing to speak privately to a journalist traveling with us — Emily Wax of the *Washington Post*. She told Wax that if anyone found out she had been raped, no man would be willing to marry her.

One goal of the Janjaweed, which comes from the government of Sudan, is to purge the region of darker-skinned Africans. They have turned millions of Darfurians into refugees by dropping bombs from Antonov bombers onto hundreds of villages. The helicopter gunships with huge Gatling guns mounted on each side come in and gun down the villagers as they race out of their camps with their children. The Janjaweed then come galloping in on horses and camels to finish the job by killing, raping, plundering, and torching huts.

Sam Brownback and I visited the refugee camps, sprawling tent cities packed with up to seventy thousand displaced people and fast becoming breeding grounds for disease. They were grim places. We drove past dozens of pillaged villages and walked through what was left of four that were burned to the ground. We heard countless stories of rape and plunder, and even watched the barbarous men who carried out these attacks sitting astride camels and horses or striding arrogantly through the marketplace of Geneina, guns slung over their shoulders, a short distance from where young and old had sought what they had hoped would be a safe harbor.

We watched mothers cradle their sick and dying babies, hoping against all odds that their children would survive. We saw the scars on men whom the Janjaweed had shot, and victims told us of being strafed by the helicopter gunships. A villager told me a shopkeeper was shot in the head for refusing to lower the price of a watermelon. Visiting a refugee camp filled with seventy thousand people, it was hard not to step in either animal or human feces.

We were watching a nightmare unfold before our eyes.

Sam and I were trailed or escorted by a mixture of military police and government "minders." These "minders" repeatedly scolded refugees and told them in Arabic to shut up. Even with these threats, however, refugees in every camp we visited were eager to tell their stories.

Just before we left Sudan, for example, we were handed a letter from a group of women who had been assaulted. The translation of this letter broke my heart:

> We are forty-four raped women. As a result of that savagery, some of us became pregnant, some have aborted, some took out their wombs and some are still receiving medical treatment.... We have high hopes in you and the international community to stand by us and not to forsake us to this tyrannical, brutal and

racist regime, which wants to eliminate us racially, bearing in mind that 90 percent of our sisters are widows.

We knew these rape victims had nowhere to turn. Even if they reported the attacks to the police, they knew nothing would happen. The police, the military, and the Janjaweed all appear to be acting in coordination.

Over the course of three days, we had seen the worst of man's inhumanity to man, but we also saw the best of what it means to be human: mothers waiting patiently for hours in the blazing sun in an effort to save their precious babies; tireless NGO aid workers and volunteer doctors feeding and caring for the sick and the dying; and the courage of the men, women, and children defiantly eager to speak with us so that we would know their stories.

Dan had taken many photos of the Antonov bombers, the Hind helicopters, the swaggering Janjaweed, the torched villages, and the refugees living in the camps. When we were leaving Darfur via the local airport, government handlers tried to confiscate the film. Dan refused to give it up, and there was something of a tussle over it. But Dan is a smart guy. When the handlers left the plane for a minute, Dan quickly removed the film and replaced it with unexposed film. When the handlers returned and grabbed the film, they got a lot of nothing.

When I got home, I called Kofi Annan, the head of the United Nations, and urged him to visit Darfur. He did go and visit a refugee camp. I later asked him to announce that unless the U.N. did certain things to help the suffering Darfurians, he was going to resign. His term was ending, anyway, and I thought it would be a very dramatic thing for him to do to shine a spotlight on Darfur. But he didn't do it. Of course, he had been head of the peacekeeping forces at the U.N. when the slaughter in Rwanda took place, and he didn't do much about that, either.

I spoke out often on the House floor about Sudan, trying to jump-start some action. So did several others, particularly Don

Payne of New Jersey, assisted by his able staffer Ted Dagne, who is an expert on Sudan. Sam Brownback spoke time and time again in the Senate about Sudan, as did Senator Bill Frist of Tennessee.

In July of 2004 the U.S. House of Representatives unanimously passed a resolution declaring "that the atrocities unfolding in Darfur, Sudan, are genocide." The Senate also unanimously passed legislation calling the carnage in Darfur by its rightful name.

I cosponsored the Darfur Peace and Accountability Act in June of 2005. By this time there had been a great deal of publicity about what was happening in Sudan, including huge rallies on the Mall, and members and senators were pretty much on board with the issue. President George W. Bush, who became the first American president in history to declare a hot conflict to be genocide, signed the Act into law in 2006, putting pressure on the Sudanese government for its involvement in the Darfur genocide. It also denied visas to, and froze the assets of, Sudanese officials. Despite the international outcry, however, the genocide tragically continues.

Along with more than 160 other members, I signed a letter to President Bush on July 5, 2006, urging him to appoint a presidential special envoy for peace in Sudan. "As you know, following the signing of the Darfur Peace Agreement on May 5, violence intensified in Darfur," we wrote. "Civilians were the targets of attacks by the government-sanctioned Janjaweed militias.... Without the presence of a strong peacekeeping force, civilians will continue to suffer."

President Bush (who had become used to receiving regular missives from me over the years) responded by appointing Andrew Natsios, who traveled regularly to Sudan to pressure the Khartoum government on human rights and autonomy for the South. He was tremendously effective. When Natsios retired in 2007, Bush appointed Rich Williamson as the new special envoy to Sudan, who also pushed hard at the Khartoum government.

You may be wondering why, given the scope of the tragedy, the United Nations is failing to do anything to help Darfurians, such as sending in peacekeeping troops to stop the violence and dealing with Sudanese president Omar Hassan al-Bashir. The answer is China. China's lust for Sudan's oil is the reason why the Chinese block the United Nations from doing anything substantive in Darfur. The largest foreign investor in Sudan, China provided Khartoum a few years ago with a seventeen-million-dollar, interest-free loan with which to build a new presidential palace.

Darfur got a burst of much-needed attention when film stars such as George Clooney, Angelina Jolie, and Mia Farrow began to speak out. But overall, interest by the West seems to have faded away; the Darfurians are once again a forgotten people in a remote corner of the world.

Tragically, we Westerners have a short attention span.

On March 4, 2009, the International Criminal Court issued an arrest warrant for Sudanese president Bashir, charging him with seven counts of war crimes and crimes against humanity. He "has selected his weapons; they are: rape, hunger, fear," announced the ICC prosecutor. It was the first warrant of arrest for a sitting head of state, and it was about time. In response, President Bashir immediately expelled more than a dozen foreign aid groups. This development had dire consequences, leaving over a million people without food, medical care, and drinking water. Without the lifesaving assistance these groups deliver, millions of lives hung in the balance.

Nearly three million Darfurians, living in refugee camps, face daily hunger and disease. And according to the United Nations, Sudanese military jets and helicopter gunships occasionally still attack innocent civilians, and Sudanese forces continue to expel human rights activists and aid workers. The United Nations – African Union peacekeeping force is now in Darfur but, underequipped and underfunded, is unable to protect the vast camps filled with millions of refugees.

. . .

Just minutes from the White House sits the world-renowned Holocaust Museum, a fitting tribute to millions of innocent victims who perished in Hitler's Germany. The world cries out, "Never again," yet genocide and crimes against humanity are alive and well in Sudan, as I learned during my five visits there.

Which is why I was livid when I discovered, in October of 2009, that a U.S. lobbying firm was seeking to represent Khartoum in Washington. I immediately sent a letter to President Obama, urging him to direct the Treasury Department's Office of Foreign Assets Control to deny any requests by U.S. companies seeking to represent the government of Sudan.

"A modern-day accused war criminal is the sitting head of state of the government of Sudan," I wrote. "In March the International Criminal Court (ICC) issued a warrant for the arrest of President Omar Bashir. He is accused by the ICC of five counts of crimes against humanity (murder, rape, torture, extermination, and forceful transfer of civilian population) and two counts of war crimes (for directing attacks against the civilian population and pillaging).

"It is unconscionable that any government with blood on its hands would be permitted the privilege of having a Washington lobbyist on retainer," I added. "This would be a disgrace and must not be permitted to take place under any circumstances.

"Sudan remains on the State Department's list of state sponsors of terrorism, with the 2008 Country Reports on Terrorism saying, 'Elements of designated terrorist groups remained in Sudan....' There have been open source reports that arms were purchased in Sudan's black market and allegedly smuggled northward to Hamas," I pointed out to Obama.

"I implore you to remember the woman in Darfur who fears rape and brutalization every time she leaves the confines of her camp to collect firewood," I finished. "Who speaks for her in our nation's capital?"

As a result of all the bad publicity, the lobbyists decided to drop Sudan as a client.

In July of 2010, in a major speech on the House floor, I urged President Obama to find his voice on human rights and condemned his administration's missed opportunities. I reminded him of the words of *New York Times* columnist Nicholas Kristof, who had recently warned, "If President Obama is ever going to find his voice on Sudan, it had better be soon."[1]

It is indisputable that President Bush and former special envoy John Danforth were instrumental in securing, after two and a half years of negotiations, the Comprehensive Peace Agreement, which brought about an end to the brutal twenty-year North-South civil war in which more than two million people, mostly civilians, perished.

I'm not the only one who worries about Obama's apparent lack of interest in Sudan. On July 14, 2010, the Associated Press noted that "the words of the Obama administration were unequivocal: Sudan must do more to fight terror and improve human rights. If it did, it would be rewarded. If not, it would be punished. Nine months later, problems with Sudan have grown worse. Yet the administration has not clamped down. If anything, it has made small conciliatory gestures."[2]

And in the *New York Times*, Dave Eggers and John Prendergast warned that "this is President Obama's Rwanda moment, and it is unfolding now, in slow motion. It is not too late to prevent the coming war in Sudan, and protect the peace we helped build five years ago."[3]

The U.S. Intelligence Community's Annual Threat Assessment recently predicted that between 2010 and 2015, "a new mass killing or genocide is most likely to occur in Southern Sudan" — more so than in any other country.[4]

The bottom line is, the violence and suffering are still going on.

In July of 2010 the International Criminal Court officially charged Bashir — long an indicted war criminal — with orchestrating genocide in Darfur that month. And yet, astonishingly, Special Envoy Scott Gration actually said that the genocide charges against Bashir would make his job harder.

What are we supposed to do? Keep quiet when genocide occurs, and let the murderer of millions go on his merry way?

If we really want to help the people of South Sudan, we ought to provide them with what they say they desperately need: an air defense system, such as mobile, truck-mounted missiles, technical support, and other assistance. President Bush reportedly approved this in 2008, but Obama has never followed through.

In 1994 the world stood by and watched as extremist Hutus systematically slaughtered more than eight hundred thousand ethnic Tutsis in Rwanda. When the killing finally died away after one hundred days — and journalists broadcast around the globe the horrific images of what had taken place — world leaders acknowledged it was genocide, apologizing for failing to intervene, and vowing, "Never again." That pledge from the international community has been put to the test during the last two decades in Sudan — and will likely challenge us in the near future.

The question is, how vigorously will we respond — assuming we care enough to respond at all?

In January of 2011 the people of South Sudan had the opportunity to vote, as guaranteed by the peace agreement, to separate from the North, which had inflicted so much suffering on them for so many years. The South voted overwhelmingly for independence.

We must hope and pray that the North honors this vote — and that in its wake, we will see the beginning of a more hopeful future for the people of South Sudan.

CHAPTER NINE

THE ELIZABETH MORGAN CASE

Woe to those who make unjust laws, to those who issue oppressive decrees.

Isaiah 10:1

Either you tell me where your daughter is, or you go to jail.

Judge Herbert Dixon

MY CAREER IN CONGRESS hasn't just been about traveling to odd corners of the globe. In fact, one unforgettable human rights case I got involved with happened right here in Washington, D.C. It involved Dr. Elizabeth Morgan and her daughter, Hilary — the child who was at the heart of one of the most notorious child custody battles in American history.

I want to make clear that I do not make a judgment on the abuse charges that Morgan leveled at her ex-husband, Eric Foretich. Nor do I want to get into the details of the case, which can be found elsewhere, including family law textbooks. I simply got involved to help a mother and a daughter who I felt were being treated unfairly by a judge.

Elizabeth Morgan's decision to go to jail rather than reveal the whereabouts of her five-year-old daughter revolved around her belief that the child's father, Dr. Eric Foretich, was sexually abusing her. The *Morgan v. Foretich* custody case began in November of 1984, when Hilary was just two years old. District of Columbia Judge Herbert Dixon eventually ruled that Morgan had not proven her allegations of sexual abuse of her daughter, and so Dixon refused to suspend her ex-husband's right to unsupervised visits with Hilary.

There was a lot of back-and-forth court action between Morgan and her ex-husband, but in the end, Judge Dixon found allegations of the abuse inconclusive. (Foretich had passed three polygraph tests.) So he ordered Morgan to allow Hilary to resume unsupervised visits with her father.

Morgan reluctantly complied. But she told others that Hilary began showing signs of stress, wetting her bed, attacking her pre-school classmates, and having nightmares. Morgan attributed this behavior to abuse.

Morgan's extended family believed that Judge Dixon had a grudge against Dr. Morgan. Hilary's grandfather, William Morgan, wrote letters to congressmen and Virginia's governor, angrily condemning the judge's "corruption and obstruction of justice."[1]

Paul Michel, a federal appeals court judge who had become engaged to Morgan in August of 1987, was also disturbed by Dixon's rulings; he told *People* magazine that he deeply regretted the two occasions on which he drove Hilary to visit her father because Morgan told him she found it too painful to endure her daughter's tears. "There is nothing I regret more than those two acts," Michel said.[2]

Morgan, concerned about her daughter's safety, again stopped allowing her daughter to see her father. After hearing new evidence in the ongoing visitation and custody hearing, Judge Dixon ordered Hilary's visits with her father to resume. Morgan refused to comply, and Dixon ultimately found her in contempt, jailing her for two days in February of 1987. After her release, Morgan reluctantly obeyed Dixon's order to allow Foretich to have Hilary on overnight visits.

It was the last straw for Morgan, who said she could no longer endure seeing her daughter suffer. According to "Family Law Armageddon: The Story of Morgan v. Foretich," by June Carbone and Leslie Joan Harris, "By then Morgan had come to believe that

Judge Dixon would never rule in her favor and that he was determined to order unsupervised visitation. She had also come to 'a profound spiritual awakening': She had decided that she would do whatever was necessary to protect her child."[3]

As Morgan recalled by email when I recently asked her for her memories of this time in her life,

> My spiritual awakening was a strange one. As I saw my child suffering and my failures increase together, I became an angry woman.... One day a stranger, a Christian missionary from Africa, came to my home saying God had sent him to save my soul. Feeling foolish, I agreed to be re-baptized as a born-again Christian after resisting since it required me to set aside my rage.
>
> The subsequent spiritual awakening shocked me. I had a vision, seeing that all my legal efforts had been misplaced because I was caught in a struggle beyond my understanding. For Hilary's life to improve, I had to put my faith in God alone. Thinking I was becoming unbalanced by stress, nevertheless I did, finding an unexpected inner peace and conviction that forces beyond my control had taken over.
>
> Over the next six weeks, obstacle after obstacle was overcome with no effort on my part. Unable to pay my lawyers any longer, a prominent law firm took over my case pro-bono. My divorced parents reconciled. My mother, dying from a wasting illness, was diagnosed, treated, and began to recover.

It was time, Morgan decided, to send Hilary into hiding. Since Judge Dixon had confiscated Morgan's passport, she was unable to take Hilary out of the country herself. She therefore turned to her elderly parents, Antonia and William Morgan, for help. Both were retired psychologists, and William had served in the Office of Strategic Services (later to become the CIA), training spies in London during the Second World War. One night, at Morgan's request, they agreed to take five-year-old Hilary out of the country. In August of 1987, a week before Hilary was scheduled to be turned over to her father, Morgan drove Hilary to a diner parking lot in Virginia, where Bill Morgan was waiting, and hugged her little girl goodbye. Hilary and Bill met Antonia, boarded a plane, and left Washington, D.C., behind.

And then Morgan was hauled back into court.

"Either you tell me where your daughter is, or you go to jail," Dixon said.

"That's not a problem. I'll go to jail," Morgan responded.[4]

On August 28, the start of her third jailing, Morgan was now considered a "crazy lady" by members of the press and the public, Morgan recalled in 2010.[5] She was strip-searched, hosed down, and given the orange jumpsuit that would serve as her wardrobe for the next twenty-five months. Her new neighbors at the D.C. jail were murderers, prostitutes, robbers — and rats. Not content with locking her up for contempt, Dixon also ordered that the $200,000 bond Morgan had previously posted be forfeited at the rate of $5,000 per day. The money was gone just forty days into Morgan's 759-day sentence. The judge then ordered Morgan's home be sold. The appeal took years, but in the end, the D.C. Court of Appeals ruled that the terms of the bond did not allow the sale of the home on Judge Dixon's orders and ordered the house returned.

Morgan continued her legal battle from jail. A year after she was first locked up, the District of Columbia Court of Appeals denied her appeal. Morgan then appealed by writ of certiorari to the U.S. Supreme Court, but the Court denied her petition. She would stay there, Morgan declared, until Judge Dixon agreed not to force her daughter to visit her father — something Dixon refused to do.

Morgan's attorneys argued that it was, by now, abundantly clear that nothing would induce Morgan to reveal her daughter's where-abouts and that her continued incarceration had thus become puni-tive rather than remedial. "In other words," note Carbone and Harris, Morgan was "effectively being held for criminal rather than civil contempt without having had the procedural safeguards mandated by statute and the Constitution. Judge Dixon rejected her claim."[6]

By now the Child Custody Case from Hell had generated mas-sive publicity. Women sympathetic to Morgan formed a group called Friends of Elizabeth Morgan, picketing the D.C. courthouse, holding candlelight vigils, and doing everything they could to generate publicity about Morgan's plight. *Glamour* magazine named Morgan their Mother of the Year for 1989, and dozens of other publications ran articles sympathetic to Morgan.

In addition to the proceedings before Judge Dixon, Morgan had filed a civil suit against Eric Foretich and his parents, alleging they had abused Hilary, charges that Foretich and his parent vehemently denied. Because Morgan was still incarcerated when this case was tried, she was unable to testify. The judge in the case refused to allow Morgan to present evidence that she argued would support her allegations, and the jury ruled against Morgan. In 1988 a federal appellate court unanimously reversed this verdict, holding that the trial court had erred in excluding Morgan's evidence, including Hilary's own statements, a new trial was ordered. In the end, no new trial took place, for Morgan would not allow Hilary to be brought back to testify. But Morgan was no longer considered a "crazy lady," as many had labeled her. The press took a new look at the case now that three federal judges, one a retired Supreme Court judge, had weighed in on her side.

Early in 1989 Prison Fellowship founder Chuck Colson sent staffers to visit Morgan in jail and wrote a column asking readers to contact their representatives on her behalf and to also contact Rep. Ron Dellums, chairman of the House committee that oversaw the D.C. judiciary. Chuck also contacted his friend, Dr. James Dobson of Focus on the Family, and suggested he devote a radio program to interviewing Morgan, which he did. Texas billionaire Ross Perot, who believed that Judge Dixon was exceeding his authority, also got involved, lobbying senators on Morgan's behalf.

Elizabeth Morgan had no idea where her parents would take her daughter. Around the world, as it turned out. William Morgan's experiences in the O.S.S. during World War II helped the couple escape with their granddaughter under the noses of police (who suspected the Morgans might flee with Hilary, and were watching William Morgan's house) and managed to keep detectives and law enforcement agencies worldwide from discovering their whereabouts for two and a half years. So did Antonia Morgan's cool head and British discretion. In her view, they were not fugitives but doting grandparents; they all traveled on their own passports, under their own names, but quietly.

The Morgans first took Hilary to a beach cottage in Nassau, which proved too expensive, then to Canada, which they soon left, fearing that their proximity to the U.S. would put them at risk of discovery if Canadians happened to see American television broadcasts about what had by now become a world-famous custody dispute. The trio then headed for England for eight months, where Mrs. Morgan held dual citizenship, but, fearing Foretich would think of looking for Hilary there, the Morgans took their granddaughter to New Zealand, which Antonia had visited in the past and which she believed offered the peace and safety that the child needed.

Like everyone else, I had followed the Morgan-Foretich custody case in the press. But I became personally involved almost two years into Morgan's sentence when Chuck Colson contacted me. He told me Morgan was having a tough time in jail. She was suffering from exhaustion because the constant noise at night prevented her from sleeping, and her teeth were loosening because of the bad food.

Chuck was outraged that Morgan could be kept in jail for years without having been convicted of any crime. "Would you look into this?" he asked.

Because of my respect for Chuck, I did look into the case. It seemed wrong to me that someone could be held in contempt indefinitely, so I decided to try to do something to help Morgan get out of jail.

In April of 1989 I put in a bill to amend the D.C. code to free Morgan. The bill, called the District of Columbia Civil Contempt Imprisonment Limitation Act of 1989, followed Morgan's fact pattern — that is, I set it up in such a way that the only person those facts would apply to was Elizabeth Morgan.

The bill said that no one could be imprisoned on civil contempt charges for more than twelve months for failing to comply in a child custody dispute. The law expired eighteen months after it was passed, to address concerns by other lawmakers. (According to Senator Warren Rudman, "Since it makes no legal sense to assert that judges presiding in custody cases should have less power to enforce their orders than judges in all other cases, the bill is a disturbing precedent in the area of civil contempt."[7])

I got the bill passed unanimously in the House, and then, with the help of Sen. Orrin Hatch of Utah, it passed unanimously in the Senate. President George H. W. Bush promptly signed the bill into law, and Morgan was released two days later, on September 23, after more than two years behind bars.

· · ·

The case took another twist just four months later. Both Interpol and Eric Foretich's private detectives were hunting for Hilary, and in February of 1990, after two and a half years of Hilary Foretich and her grandparents being on the run, detectives found the eight-year-old in Christchurch, New Zealand, where she was living under the name of Ellen Morgan in a motel with William and Antonia.

Learning that the child's father had discovered their whereabouts and filed for custody of Hilary, the child's maternal grandparents promptly went to a New Zealand court, asking for, and receiving, a temporary custody order. The court also prevented Foretich from seeing Hilary until it could determine if such a visit would be psychologically harmful.

Later that year, the New Zealand family court ruled that Hilary, now called Ellen, should stay with her mother, who had flown to New Zealand as soon as Hilary's whereabouts were revealed. Hilary's physical, spiritual, educational, and emotional needs were being met, the court found. The court "made no finding on the sex abuse allegations, but it concluded that Ellen believed that Foretich and his parents had abused her, whether or not it was true, because she had been told this so often. The court therefore forbade Foretich from visiting to prevent disruption of her emotional security."[8]

Elizabeth Morgan and her daughter, Ellen, continued to live in New Zealand because Judge Dixon's custody order was still in effect in Washington, D.C., and also because the court would not allow Morgan to take Ellen out of New Zealand without its permission. That's how things remained for the next seven years.

In 1997 I again became directly involved with Elizabeth Morgan's custody battle. Morgan's mother, Antonia Morgan, came to see me one day and told me that Elizabeth was having serious health problems. She had undergone emergency surgery and was unable to work; she and Hilary were now on welfare. She had asked her mother to return to New Zealand to take care of her and look after Ellen.

Elizabeth Morgan also told me later that Ellen, whose life had settled down, was destabilized by seeing her mother almost die, and stigmatized at school by being on welfare. Ellen knew she faced losing her mother and becoming destitute in a foreign land. Distraught, she became a rebellious teenager. She began skipping school and hanging out with people who Morgan feared were involved in drugs. Morgan wanted to return to the U.S. for medical care and because she felt her daughter would be better off in America.

Antonia Morgan also told me that her husband, who was living in Maryland, was very sick and that Elizabeth wanted to see her father before he died. She asked me if there was anything I could do to help.

I was at that time the chairman of the Transportation Appropriations Subcommittee. The chairman on the Senate side was Senator Mark Hatfield, who was a strong Christian. We had a very friendly relationship, writing and negotiating various bills. At the end of the negotiations, we had reached all the agreements for transportation, for funding for rail, funding for aviation, for everything.

"Now, are we all finished?" Hatfield asked.

"There's one more thing," I said. "There's this lady ..." And I told him what was going on with Elizabeth Morgan.

Hatfield leaned back in his chair and stared at me. "What's that got to do with transportation?" he asked.

"Senator," I said, "this is really important because her father is dying, Dr. Morgan is sick and needs treatment in the U.S., and her daughter is having unbelievable difficulties living in New Zealand."

Hatfield, to his everlasting credit, said, "Put it in the bill." So we tucked a rider into the bill that would allow Elizabeth Morgan and her daughter to come back to the U.S. without being subject to the D.C. court order demanding that Morgan turn Hilary over to her father. It was called the Elizabeth Morgan Act, and once again, we wrote it in such a way that it would apply only to Dr. Morgan.

One member of Congress, who has since died, rushed over to the floor and just gave me the dickens when he found out what was in the bill. Eric Foretich's parents lived in his district, and they were demanding that I remove this rider from the transportation bill, which I declined to do.

Once the transportation bill passed, and the president had signed it, a lot of people were pretty upset with me — again. Matt Lauer, host of NBC's *Today* show, asked me to come on his program. Dr. Morgan, who was still in New Zealand, would also take part. I didn't want to do it. It was going to be a 7:10 a.m. segment, the drive from my house to the studio in the Capitol would take an hour, and I had congressional business late the evening before. But I finally agreed.

The segment was going to be live, and once I was at the studio, I was put in a dark room, alone, looking at a TV camera.

"It's just going to be Mr. Wolf and Dr. Morgan," a Lauer staffer told one of my staffers reassuringly.

The segment began, when out of the blue appeared Jonathan Turley, a law professor at George Washington Law School who had worked pro bono with Eric Foretich — and he just ripped me apart. I was very tired because I'd been up late working the night before, and I was angry because I hadn't been told Turley would be on the show with me. And I just lost it. I lost my temper and yelled at Turley.

At that time, one of my daughters was engaged to a guy from Atlanta. His mother happened to watch the *Today* show that morning, and she was a little shocked at my behavior. Some of her friends saw the show, too. "What kind of a family is your son marrying into?" they asked her.

Back at the office, the switchboard lit up as hundreds of people called to criticize me, accusing me of being rude and mean. It didn't subside for about a week.

I realized that putting in a rider applying to just one person was an unusual thing to do. It hadn't been done before and hasn't been done since. But I felt so badly for Elizabeth Morgan and felt the courts had dealt unjustly with her. Plus, her father had died, her mother was worn out, she herself was sick, and Ellen was going through mental health problems. As the father of four daughters, I had to ask myself, "What would I want a congressman to do for me if I were in a similar situation?"

Neither of the bills I introduced took a position regarding which of the parties in this dispute was right. The question was whether it was appropriate for a judge to thrust Morgan into jail to rot, with no end in sight, simply because she refused to reveal the whereabouts of her child.

This was not a matter of Morgan denying the jurisdiction of the court or being obstinate; it was a matter of conscience: she did not want to subject her child to what she truly believed was a risk to her safety. And as an act of conscience, she was willing to suffer the indignity of being shut up in the D.C. jail like a common criminal.

Judge Dixon did have other options. Because of the seriousness of the accusations, he could have issued a temporary restraining order, keeping the child away from her father. Or he could have ordered court-supervised visits only. Instead he ordered the child to be produced so she could be handed over to her father. And he threw Morgan in jail, refusing, over and over again, to let her out, which was a ruthless act on his part and, I thought, an abuse of power.

I took this job to try to help people, and letting Elizabeth Morgan back into America wasn't going to hurt anybody. We were just allowing a woman in bad health to come home — and that's what I tell people when they holler at me for what I did. If you believe, as I do, that all people are made in the image of God and have innate dignity, you're going to support that in your actions.

I didn't set out to hurt Eric Foretich or his parents. As I noted previously, I made no judgment on the merits of the abuse charges. I just wanted Elizabeth Morgan — who had never been convicted of any crime — out of prison and able to live at home with her daughter.

On December 16, 2003, the U.S. Court of Appeals for the District of Columbia overturned the Elizabeth Morgan Act, declaring it unconstitutional. But by then Ellen had turned twenty-one and could not be forced to visit her father against her will.

The New Zealand Court allowed Dr. Morgan and Hilary to return home in 1997. When Dr. Morgan came back to the United States, she stopped by my office to thank me. A lot of feminist groups thanked me, too.

In September of 1997 I received a letter from Dr. Morgan:

Dear Congressman Wolf:

Ellen and I want to thank you very much for bringing her safely home to the USA through the legislation you introduced last year.

We finally obtained permission to come home in May and came back at once, but not to this area at first. After waiting to be sure things stayed as settled as they had been, we came home in mid-July. Ellen and I are now living in Maryland, close to my brother and his family, and to my mother as well.

Ellen today started high school. You made it possible for me to keep a promise to her that I made in 1990 — that she would be able to go to high school at home. For her, this was a dream come true, a dream in which she had never dared to believe, until today.

Your help has meant so much to me, as well as to her. We have had a hard fifteen years and it is wonderful to now be home, able to start our lives again, with confidence in a normal, peaceful future for both of us. I cannot thank you enough.

For Ellen, being reunited with her family, her friends and her homeland revolutionized her view of life and of herself. You have not only changed, but in many ways saved her life and preserved her future, not once, but twice, first in 1989, and again, last year.

For us, you have been the person sent by God to answer our prayers. I feel that I have lived a miracle.

> With the deepest gratitude, respect, and affection,
> Sincerely,
> Elizabeth Morgan, MD, PhD

. . .

Because of my admiration for William Wilberforce, I was honored when, in 1990, Chuck Colson's Prison Fellowship awarded me the second annual William Wilberforce Award, given to people "whose personal and political life mirror the service, selflessness, and sacrifice of William Wilberforce." I received it not only for my efforts to help political prisoners in the gulags of the former Soviet Union but also for "drafting the legislation that freed Dr. Elizabeth Morgan, an inmate of a D.C. jail whose rights had been sacrificed by a harsh judicial judgment."

. . .

Eric Foretich has had no relationship with his daughter since she was five years old. He lives in Virginia — in my district, as a matter of fact — and continues to maintain his innocence.

Elizabeth Morgan, now in her sixties, earned a degree in trauma psychology from the University of Canterbury in New Zealand. As of 2009 she was back at school again, completing work on a master's degree in public health from UCLA. In 2010 she settled permanently in Atlanta, opening a new plastic surgery practice.

Ellen Morgan — who now goes by the name Elena — celebrated her twenty-eighth birthday in 2010 and earned a journalism degree from American University. For a time she pursued a career as a singer in Los Angeles, and she is now a pre-med student.

Helping Elizabeth Morgan and her daughter — twice — were satisfying moments of my career, despite the fury of voters who thought I'd done the wrong thing. But reuniting a child with her mother and helping them both come home — I'd do it again in a heartbeat.

CHAPTER TEN

ADVENTURES IN IRAQ

Terah took his son Abram ... and together they set out
from Ur of the Chaldeans to go to Canaan.

Genesis 11:31

I HAVE ALWAYS FELT that if you have voted to send America's young men and women into war, you owe it to them to go see for yourself what is going on there on the ground — even if the Pentagon doesn't want you there and tries to prevent you from going. So on May 25, 2003, I found myself traveling through the Kuwaiti countryside in a Land Rover, headed for Nasiriyah in southern Iraq. Dan Scandling, my chief of staff, and I had come to get a firsthand look at what was happening two months after coalition forces had invaded Iraq and assess the humanitarian assistance the U.S. government was providing.

Coalition forces had invaded Iraq on March 20, 2003, and captured Baghdad on April 9, sending Saddam Hussein into hiding; he would be discovered eight months later by the U.S. Army's Fourth Infantry Division and members of Task Force 121, on a farm near Tikrik, hiding in a hole in the ground. Because the long years of reconstruction were just beginning, coupled with attempts to secure the country from hardcore Islamic radicals, I was warned not to go because of the danger — this time by the Department of Defense — but I decided to go anyway.

Since the Defense Department refused to let Dan and me into Iraq, we connected with a nongovernmental organization (NGO) whose name I will not mention for their own protection, and flew to meet them.

As we drove several hours from Kuwait into Nasiriyah, Iraq, nobody knew we were there except the guy with the NGO and the driver. Even the NGO people we stayed with didn't know I was a congressman; they'd been told we were businessmen who supported the NGO. As we crossed the border from Kuwait into Iraq, I saw the words No to Saddam Yes for Bush spray painted in green letters on the side of a building.

Some of the heaviest fighting of the war had taken place in Nasiriyah, the town where army Pfc. Jessica Lynch, a supply clerk with the 507th Maintenance Company, had been captured following an ambush by Iraqi forces. The ambush led to the crash of the Humvee on which Lynch was riding, causing her injuries: a broken arm, broken thigh, and dislocated ankle. When we arrived in Nasiriyah, Lynch had just been rescued a few weeks before by U.S. Special Operations Forces and others in a videotaped nighttime raid, and the dramatic story was still very much in the news.

We visited the hospital where Lynch had been held — it had been called the Saddam General Hospital and was now called the General Hospital and was run by Iraqis. The staff showed us the sand-filled bed where she'd lain, recovering from her injuries. (Sand helps prevent bedsores.)

Conditions at both the General Hospital and another we visited, while dramatically improved from the previous month, were pitiful. At the General Hospital there were no screens, which meant that every time a door was opened, flies and other bugs came streaming in to swarm over the empty beds in the emergency room. We saw no monitoring equipment for these emergency room beds; in fact, there was almost no monitoring equipment anywhere in the hospital. Medicine was also in short supply.

We saw very sick children, who probably died from cholera and malaria (spread by mosquito larvae) shortly after our visit. Bites from sand fleas are the cause of visceral Leishmaniasis, which attacks internal organs and has an 80 percent fatality rate for young children unless they are treated with a twenty-one-day shot routine.

I saw a young boy about ten years old who had been brought into the emergency room just minutes before we arrived. He had been playing outdoors and came in contact with either a land mine or unexploded ordnance. His face was severely burned, and a piece of shrapnel was deeply embedded in his right eye. Blood was streaming down his face onto his chest and pants, and yet the boy never cried. It was a terrible sight.

Dan and I went down into the hospital's basement, which during the war, we were told, had been a base of operations for Ali Hassan Majeed, a military commander better known as Chemical Ali. The basement was now used to store medical supplies, which were piled up against the walls — but the sand tables, where Ali had plotted his maneuvers, were still there.

Our driver, a young Iraqi who'd been hired to work for the NGO, took us to see what was left of one of Saddam Hussein's infamous torture chambers; the stark white building had been bombed into rubble. Survivors told me ghastly stories about the brutality of Saddam's regime: horrific torture, the disappearance of neighbors, family members dragged from their beds in the middle of the night and taken away, and the mass graves of Saddam's victims.

As we drove through the rubble-strewn streets of villages and towns, I saw many paintings and posters of Saddam, which Iraqis had defaced by throwing black paint on them. Statues of the former ruler had also been defaced or destroyed, and his name had been scratched off or punched out of signs and buildings — a visual reminder of how much the Iraqi people had hated Saddam.

I saw for myself the amazing results of precision-guided bombing. In once instance, I was taken to what was left of the home of a Baath Party leader, a house sandwiched between other houses. The

Baath Party leader's home had been reduced to rubble, but none of the surrounding houses had sustained the slightest damage.

Dan and I had been invited to stay at the home occupied by an NGO guy, who'd also been told we were businessmen interested in assisting the NGO. After a simple dinner of rice and bread, along with a tasty concoction we dipped the bread into, we climbed into comfortable beds for the night.

The next morning we left Nasiriyah, traveling by Land Rover northeast to Al Kut, then south to Al Amarah and through the outskirts of Basra. I talked with Iraqi citizens, whose words were translated by someone with the NGO. In towns with a U.S. military base, we spoke with officers and enlisted men and women. Since we hadn't exactly been invited to Iraq, we couldn't just drive onto the military outposts. So whenever we arrived at an outpost, we'd get out of the Land Rover, walk up to the barbed-wire fence, and holler to the soldiers until they came over to the fence to see what we wanted.

"I'm an American congressman," I announced, holding my congressional ID up to their surprised faces. They couldn't believe I wasn't traveling with a delegation escorted by heavily armed troops.

The soldiers, airmen, sailors, marines, and Coast Guard members who served in Operation Iraqi Freedom were the best of the best. They were doing an incredible job under extremely difficult conditions. The heat in Iraq and Kuwait was over 100 degrees during our May visit, and it would only get worse as summer approached—upwards of 140 degrees in July and August. Living conditions for most of the soldiers and marines were primitive.

It was clear, as we continued driving around southern Iraq, that life there was difficult. The water was putrid. Buildings were dilapidated, and trash and rubble littered the streets. The residents had cut down trees and used them for firewood because propane was so scarce under Saddam's rule.

Much of the blame for this could be laid at the feet of Saddam Hussein, who had done everything in his power over the previous decade to make life in towns like Nasiriyah as miserable as possible because of the uprisings following the first Gulf war.

Security remained a real concern for both coalition forces and the general public. Looting was a problem in some parts of Iraq, and I heard several stories about robberies and carjackings. Many Iraqis were afraid to go back to work, for fear that their homes would be looted or that they would be robbed. Several people told me that hearing random gunfire after sundown had become commonplace.

The NGOs experienced their own problems. It was not unusual, they said, for their vehicles to be pelted with rocks in some parts of the country. Civilian convoys were threatened, and nobody dared travel after sunset.

The lawlessness could also be placed at the feet of Saddam, for just prior to the start of the war, he threw open all the prisons, releasing both political prisoners and hardened criminals: murderers, rapists, and robbers. Looters continued to target electrical substations in southern Iraq (which provide much of the power for Baghdad), stealing the copper wire and oil from the pipeline to sell on the black market.

One thing became clear to us: security was Job Number One. It was the linchpin to winning the peace in Iraq — security for coalition forces, for the NGOs, for the contractors, and for the Iraqi people.

After finishing our visit, we began the drive back to Kuwait. It was getting dusky, and the car I was riding in, driven by a Kuwaiti, was lagging pretty far behind the other car. One of the NGO guys, a burly former British security specialist who had worked in dangerous places all over the world, didn't like this.

"Pull over," he ordered the driver. He switched places with the driver, then jammed his foot on the accelerator and didn't let it up again until we were in sight of the other car.

A few miles later we saw an ominous sight: somebody had piled rocks across the road. We'd been told that criminals did this as a way to get people to stop, so they could rob or hijack them. Both drivers, already barreling along at a pretty high speed, knew exactly what to do. They stepped on the gas — hard — and shot through the rocks. We all got bounced around a bit, but we were fine.

. . .

When I got back to Washington, I noted in a report that the reconstruction of Iraq would be long and arduous, but we could not leave the Bush administration to do it alone. We had won the war at that time and needed to be careful not to lose the peace. A well-developed plan for reconstruction was imperative, and congressional involvement would help the Bush administration to keep from steering off course as it worked to rebuild Iraq.

I suggested that "Play to Win," the final report of the bipartisan Commission on Post-Conflict Reconstruction, be used as the blueprint for rebuilding Iraq. The report, released in January of 2003, was produced jointly by the Association of the United States Army and the Center for Strategic and International Studies. Its seventeen recommendations provided an excellent model to follow.

We also needed to reestablish a fair and just judicial system there, improve communications and banking systems, find and remove unexploded ordnance, protect the rights of religious minorities, and improve health care, particularly for women, who suffered from the poor quality of medical care when delivering their babies.

I urged other members to visit all parts of Iraq. Safety was obviously an issue, but congressmen could travel in small groups without publicity. The only way to get a feel for what was happening, I told them, was by visiting the towns and cities and by talking to the people living in them.

. . .

Blue-flowered tablecloths covered a long row of tables boasting plates of roasted lamb, vegetables, rice, and flatbread, filling the night air with the delicious odors of spicy cooking. Rows of light-bulbs were strung above the wedding banquet, keeping the evening darkness at bay.

At the appointed hour, the groom motioned to the hundreds of men and boys gathered in the alley. They immediately came to the tables to partake in the feast. Meanwhile, the bride, completely swathed in white, including her face, went to a nearby house following the wedding to feast with the women of the neighborhood.

After the meal, which I was invited to enjoy, the men followed the bride and groom to the home where they were to spend their wedding night. The bride disappeared into a private room while the groom's friends noisily toasted him with songs and shouts, fir-ing bullets into the sky. It was a joyous evening in a town that had suffered so much under Saddam Hussein.

I was back in Iraq, this time with Rep. Chris Shays of Connecti-cut, eager to see the progress that had been made since my trip six months previously. At that time, our government had a policy of not allowing congressional delegations to spend the night in Iraq. We'd been told that if we wanted to travel to Baghdad, we'd have to be brought in by C-130 aircraft from either Jordan or Kuwait and stay in the Green Zone "bubble." U.S. and Iraqi officials would be brought to us, we'd talk, and then we'd be flown back to Jordan or Kuwait the same day.

We didn't want to do that. We wanted to get out into the coun-tryside and speak to ordinary Iraqis and the NGOs working with them and find out what was really going on.

Paul Bremer, special U.S. envoy to Iraq, and his people were strongly opposed. "If you want to go through with this, you'll have to get there under your own steam," one of them warned us.

So Chris Shays and his aide, Dr. Nick Palarino, my chief of staff, Dan Scandling, and I flew to Baghdad from Jordan as the guest of the NGO Mercy Corps in a small plane operated by AirServe of Warrenton, Virginia, which charters planes to go into tough neigh-borhoods, which Baghdad certainly was at that time.

Even before we touched down at the airport, it was clear that security was still a major problem. Our plane had to make a cork-screw-pattern landing, spiraling rapidly down to the tarmac, which pilots regularly did in order to avoid enemy surface-to-air missiles.

We met our NGO escorts at a staging area a kilometer outside of Baghdad International Airport. All of us were wearing old clothes so we would not appear to be the U.S. congressmen and congressional aides that we were. Dan and I climbed into a battered car that had baby shades in the back window, both to cut the glare and to conceal us. The cars were also beat-up for security reasons: we wanted to blend in with ordinary Iraqis. In the front seat of my car were two Iraqis who worked with the NGO. In the other car went Chris and his aide, an American named David Holdridge from Mercy Corps, and the Iraqi driver, who was David's Mercy Corps Baghdad manager.

As we drove through the chaotic streets, we saw cartons of smuggled goods piled up on the sidewalks. Peering up through dirty car windows, we saw one damaged, crumbling building after another.

Few, if any, drivers obey traffic signals in Baghdad, and there were no police to direct traffic through intersections. Shortly after we started out, we got snarled up in the mother of all traffic jams in a traffic circle. Drivers were jumping out of cars, shouting, smacking each other's cars, and shaking their fists at one another. We slunk down, afraid someone would spot the Westerners in the backseat, traveling without bodyguards. Americans weren't too popular with many Iraqis at the time, and we weren't sure what would happen, but in this volatile situation, we suspected that if anybody saw us, they would drag us out of our cars and beat us up. There were no U.S. or Iraqi soldiers to protect us, and we had no weapons.

After a few tense minutes of our being, in effect, parked in the middle of the intersection, several men, including our driver, got out of their cars and finally managed to get traffic moving again.

We drove southwest for two hours until, as the sun set over the

Tigris River, we reached David's house in Al Kut, which is in the Shia heartland. There were no armed guards at the gate, and we noticed a sign in the hallway reading, No Arms Allowed.

Darkness fell as dinner was being prepared, and almost at once we heard grenade blasts nearby as vigilantes destroyed the homes of Baathists.

Among our dinner companions were other Mercy Corps people: a young engineer from Walla Walla, Washington, a young woman from Portland, Oregon, whose job was evaluating and monitoring the work, and a former Vietnam platoon leader from New England. Chris said grace over the chicken and rice, and we began firing questions at them.

As David recalls of that evening, "We got the most nonstop, intense interview of our respective lives. 'How can you live without arms?' 'The neighborhood protects us,' we replied. 'And the religious sheikhs?' We told them about the famous fatwa from Ayatollah Sistani that had been read all over at Friday prayers. That we were okay—not part of the occupation. 'Can you go to the souk without guards?' 'See this haircut?' I responded. 'Yesterday in the souk.'

"And so on deep into the evening, as the windows rattled now and then from the grenade blasts. But, and here was and is the essence, 'Our life is not sustainable,' we told them. 'As instigators, insurgents, and zealots roam the void, the official Americans react predictably.... The U.S. military and their civilian staff raise their perimeter walls even higher — only to sortie out in armed convoys.'

"The next couple of days, they [Chris and I and our aides] lived like us. A trickle of tepid water for the morning ablution, greasy eggs, sitting cross-legged on hard floors before every religious and tribal sheikh we could muster up. And then, without warning, a quick detour into the slums — down by the burning fields of rubbish — quick in with Mr. Wolf and Mr. Shays to ask a hundred questions of the squatters who were totally bewildered as they rushed to make tea; quite incomprehensible to them that Americans were sitting before them, with nary a weapon in the vicinity."

As Chris and I met and talked with dozens of ordinary Iraqis over the next few days, none of them knew that we were congressmen. They assumed we were supporters of the NGO working in this region. All of them expressed their gratitude to the United States for removing Saddam from power. Unlike the Iraqis in the streets of Baghdad, who we feared might kill us, these Iraqis were grateful for the help the American NGOs were providing.

Resentment toward America did seep out now and then, however. One young man told me accusingly, "You Americans abandoned us after the first Gulf war." A prominent religious sheikh we met in Al Kut told us that while he bore no ill will toward the American people, he was concerned by our government's policies.

During our time in Al Kut, we visited one neighborhood where an NGO worked with the community to fill in what had once been a garbage dump and de facto collecting point for raw sewage. The sewage was about a meter deep before it was removed, and the local children were often sick and rarely played outside because of the smell. The area was drained, and new soil was brought in and leveled. The goal was to make the area a playground.

Many Americans were critical when they heard that tax dollars were being spent on garbage trucks for Iraqis. What they didn't realize was that if a reliable system of neighborhood trash collection was not quickly implemented, plots of land like the one in Al Kut would quickly revert to dumping grounds. Since Iraqis don't have trash service, most of them just throw their garbage into the streets. So not only did they need garbage trucks; they also needed Dumpsters to prevent trash piles from becoming breeding grounds for disease.

Coalition Provisional Authority (CPA) officials working in Al Kut were very upbeat. They were busy making repairs to the "canal system" that runs through the town. (There are no sewers in Al Kut. All sewage runs through these "canals" — essentially, the middle or side of the street — into the nearby river.)

Yes, the CPA officials acknowledged, rebuilding Iraq would take much time and hard work. Aside from the security issues, another major stumbling block was getting the Iraqi people to trust one another. They had been oppressed for so long, and had become so fearful of speaking out against Saddam or the Baath Party, that they had no faith in one another.

Corruption was another problem. It had been so commonplace under Saddam that it was now endemic: for many Iraqis, lining their own pockets was their first priority.

On Saturday, December 6, Chris and I left Al Kut at daybreak to travel back to Baghdad, again riding in beat-up cars so we'd blend in. We wanted to meet with Ambassador Paul Bremer, who was then head of the CPA, so we headed for what had been Saddam's main Baghdad palace, which was where CPA headquarters was located. Bremer told us the coalition had made "enormous progress in essential services," such as restoring electricity, rebuilding roads, and opening hospitals. Turning over power to the Iraqi people on July 1, 2004 — just seven months away — would be a huge step forward.

We also met with British ambassador Jeremy Greenstock, Great Britain's top official in Iraq, and senior British and U.S. military officials to discuss conditions in Iraq and the country's future. FBI agents detailed to Iraq told us that they, as well as the military, were daily capturing and detaining people suspected of trying to undermine the efforts of the coalition. These individuals were helping make or plant improvised explosive devises (IEDs) used to blow up U.S. military convoys and kill American troops. Others tore down power lines to steal the copper wire for cash.

We took time to see the senior advisor to the Iraqi Ministry of Strategic Communications. He and his colleagues were responsible for putting together the radio and TV broadcasts to provide news and commentary to the Iraqi people — part of the public diplomacy effort to win their hearts and minds. We also had many conversations, both on and off the record, with American military personnel and government officials serving in and around Baghdad.

We were well aware of reports that Saddam Hussein had huge weapons caches scattered throughout the country. The locals were well aware of this, too, for they raided them after Saddam's troops and guards abandoned their posts. Consequently, the people living in the towns and countryside had their hands on everything from AK-47s to rocket-propelled grenades.

No wonder Iraqi citizens were still afraid to go out after sunset. I heard random gunfire both nights I spent in Al Kut, and the NGO staff I was staying with in a private home said gunfire and explosions after dark were commonplace. One of them told me that the recent attacks outside the Sunni Triangle (the area northwest of Baghdad inhabited primarily by Sunni Muslims) left them feeling that the security situation around them was deteriorating. One of their staff members was carjacked on the way back from Kuwait the day before we arrived.

When officials from USAID or other government officials visit projects in towns and villages, they arrive in armored vehicles and with a military escort. Driving back to the airport from the CPA headquarters in Baghdad, Chris and I had to travel along a stretch of road referred to as "ambush alley." As we hit that stretch of road, our drivers stepped on the gas and shot us along the roadway at around ninety-five miles per hour. No seatbelts.

As far as we knew, Chris and I were the only members of Congress to spend the night in Iraq and speak with ordinary citizens, at least at this point, which was not surprising given that we were there without permission and passing ourselves off as NGO supporters. We both believed this access helped give us a better understanding of the daunting task then ahead of us and gave us an unvarnished look into the daily life of Iraq's people. I have always found that if you stay overnight in a place, you can get a feeling for the rhythm of life there — what it's like at night and first thing in the morning. Living and eating with Iraqis provided me with a better understanding of life there, and people tended to be more candid with me.

. . .

"I've been watching the news about the protests back home," the young enlisted man told me. "I just want to know one thing: are the American people still behind us?"

It was August 28, 2005, and I was back in Iraq. It had been two years since my last visit, and I found the place dramatically altered. The political landscape at home had also changed strikingly in that time. America was engaged in a raging controversy over a war of the kind not seen since the Vietnam War four decades earlier. Good and reasonable people came down on both sides of the decision to send U.S. forces to Iraq, as well as the issue of whether they should come home immediately or stay and finish the job.

I'd voted to send American men and women to war, and I strongly believed I had an obligation to keep abreast of what was going on, so I could fully explain the situation to parents in my district — to a mother in Warrenton or a father in Berryville. It was clear to me that at the same time the Bush administration was telling Americans that the situation regarding the violence in Iraq was improving, it was actually getting worse.

Many of us recognized that mistakes had been made in the war effort. But I felt we could not abandon the mission to bring peace and stability to Iraq and its people — or turn our backs on the sacrifices of American sons and daughters in uniform.

I traveled this time as a guest of the U.S. military, visiting Baghdad, Tikrit, and Kirkuk. We went straight to the Green Zone, meeting and chatting with military personnel in the mess hall.

The next morning we were told to put on body armor and helmets, which were hot and heavy. We then climbed into a Black Hawk helicopter, and a couple of pilots flew us over Baghdad and some villages. I saw with my own eyes real progress being made on several fronts. Safe drinking water was now available in places that had never before had it. Electricity was being restored, and oil pipelines were being repaired. Schools were being renovated, hospitals and health clinics were getting built, and police stations were under construction. I watched as a team of Iraqis, under the supervision of the U.S. Army Corps of Engineers, worked on a building that would become part of the military base for the newly reconstituted Iraqi army.

Perhaps most impressive of all, Iraq had just held its first election in more than thirty years. Who will ever forget the images of this election flashed around the world — of smiling Iraqi women, holding up their forefingers stained with purple ink after casting the first votes in their lives? In late September Iraqis would vote on a constitution.

The bad news was that the security situation had deteriorated. Everywhere I went, I was escorted by a full complement of heavily armed soldiers and security personnel. Even while riding in armored vehicles, I was required to wear body armor and a helmet. It was clear that if embassy officials, USAID staff, NGOs, contractors, and the media could not move around the country without the fear of being attacked, our efforts to bring peace to Iraq would be hampered.

I was told that many contractors remained unwilling to bid on work there because of the continuing violence; those who did take on projects spent enormous sums on private security. The World Bank, a critical element to helping rebuild Iraq, refused to send staff because of security concerns.

I spent a lot of time talking with our soldiers in the mess hall and anywhere else I ran into them. Several told me they had heard about the antiwar protests at home, especially the vigil of Cindy Sheehan, whose son was killed in action while serving in the war. As I wandered through the mess halls and offices, I could see televisions all tuned to CNN, CNBC, and FOX.

"What on earth is going on back home?" soldiers asked me. "Do the American people still support us?"

"Yes, they do," I reassured them. One young enlisted guy gave me a skeptical look. I don't think he quite believed me, because he asked the question again. And he told me that when some of his fellow soldiers learned about the antiwar vigils, their morale plummeted. I wasn't surprised.

I was struck by the number of soldiers who told me they were bewildered by the news accounts coming out of Iraq. The Iraq being portrayed on the news was not the Iraq they saw every day. One young officer told me he no longer watched television news because it frustrated him so much; time and again soldiers, civilians, and even members of the Iraqi government said they wished the media would report some of the many good things happening in Iraq.

The news crews were, like everyone else, working under difficult conditions. It wasn't easy to move around the country, and more than sixty reporters had lost their lives. Many did an outstanding job, and I'm sure they too wanted to report good news more regularly. But their reports were often overtaken by the events of the day — such as the tragic stampede over a Tigris River bridge in Baghdad on August 31 of that year, in which more than nine hundred innocent people were killed fleeing from a mosque that was rumored to be the target of a suicide bomber. Foreign suicide bombers were pouring into Iraq in hopes of undermining our progress and turning the Iraqi people against us. Attacks such as these were the reason why most of the reporters were locked in the Green Zone, the safest part of Baghdad and heavily guarded by our troops.

On my second day in Baghdad I met with Lt. General David Petraeus, then commander of the Multinational Security Transition Command in Iraq, in his office. He's like an Eisenhower, and I was very impressed with him. While the general was extremely upbeat about the progress being made, he cautioned that there was still a long way to go. In that prediction, he turned out to be correct.

I also attended a lunch meeting with U.S. ambassador Zalmay Khalilzad and several members of the Iraqi government. Our meeting took place just hours before the Iraqi government announced it had reached an agreement on Iraq's constitution, and it was amazing to watch all sides involved in the process talk about compromise. Each of them acknowledged that no one was entirely satisfied with the constitution, but realized that each party involved had had to give up something in order to move the process forward. They all agreed that it would be a mistake for the U.S. to leave before Iraq was safe — and that no timetable should be set for U.S. troops to be withdrawn.

The one question I asked everyone I met was, "What would be the ramifications if we fail?" The answers were chilling: Slaughter in the streets of Baghdad, with the country splintering into a bloody civil war. Ethnic cleansing and chaos along the lines of what had happened in Somalia and the former Yugoslavia. Iraq would become a safe haven for terrorists, as Afghanistan had been. The U.S. would be perceived as a fair-weather friend, not to be depended on, and the fragile seeds of democratic reform would be crushed before they had a chance to take root.

Such a civil war had the potential to destabilize or even overthrow the governments of neighboring Jordan and Saudi Arabia. If the U.S. left Iraq too early, we would almost certainly have to return later, probably facing an even stronger and more determined enemy.

No one I spoke with during this trip believed we would lose the war on the ground in Iraq. But they feared that — as happened with the Vietnam War — the war would be lost at home. One general told me point-blank that the "center of gravity" for our success in Iraq was the American public.

.   .   .

A Black Hawk helicopter carried us over the Al Fathah Tigris River bridge/pipeline project just south of Kirkuk. Coalition forces had bombed the bridge during the war to restrict enemy movement and contain the old Iraqi army. Suspended under the bridge deck were critical pipelines that carried oil from the Kirkuk oil fields to

the Iraq-Turkey pipeline and then north, south, and west to petro-
leum-processing facilities across Iraq.

Repairing this vital pipeline, considered to be the principal
component of the Iraqi oil infrastructure, had been a challenge.
The insurgents were fully cognizant of the importance of this pipeline and regularly attempted to disrupt progress on the project.
There were bursts of small-arms fire almost daily at the site.

It was clear to me that Americans needed to manage their
expectations when it came to rebuilding Iraq. Almost an entire generation of Iraqis knew nothing but the brutal, murderous regime
of Saddam Hussein. While Saddam, his two sons, and other loyal
supporters had lived lavishly in Baghdad, everyone else had lived
in extreme poverty. Saddam spent millions on ornate palaces and
tributes to himself and invested only the bare minimum in keeping the country's infrastructure in place. Consequently, the task of
repairing oil pipelines, electric-generation plants, roads, and the
country's rail system would be much greater than many Americans realized. And the rebuilding would have to take place on
Iraq's timetable, not America's. This, I felt, was a key point — one
the Bush administration needed to do a better job of explaining.

The need to reevaluate our Iraq policy was brought home to
me during a visit to a hospital in Tikrit that was being rebuilt. Dan
and I were being taken around in a bulletproof Suburban in a heavily armed convoy, and everywhere we went, the private security
guards went in before us and behind us. In the hospital, they went
into the halls and the patient rooms ahead of us, pointing guns at
people, even the patients. Finally, I said, "That's it, we're leaving; we
can't be waving guns around in a hospital." You can bet this kind
of thing did not endear Americans to the Iraqis. This was one of
the defining moments for me. The security situation was so bad
that our military felt we had to be guarded like this, even when we
toured a hospital.

I could not help thinking of that hospital on the long flight
home, and of constant car bomb explosions and gunfire that

made life terrifyingly difficult for Iraqi citizens. I thought about the steady stream of American casualties who were flown into the Green Zone for treatment — or who would be flown home in flag-draped coffins. I thought of the tens of thousands of innocent Iraqis being killed by insurgents, and of the growing skepticism of the American people about the value of continuing to fight in Iraq. It was time, I thought, to bring fresh eyes to our Iraq policy.

So when I returned from my third trip to Iraq, I began calling for a "fresh eyes on the target" assessment of our Iraq policy. As I explained to the *Washington Post*, "If you ordered an Erector Set and you were trying to build it before Christmas and you got stuck and someone else came along, they might just see immediately what needs to be done.... It's all about fresh eyes on a target."[1]

The Iraq Study Group (ISG) would examine each and every operation, from how we were dealing with the insurgency to the status of the thousands of reconstruction projects being undertaken to what we were doing to improve America's image through public diplomacy in the region, and, in doing so, perhaps offer different perspectives in addressing what was a very complex issue.

The panel would answer such questions as how accurate a picture did we have of the insurgency? What could we do to get better tactical intelligence on the enemy? What role were Iran and Syria playing in the evolving political and security situation in Iraq? Was there an antisabotage strategy to protect the energy infrastructure? In short, a "fresh eyes on the target" group could help ensure that we were successful in Iraq.

My motive behind the appointment of this group was not to find fault with the U.S. effort there. Such an independent, comprehensive review could, I felt, help to assure Americans — no matter what their position was on the war — that every effort possible was being made to protect our troops and realize our goal of a secure and peaceful Iraq.

I knew that the Bush administration had sent other teams to Iraq to assess the ongoing situation. But a fresh-eyes review, as

I envisioned it, would not just report back to the president, the secretary of defense, or the secretary of state; it would also report directly to the American public.

I met with other members and senators to promote forming a nonpartisan review group, and they were enthusiastic about it. I then wrote an op-ed piece for the *Washington Post* on September 24, 2005, recommending the creation of a panel made up of ten distinguished individuals — five Democrats and five Republicans, some with a military background and others with extensive foreign policy experience — to go to Iraq and other parts of the Gulf region to comprehensively review our efforts, to talk to everyone from general officers to NCOs to privates to civilian contractors.[2]

The idea was to choose people of a very high moral caliber who, when they spoke, had a lot of credibility, and people would listen to them. We didn't want anybody connected either to the White House, the Democratic Congressional Campaign Committee, or the Republican Congressional Campaign Committee. Most important of all, we wanted people who loved their country more than they loved their political party.

On November 10, Rep. Chris Shays and I, along with five other House Republicans, wrote to President Bush about our proposal. I met with both Condoleezza Rice and National Security Advisor Stephen Hadley, urging them to support the panel idea, which they did. I then initiated the legislation authorizing and funding — to the tune of one million dollars — what became the Iraq Study Group, which was set up in March of 2006 through the U.S. Institute of Peace.

"U.S. operations to liberate Iraq and bring stability to the country have reached the three-year mark," I reminded my colleagues in a speech on the House floor. "From my firsthand looks at the situation there, I strongly believe it is time for a select group of capable and distinguished Americans to go to Iraq and comprehensively review our efforts. Last September, soon after I returned from my most recent trip, I wrote an op-ed for the *Washington Post* in which

I recommended the creation of a panel to essentially provide 'fresh eyes on the target.' The target, of course, being how to bring about success in Iraq. The group would be tasked with looking forward, not back, and with explaining to the American public the ramifications of failure of our mission in Iraq.... Over the past few months, I have had extensive conversations with the White House, the State Department, various administration officials, and other members of Congress about the merits of a 'fresh eyes' group. We need a bipartisan group of men and women of honor who love their country more than their political party to go to Iraq and provide an independent assessment."

Three groups — the Center for Strategic & International Studies, the U.S. Institute for Peace, and the Center for the Study of the Presidency — oversaw the process, beginning with selecting the panel's co-chairs: former secretary of state and the treasury James Baker and former congressman Lee Hamilton, who also co-chaired the 9/11 Commission. They were good choices, and I knew them both. Hamilton and I had served in the House together, and I'd worked on human rights and Sudan policy with Baker when he was secretary of state.[3]

"In recent months there has been no shortage of heated rhetoric, on both sides of the proverbial aisle, surrounding U.S. policy in Iraq," I noted. "Debate on the issues of the day is not only acceptable but also desirable in a vibrant democracy. But short-term criticism absent discussion of long-term viable alternatives is unhealthy and potentially dangerous....

"It saddens me that in my twenty-six years of public service, I do not think I have ever seen the country more divided, or Washington more partisan. But I am hopeful that this panel, comprised of honest, ethical, and experienced patriots, will offer a realistic and frank assessment of the situation in Iraq and will ultimately lead us to common ground from which we can move forward as a nation."

The Iraq Study Group held extensive meetings and traveled to Iraq, where the military put them into bulletproof vests before letting them loose, and where they slept (or didn't sleep) to the sounds of car bombs rattling the windows of their trailers. They met with members of the Bush administration and with all sorts of high-level people in Iraq.

President Bush, Secretary Rumsfeld, Secretary Rice, Chairman of the Joint Chiefs of Staff General Peter Pace, and others in the Bush administration cooperated with the Iraq Study Group; not all of them were wild about it, but they cooperated.

The team labored for more than eight months, supported by expert working groups and senior military advisors in the areas of economy and reconstruction, military and security, political development, and strategic environment. According to press reports, there was a certain amount of quarreling between the liberals and the conservatives in the Iraq Study Group. For instance, former defense secretary William Perry wanted to call for a timetable to withdraw U.S. troops, while Baker was adamantly opposed to this. In the end, Baker, Perry, and the other group members agreed to recommend removing combat troops by early 2008. But this was to be a goal, not a timetable.

The group released its report — signed by all members — in December of 2006, right after the November elections, to a packed audience (including press from around the globe) in a Senate hearing room. The group then celebrated over crab cakes at Vernon Jordan's home. The report was widely hailed as an important opportunity to chart a new course for Iraq.

As the *Washington Post* noted of this difficult process, "The fissure and its resolution culminated a process marked by that rarest of qualities in a polarized era: bipartisanship. At a time when Washington prefers confrontation to compromise, five Republicans and five Democrats sat down to tackle the country's most urgent crisis and came up with a document they all could sign. It proved to be a nine-month study on how to bridge not only Iraq's deep divide but also America's."[4]

For instance, the group embraced the idea of a surge —

immediately sending some twenty thousand more troops to Baghdad — that retired general John Keene and historian Frederick Kagan had come up with. Former senator Chuck Robb of Virginia, a former marine who'd been the only group member to leave the Green Zone to look around the rest of Baghdad, especially advocated this idea.

Many people now believe that the Iraq Study Group findings were a moment of truth and helped lead us to where we are today. It brought the country together, because when the ISG report came out with its recommendations, there was tremendous support for them in both political parties, although not everyone agreed with its conclusions.

The group kind of forced the Bush administration to rethink what direction we should take in Iraq at a critical juncture. An article in *Foreign Affairs* had just analyzed public support for the war in Iraq compared with previous extended ground combat situations and concluded that "the American public places far less value on the stakes in Iraq than it did on those in Korea and Vietnam."[5]

But the stakes had arguably never been higher. Steven Weisman of the *New York Times* painted a grim picture that would likely ensue if the already fragile Iraq spiraled into civil war, with the Shiite factions drawing Iran into the regional chaos, Sunni countries such as Saudi Arabia, Jordan, and Kuwait coming to the defense of Iraq's Sunni population, and Turkey entering the fray on behalf of the Turkoman population in the north.[6]

Weisman was not alone in his speculations. Countless well-respected analysts have all come to the conclusion that failure in Iraq would have devastating regional consequences and a direct impact on American national security. Al-Qaeda and other terrorist groups would like nothing more than to have a new base from which to operate, much like Afghanistan in the 1990s after the Soviets were defeated.

Although we have officially finished combat operations in Iraq, there is no denying that the terrorists have designs on the United

States and, as one U.S. officer told me, "We must win the war so we don't fight the next war in America."

. . .

When I think back on my visits to Iraq, I don't just picture soldiers at war. The patriarch Abraham came from an Iraqi city called Ur. Isaac's bride, Rebekah, came from northwest Iraq. Jacob spent twenty years in Iraq, and his sons, the twelve tribes of Israel, were born in northwest Iraq. The biblical book of Jonah describes a remarkable spiritual revival in Nineveh, which is in Iraq. And Nineveh — once the capital of the Assyrian empire — is where American troops are based today, although we now call it Mosul. Queen Esther pleaded for the lives of her people in Iraq, and Daniel walked into an Iraqi lions' den. On my first trip to Iraq, an army officer took me out to the ancient site of Ur, the home of the biblical Abraham. I even saw the purported site of his house and climbed on the ziggurat built in 2100 BC.

Iraq is still home to ancient Christian communities. In fact, with the exception of Israel, we find more biblical references to the cities and regions of Iraq than any other place. But tragically, Iraq's ancient Christian community, Chaldean Catholics who still speak Aramaic, the language of Jesus, is facing extinction. Shockingly, more than five hundred thousand Christians, roughly 50 percent, have fled Iraq since 2003. Even though Christians make up only 3 percent of the country's population, according to the U.N. High Commission for Refugees, they comprise nearly half of all refugees leaving Iraq. As Iraq continued to stabilize as the war wound down, minority populations are dwindling and increasingly vulnerable to marginalization and vicious targeted attacks by Islamic extremists. Among them were the coordinated attacks on July 12, 2009, in which bombs were exploded outside five Baghdad churches, killing four and wounding over thirty. Rep. Anna Eshoo, a California Democrat, and I are co-chairs of the Congressional Religious Minorities in the Middle East Caucus, and we immediately sent a letter to Iraqi prime minister Nouri Al-Maliki, expressing our sorrow over this event.

Even more horrifying was the attack in October of 2010, on worshipers at Baghdad's Our Lady of Salvation Church, in which fifty-eight people were slaughtered by members of an al-Qaeda affiliate who gunned down some worshipers, killed others with grenades, and murdered still more when the attackers, hearing security forces arriving, detonated suicide vests.

I wrote to high-ranking members of the Bush administration, and later the Obama administration, after each attack, urging that they take dramatic action on behalf of this hurting population. We need, I wrote, "a comprehensive policy or even a point person at the embassy in Baghdad to address the unique situation of these defenseless minorities." If we do not, they will be driven off their ancient lands or obliterated. How, I wondered, could we celebrate the fact that we freed twenty-five million people from a vicious tyrant if we then turn a blind eye to Iraqi Christians being persecuted and put to death for their faith?

. . .

During my 2005 trip to Iraq, I was particularly moved by something army chaplain J. D. Moore told me. Moore, who hails from Gloucester, Virginia, told me that one of his duties is to accompany troops assigned to recover the remains of fallen soldiers — called "heroes" in the field by their comrades and treated with respect and honor. He explained that as the body of the fallen soldier is put onto a helicopter to be flown back to a base camp, the soldiers on the ground salute and then stand at attention until the helicopter takes off. Moore said he will often look back and see the soldiers still standing at attention even though the helicopter is more than a mile away.

I want to close this chapter with an excerpt from an essay by Chaplain Moore titled "Hero Mission." Whenever I read it, it reminds me of the high cost of every war upon which America embarks:

When I arrived to see the Battle Captain, he told me that I was given a Hero Mission for a young soldier who had died in battle only hours before. I had about twenty minutes to ready myself and to go by Black Hawk with Specialist Toussaint to recover the soldier's body from his unit and to escort the Hero to another base where he would be sent home to his family. I found Specialist Toussaint, gathered my gear, and made my way to the flight line to board the aircraft.

When I arrived, everyone was as somber as I. I prayed over the aircraft, received our mission briefing, and then we departed. Once arriving to the location of the unit, I found the fallen soldier's unit neatly and sharply in formation next to the landing zone. Their clothes were muddy and their faces were downcast. Immediately you could sense their pain....

The soldiers carefully opened the back of the vehicle and solemnly and with honor removed their fallen friend from the vehicle. The black body bag hung in the hands of his friends.... We slowly and reverently followed the soldiers and their fallen comrade to the aircraft. Once arriving to the helicopter with the blades still churning and whirling, we all carefully placed the Hero in the aircraft. The crew chiefs of the aircraft gently situated the new crew member, our Hero. We stopped and prayed.... I turned back to see the rest of the America's Sons. Their chaplain, Chaplain Fisher, came to me, embraced me tightly, and with a shattered voice said, "Thank you for being here and escorting our friend part way home...."

I then boarded the aircraft, and we began our ascent. As the aircraft blades aggressively moved the air and we began to rise off the ground, I looked to my right out of the window to see the unit being swayed by the turbulence but still saluting their fallen hero....

I certainly will never forget this Hero Mission. I was very quiet all the way back to Speicher and could only think about the pain a family back home was getting ready to experience. I prayed for the family.[7]

I pray for those families, too, and for the soldiers who go into harm's way, answering the call of their country.

CHAPTER ELEVEN

KITES IN THE SKIES: AFGHANISTAN

What does the LORD require of you? To act justly and to love mercy.

Micah 6:8

THE SMOKE WAS STILL RISING from the rubble at Ground Zero when I decided it was time to visit Afghanistan. Since I had voted to send American troops to fight there, I thought I ought to go see what was going on. But, as usual, when I asked the Department of Defense if I could visit with the troops in Afghanistan, they said no.

Tony Hall and Joe Pitts, who are in my congressional prayer group, and I decided to go anyway. Since the Department of Defense wouldn't take us, we flew to Pakistan on a commercial jet and then transferred to a World Food Programme airplane, which took us on to the Bagram Air Force Base. Flying into Afghanistan was majestic, but the beauty of the spectacular, snowcapped mountains belied the situation on the ground. Once you land, it becomes clear that the entire country is a war zone.

A guy from the U.S. Agency for International Development met our plane and drove us into Kabul along a road littered with hulls of tanks and trucks — some the rusted-out remains of the war with the Soviets, and others recently bombed by U.S. planes. Unexploded ordnance sat randomly on the barren land. The vehicles we traveled in had to ford a stream because U.S. precision-guided bombs had taken out a bridge. When we arrived in Kabul, we could see that much of the city had been leveled, not by coalition troops but during the war with the Soviet Union.

Afghanistan is sandwiched between the Middle East, Central Asia, and the Indian subcontinent along the ancient Silk Route. Consequently, despite its rugged and forbidding terrain, it has long been fought over for its strategic position. Afghanistan was at the center of the so-called Great Game in the eighteenth century when Imperial Russia and the British Empire in India vied for influence. It became a key Cold War battleground after thousands of Soviet troops intervened in 1979 to prop up a pro-Communist regime, leading to a major confrontation that drew in the United States and Afghanistan's neighbors.

After the Soviets withdrew in 1989, the outside world lost interest, and the country descended into civil war. The official government was ousted in 1992, and a new government was never really established; groups that were formerly allies against the Soviets split into several factions, essentially led by warlords all vying for control of portions of the country.

Eventually, the Taliban, which originated in Pakistan, swept across most of the country to gain control. While Afghanistan became relatively stable under Taliban rule, the regime proved to be one of the harshest and most repressive in modern history. Life under the militant, extremist Islamic Taliban regime permanently scarred the country and its people. More ominously for America, the Taliban allowed Osama Bin Laden and the al-Qaeda network to move to Afghanistan and begin operations there.

Then 9/11 happened.

After coalition forces routed the Taliban, the world was shocked at the reality of life in this desperately poor country. Widespread land mines killed innocent civilians, and during a security briefing before we entered the country, Tony, Joe, and I were warned not to venture off any hard road surfaces for fear of these mines.

We were the first congressional delegation to reach the country after the war broke out, and in addition to meeting with the troops, we wanted to witness firsthand the ongoing humanitarian crisis in Afghanistan, which some considered the most dire in recent history. Almost four million Afghans had been uprooted by war and drought. Food and medicine were in short supply, and an entire generation of children knew nothing but war, hunger, and despair.

Perhaps the most depressing part of our trip was our visit to the Indira Gandhi Pediatric Hospital in Kabul. Of all the war-torn and impoverished places I have been in the world — including Chechnya, Bosnia, Ethiopia, Sudan, and East Timor — the conditions here were among the worst: Little to no heat. No medicine or medical equipment. Scarce food. And the doctors had not been paid in more than five months.

We walked into a ward room where mothers and their severely malnourished children slept two and sometimes three to a bed. Some of the babies were laboring just to catch their breath; others were wailing in pain. One child never blinked. One out of every three babies died that night — something that, tragically, happened every night.

Incredibly, we were told this was the best hospital in Afghanistan. But it was hard to imagine anything worse.

· · ·

The Taliban, as most Americans now know, forbade women from attending school — but the Dorkhanai High School for girls had just reopened a week before we arrived in Afghanistan. The girls at the Dorkhanai had a great desire to learn, despite pitiful conditions and the lack of resources. There were no pens or paper, few books, and no desks, which meant the girls had to sit on the cold, dirt floor. A classroom on the second floor had been completely destroyed by a bomb that hit during the war with the Soviets. The United Nations estimated that two thousand Afghani schools had been destroyed by more than twenty years of war.

Education, for both boys and girls, will play a pivotal role in the future of Afghanistan. The minister of education told us that few teachers are left in Afghanistan; most either fled the country or died in the war or as a result of war.

This problem extends through the entire region, especially Pakistan. Often, families with no means to educate their children through conventional schools resort to the only option available: enrolling their children in madrassas, some of which have been linked to recruiting and training students for militant causes and which have been characterized by some as "holy war" factories. According to recent reports, Pakistan has an estimated 7,000 madrassas with an enrollment of more than 650,000 students. If all that exists — or is allowed to exist — are schools that teach extremism and breed terrorism, we will never win the war on Islamic extremism.

. . .

Tony, Joe, and I visited the Allaudin Center Orphanage in Kabul, where more than 850 children lived. Most of the children's parents were killed during the war with the Soviet Union, which led to the opening of the orphanage. Others were killed during the ensuing civil wars or by the Taliban. Some of the children were simply abandoned by their parents.

Firefighters and police officers from New York City had visited this orphanage just before Christmas, bringing desperately needed food, clothing, and other supplies. As we met with the children during lunch, we were moved to see one smiling young boy wearing an FDNY baseball cap.

Next we visited the site of the former Soviet Union Embassy compound, which was serving as a makeshift refugee camp for twenty-five thousand Afghans from the Shomali Plain, north of Kabul. The living conditions of these people who had resisted the Taliban were extremely grim, and security was a major concern.

We also drove by the house where American missionaries

Heather Mercer (who grew up in my district), Dayna Curry, other aid workers, and a journalist had been held for four months. The women were eventually freed by anti-Taliban forces.

One of our final stops in Kabul was to a "woman's bakery." Inside a dark, mud-walled bakery, women toiled seven days a week baking the traditional Afghan bread called *nan*. (Fortified wheat for the bread was provided by the World Food Programme.) We observed two women making the dough, then weighing it on old metal scales. Four other women rolled it out by hand, forming it like a pizza. Another had charge of the red-hot wood-burning oven. After the bread was baked and cooled, the women took it outside, where children sorted it into piles, wrapped it in cloth, and then left through an alley to sell it on the street.

The bakery women made twenty dollars a month, a pricey sum at the time. We were told doctors and lawyers had been asking to work in the bakeries because they had not been paid in months.

I saw only a few women walking the streets of Kabul without a burka, the full-body covering women wore in public. They remained extremely fearful that the Taliban were still lurking in the city and that they would be beaten or have acid thrown in their faces if they appeared without the burka. Clearly, the psychological scars left by Taliban rule are deep.

It was also clear that something had to be done to rein in the remaining warlords who controlled different provinces around the country. And the ongoing drought only exacerbated the problem.

The Afghans are proud people; they did not want handouts. They wanted to be self-sufficient. I was impressed by the level of business being conducted on the streets of Kabul. The city was very much alive, but if the drought continued, the situation would continue to deteriorate.

We met with Hamid Karzai, the leader of Afghanistan's interim government, in his office in downtown Kabul at night and then traveled back to Pakistan. The next day, we were standing in the lobby of a restaurant with a television set tuned to a U.S. news station, airing footage of nine U.S. senators — including John Edwards — standing on the back of a plane at Bagram air base, claiming to be the first congressional delegation to get to Afghanistan.

Their visit was nothing like ours. They never actually left the air base, which was controlled by Americans, and Afghan president Hamid Karzai had to drive from Kabul to Bagram to meet with them, so the senators never saw all that we saw — the destroyed tanks and cars where our laser-guided bombs had hit them, and the devastation in and around Kabul. But when John Edwards got back home, he made a point of telling people about how he'd been "on the ground" in Afghanistan.[1]

· · ·

When I returned to Afghanistan in September of 2005, five and a half years after my previous trip, I was amazed at the differences I saw.

Colorful kites were flying in the skies of Kabul — a longstanding Afghan tradition that had been forbidden by the Taliban. Shoppers and young children crowded the streets. Both boys and girls were attending schools. Hospitals were being improved, and health clinics were opening in villages that had never seen any form of health care. New roads were being built. The country had elected its first president and would shortly elect a national assembly. Five years earlier women were being executed in soccer stadiums. Now many walked the streets free of a burka.

I met again with President Karzai, as well as Ambassador Ronald Neumann and Lt. Gen. Karl Eikenberry, commander of the combined forces. I also spoke with members of the FBI and of NGOs operating there, and nearly everyone seemed pleased with the progress made to date, but stressed that there was still a long way to go. Security remained an issue, both internally from some of the militias that continued to exist and externally from al-Qaeda.

Aside from security, there were two other threats to Afghanistan's future: corruption and drug trafficking. Almost half the country's GDP came from the sale of illicit drugs, mostly from their huge poppy fields, the profits from which were helping fund the global terrorist network. The government needed to get a better handle on both of these problems.

The Afghans were enthusiastic about the upcoming elections. I wish C-SPAN had been with me to capture the excitement in the air. Candidates were going to people's homes to solicit votes and holding campaign barbeques. Campaign posters were plastered on signposts and storefronts all over Kabul.

As with Iraq, patience was the key to success in Afghanistan, which had known nothing but war for twenty-five years. It was slowly making the transition to a democracy, but its future was very much tied to the commitment of the United States — and its coalition partners — to seeing it through to the end.

. . .

Five years later, in the summer of 2010, it was clear that our Afghanistan policy was adrift. Bin Laden had not yet been killed, and Mullah Omar, spiritual leader of the Taliban, still directed their operations. By all accounts, the Taliban had reconstituted, taking back areas once held by coalition forces. They had studied our tactics and were adapting. Low election turnout and allegations of fraud weakened the Karzai government. Narco-trafficking was fueling the insurgency. And July of 2010 had been the deadliest month ever for U.S. troops there: sixty-six dead.

There had been a palpable shift in the nation's mood regarding the war in Afghanistan. A July 2010 *CBS News* poll found that 62 percent of Americans thought the war was going badly.[2] That month, 102 Democrats voted against the war spending bill — sixty more than had voted this way the previous year — and they were joined by twelve Republicans.

I remained unequivocally committed to the success of our mission in Afghanistan and to the more than one hundred thousand American troops and their families sacrificing toward that end.

But I felt it was time to evaluate U.S. strategy in both Afghanistan and Pakistan and clarify the U.S. mission, goals, and objectives for success. We also needed to examine our efforts in the region holistically, given the Taliban's presence in Pakistan, and that country's strategic significance to our efforts in Afghanistan, especially in the border areas.

On August 4, 2010, I wrote to President Obama, telling him I thought it was time for him to immediately convene an Afghanistan-Pakistan Study Group to achieve these goals, modeled after the Iraq Study Group. I told him I had recently spoken with senior diplomats, public policy experts, and retired and active-duty military. Many of them believed that our Afghanistan policy was falling apart, and all agreed that there was an urgent need for a study group.

"We are nine years into our nation's longest-running war, and the American people and their elected representatives do not have a clear sense of what we are aiming to achieve, why it is necessary, and how far we are from attaining that goal," I wrote. I reminded President Obama of his own words of a year before, as he was speaking before the Veterans of Foreign Wars National Convention, when he said, "Those who attacked America on 9/11 are plotting to do so again. If left unchecked, the Taliban insurgency will mean an even larger safe haven from which al-Qaeda would plot to kill more Americans. So this is not only a war worth fighting... this is fundamental to the defense of our people."

The implications of failure in Afghanistan were chilling: an emboldened al-Qaeda, a reconstituted Taliban with an open staging ground for future worldwide attacks, and a destabilized, nuclear-armed Pakistan.

An Afghanistan-Pakistan Study Group could have strengthened many of our NATO allies in Afghanistan who were also facing dwindling public support (as evidenced by the recent Dutch troop withdrawal) and would have given them a tangible vision to which they could have committed. Such a study group had helped force a moment of truth regarding what we needed to do in Iraq; maybe it would work again for Afghanistan.

Obama did not respond to my letter, but I continued to press the idea of a study group. On September 28, 2010, I wrote to Obama for the third time. I was deeply concerned by a *Washington Post* piece adapted from Bob Woodward's new book, *Obama's Wars.* It was clear that discussions of the war strategy were infused with political calculations involving Obama's reelection. Woodward painted a picture of a president who quite simply refused to listen to his most experienced military advisors — the generals who knew most about what we were dealing with in Afghanistan.

"Even at the end of the process," Woodward informed us, "the president's team wrestled with the most basic questions about the war, then entering its ninth year: What is the mission? What are we trying to do? What will work?"[3]

Sobering questions that still have to be answered.

CHAPTER TWELVE

THE BEIJING OLYMPICS

Having heard all this you may choose to look the other way, but you can never again say that you did not know.

William Wilberforce, regarding the horrors
of the British slave trade

On this spot in 1989, nothing happened.

A plaque on Tiananmen Square
in an episode of The Simpsons

IT WAS THE SUMMER OF 2008, and the eyes of the world were focused on the Beijing Olympics — which is exactly where the Chinese government wanted them. They had spent a whopping forty billion dollars preparing for the Games and planned to dazzle the world with their gymnasts, their "Bird's Nest" stadium, and spectacular opening ceremonies. China's leaders wanted everything to be perfect, which is why they were less than delighted when a couple of troublemakers named Frank Wolf and Chris Smith showed up in Beijing shortly before the Games began.

It had been seventeen years since Chris and I traveled to China in 1991 to visit with dissidents and find out what happened to the Tiananmen Square protesters. Now, with the global spotlight on China, we decided to try to divert at least a little attention to the plight of people whom the Chinese government was carefully keeping out of sight of the Western media: human rights activists, persecuted Christians, and others who had run afoul of the Communist regime.

We also wanted to witness firsthand the human rights conditions that had — according to groups like Human Rights Watch

233

and Reporters Without Borders — become nothing less than deplorable. We knew through our contacts in the human rights community that in the run-up to the Games, Chinese security forces had unleashed a series of systematic and brutal crackdowns on underground house church leaders, members of the Falun Gong spiritual movement, human rights and democracy activists, and anybody else the Chinese government believed would disrupt the mirage of harmony and peace it sought to display for the world.

Amnesty International reported that the Chinese government had rounded up people who might "threaten stability" during the Games and detained them without trial. Local governments were under strict orders to quickly shut down public demonstrations after an antigovernment protest in southwestern China involving thirty thousand people turned violent.

Chris and I planned to meet with dissidents and human rights lawyers, attend services at an underground house church (faithful Christians whose leaders are regularly harassed, detained, and jailed because they refuse to be accountable to the government), and visit an internet café to see if access to certain websites was blocked. But China's leaders were still smarting over my undercover visit to Tibet, which led to worldwide publicity about their brutal oppression of the Tibetan people. They also hadn't been thrilled with our work over the years with Chinese dissidents in the U.S., exposing China's brutal policies, and they didn't want us crashing their Olympic party. After all, part of the purpose of the Beijing Olympics was to erase the memory, among Western viewers, of the Tiananmen Square massacre.

So Chris and I weren't too surprised, when we asked for visas, that the answer repeatedly was no. But a very determined young woman who works in my office refused to give up. She kept after the Chinese, hounding them for weeks in an effort to wear them down.

At ten o'clock the night before we were supposed to leave, the Chinese Embassy finally called to say, "Okay, you can go." They probably thought we wouldn't be prepared to jump on a plane and travel seven thousand miles on just a few hours' notice, but we were. In the end, I think they were kind of embarrassed over how they were treating us. They'd invited President Bush to attend the Olympics, and here they were, turning down a couple of congressmen.

As it turned out, our flight was canceled, and we rescheduled for the next day. When we arrived at Dulles Airport that morning, we found an unexpected send-off committee: the Chinese ambassador. He glowered at us. "No funny business, no surprises when you are in China," he told us sternly.

Chris smiled at him. "Life's full of surprises, isn't it?" he said cheerfully. And then we boarded the plane.

Stepping off the plane onto the tarmac in Beijing, I inhaled the badly polluted air. Nobody was there to say, "Welcome back, Frank," which wasn't surprising.

As a U.S. Embassy car drove us to our hotel, we noticed many changes in Beijing. Gleaming office towers now soared high over the city. Luxury hotel chains such as Marriot, Radisson, and Fairmont had invaded this once-closed society, along with upscale shopping malls. The thousands of bicycles I'd seen on my previous trip had been largely replaced by foreign-made cars, and around the city we saw the "Dancing Beijing" emblem of the Games, intended to depict a dancing figure on a red background. The emblem was unintentionally humorous, however, to many in the human rights community, who thought it looked less like a dancer than like a dissident trying to run away.

Our first stop the next morning was an underground Protestant house church, located in a high-rise apartment building. These illegal congregations meet secretly in private homes, and despite severe persecution, including imprisonment and sometimes death, the house church movement is vibrant, with millions of Protestants and Catholics worshiping covertly.

We were amazed when the pastor (whom I will call Mr. Wong

for his own protection) prayed for government authorities — the very people who had so badly treated him. He was praying for his persecutors, exactly as Jesus commands us to do. We stayed at the service only briefly because we had been followed by the Chinese state security services. The congregation urged us to stay anyway, but we didn't want to put them at risk of being targeted for punishment. We found out later that, as retaliation for hosting us, the government placed Pastor Wong under house arrest.

We then attended Mass at the beautiful Cathedral of the Immaculate Conception in Beijing, a historic Roman Catholic Church. While parishioners are able to meet openly in this state-registered church, registered Catholic bishops are forced to "exercise their faith according to Party-dictated terms," according to the Congressional-Executive Commission on China (CECC), which monitors human rights in China.

Everywhere we went in Beijing, the Chinese security police followed us, and we knew they were also listening in on our phone calls. One afternoon Chris and I were traveling to Tiananmen Square in a car, and I was talking on a cell phone to a friend back in the U.S. As a joke, I said, "We're approaching Tiananmen Square. When we get there, we're going to jump out of our car and unfurl the freedom banner."

Twenty minutes later our embassy got a call from an irate Chinese official saying they were going to crack down on us, but good, if we pulled a stunt like that.

Such eavesdropping is typical. They followed us everywhere and bugged our hotel room. We had to be careful where we left our papers. They spy on businessmen, diplomats, members of Congress, and even our cabinet members.

When we arrived at Tiananmen Square, we got out of the car to take a look. It was huge. A large banner of Chairman Mao flew over the Square. There were guards every few feet, keeping people moving. I looked around, trying to figure out where "Tank Man" had stood. You may remember the famous photograph of a courageous man standing alone in the Square, facing down a row of Chinese tanks and forcing them to a halt. After a standoff, two policemen dragged him away. The young man, identified by British journalists as a nineteen-year-old student named Wang Weilin, was never seen again.[1]

I thought of the men I had visited in Beijing Prison Number One during my last trip to China, many of whom had taken part in the Tiananmen Square protests. Some of them were still in prison, all these years later.

· · ·

Chris and I were planning to dine that evening with six Chinese pastors and human rights attorneys. Bob Fu, a Chinese-born pastor who'd escaped from China with his wife and now runs the CHINAaid Association out of Texas, had set up this dinner for us. Among the expected guests were Li Baiguang, a distinguished human rights lawyer. Just a few weeks earlier Chris and I had awarded Mr. Li a National Endowment for Democracy award at a reception on Capitol Hill.

But that afternoon, we began receiving word that the Chinese security police had visited the dinner guests and warned them not to meet with us. Mr. Li was taken to a town several hours away from Beijing and prevented from returning. At least two other dinner guests were placed under house arrest for several days.

In the end, just one of the guests was able to join us, Pastor Zhang Ming-xuan. As we dined, we talked about Pastor Zhang's life, his family, and conditions in China — and the next morning, Zhang too was arrested. I was thankful to learn later that all six of our would-be dinner guests were released unharmed. But Chris and I were outraged over what had happened and lost no time raising the journalistic roof. We held a press conference, and the *Washington Post* ran a lengthy story about it:

> BEIJING, July 1 — A group of Chinese human rights lawyers were detained and later put under house arrest by government

security officials to prevent them from attending a dinner hosted Sunday by two members of the U.S. Congress....

"China has regressed," Wolf said in an interview Tuesday, adding that there had been "absolutely, positively no progress" on human rights....

Foreign Ministry spokesman Liu Jianchao criticized the congressmen for not respecting China's laws and regulations but refused to discuss what law prevented foreign officials from meeting with Chinese citizens.[2]

When Secretary of State Condoleezza Rice arrived in Beijing the next day, we waited to see what she would say about the arrests. We knew she was well aware they had taken place. But instead of condemning this outrage to a worldwide audience during her press conference with the Chinese foreign minister, Dr. Rice told reporters which Olympic venues she planned to visit.

Condoleezza Rice is the daughter of a pastor, and yet she chose to keep silent when Chinese pastors were arrested for the crime of wanting to speak with two United States congressmen. Maybe she had raised the issue privately. I know she cares about human rights, but I was disappointed that she did not speak out publicly.

I knew that part of the problem was that Clark Randt, the U.S. ambassador to China, was very close to the Chinese government; there was no way he was going to aggressively raise and push the human rights cases or encourage others to do so.

Over the years, I had written Randt letter after letter about Chinese government abuses. He would write back with good things to say, and he would even stop by my office occasionally to discuss these issues, but he seldom spoke out publically about them. During our meeting with him on Monday, he listened politely to our concerns about China's treatment of dissidents and about their brutal one-child policy, but he made no promises.

Randt, a fraternity brother to George W. Bush, is a nice man, but I always had the feeling that he didn't want to criticize the Chinese government. At the time, I thought that perhaps he wanted to stay on their good side because he hoped to get a job representing Chinese interests after he retired from diplomatic service.

This is, in fact, exactly what he did. Randt is now a special advisor to a Chinese private equity fund called Hopu Investment Management.

Most of our diplomatic personnel around the world are dedicated public servants who serve our country well. But some become more concerned about the wishes of their host government than those of their own government — and they frequently hope to obtain jobs with their host countries after their diplomatic stint is finished. This is regrettable, especially when it comes to countries like China. I have always believed that our embassies should be islands of freedom in oppressive regimes, not places where diplomats essentially back up the attitudes of the host country.

During our time in Beijing, Chris and I also spent two hours meeting with Ambassador Li Zhaoxing, the former Chinese foreign minister who was now chairing the Foreign Affairs Committee of the National People's Congress. Chris and I pressed him for the release of detained individuals and presented him with a list of 734 other political prisoners, compiled by the Congressional-Executive Commission on China (CECC) — people who'd committed the "crimes" of promoting democracy, religious freedom, and labor rights. "We'd like to see them released, too," we told Li. Ambassador Li simply talked around the issue and took no action.

Among the prisoners we were most concerned about was Zhang Rongliang, an unregistered Protestant church pastor. Zhang was a leader of the China for Christ Church, whose network of house churches included up to ten million members. Zhang had lived in hiding for several years prior to his 2004 arrest, when he was sentenced to seven and a half years for fraudulently obtaining travel documents and illegally crossing the border. According to the CECC, Zhang had been subjected to electric shock and suffered from hypertension and diabetes. His family relied on donations from church members to survive.

Protestant pastors are not the only religious believers the Communist government persecutes. Catholic bishops, Muslim Uyghurs, Falun Gong followers, and Buddhist monks have also been harassed, beaten, and jailed for practicing their faith. According to the Cardinal Kung Foundation, at the time of our visit, every one of the approximately thirty-five underground bishops of the Catholic Church was either in jail, under house arrest, under strict surveillance, or in hiding.[3] Renowned human rights advocate Rebiya Kadeer, a Uyghur who now lives in Fairfax County, Virginia, watched in exile as the Chinese government arrested and beat her sons.

All that Chris and I saw and experienced during our visit to China was consistent with the heartbreaking accounts given to us by political dissidents and persecuted people of faith in China, which is why we tried so hard to convince President George W. Bush that he should not legitimize China's barbarous regime by attending the opening ceremonies of the Games. So did many human rights groups and other members of Congress, not simply for China's abuses of its own citizens and of Tibetans but also for its complicity in the genocide then taking place in Darfur. China supported the Khartoum government and was sending them everything from armored trucks to fighter jets to howitzers in exchange for oil. These weapons, with China's knowledge, were being turned on the helpless citizens of Darfur, maiming and murdering them by the tens of thousands.

The Beijing Olympics bore some eerie parallels to the 1936 Summer Olympics in Berlin. For instance, just prior to the 1936 Games, Berlin police rounded up and interned some eight hundred Gypsies, confining them for the duration of the Games; the Chinese rounded up "troublemakers" and kept them locked up until the Beijing Games were over. The Nazis also removed Jews Not Wanted signs from Berlin lest tourists and press cameras see them; the Chinese did them one better: they simply censored their own media and put restrictions on where foreign journalists could go, whom they could talk to, and what they could report on.[4]

Many Jews and Gypsies were prevented from participating in the Berlin Games; political dissidents and religious minorities were kept out of the Beijing Games. Nazi Germany played down its anti-Semitic agenda and plans for territorial expansion, fooling the international community with an image of a peaceful, tolerant nation under the cover of the Olympic Games. China played a similar game. Finally, both the Berlin and Beijing Games were intended to strengthen nationalistic feeling and demonstrate the important place of each country in the world. Neither should have been allowed to use the Olympics to do it.

. ` . .

Before leaving Beijing, Chris and I held another press conference at the U.S. Embassy, during which we appealed to the Chinese government to free its prisoners of conscience, stop harassing dissidents, and respect fundamental human rights. We pointed out that Chinese men and women were being tortured and jailed simply for exercising their fundamental freedoms — freedoms guaranteed by both the Universal Declaration of Human Rights and the Chinese Constitution. We reminded journalists of the words of Liu Jingmin, vice president of the Beijing Olympic bid committee, who claimed that giving China the honor of hosting the 2008 Summer Games would promote "the development of society, including democracy and human rights."[5] Tragically, just the opposite happened: the Games triggered a brutal crackdown on those whose views differed from the official party line.

I again called on President Bush to boycott the Games until China dramatically improved its treatment of dissidents, including prisoners of conscience, as China had promised to do as a condition of being allowed to host the Games. I tried to convey to President Bush that Chinese political prisoners and dissidents would be demoralized by what the Chinese government would surely portray as symbolic support for its regime if senior American officials attended the Games.

When President Bush announced he would not back off on his commitment to attend the Beijing Olympics, I wrote to him again, urging him to deliver a major human rights speech in Tiananmen Square, similar to the one President Reagan gave in Moscow in 1988. In the midst of the Cold War, at the Danlov Monastery, Reagan publicly called on the Soviet Union to promote religious tolerance.

"While in Beijing for the opening ceremonies," I wrote, "you should deliver a public address calling on the Chinese government to release all the political and religious dissidents who languish in labor camps and prisons across China. The people of China, and the dissidents who sit in their jail cells day after day, week after week, year after year, should know that the president of the United States of America and the leader of the free world stands valiantly with them in their quest for liberty, and not with the repressive Communist regime of China."

As I have mentioned before, dissidents who spent years in the gulags of the former Soviet Union will tell you that life in prison gets better when Westerners advocate for them. This is especially true when someone of the stature of the American president is doing the advocating. Afterward, when letters pour in from all over the world expressing concern for Prisoner X, the warden starts giving him more food, and he's treated better.

Unfortunately, President Bush declined to make such a speech.

Finally, I urged Mr. Bush to go visit and worship with illegal house church leaders and dissidents while in China. The president chose instead to worship in a government-run church.

To his credit, President Bush did twice rebuke China over the country's political and religious oppression, but, as the *New York Times* noted, Mr. Bush "tempered his criticism with effusive praise for the country's history and embraced its hosting of the Olympic Games."[6] Yet, restrained as Bush's criticism was, Chinese leaders responded angrily, saying that America had no business "interfer[ing] in other countries' affairs."[7]

But is that really what Bush was doing? My friend Chuck Colson tells the story of how, in 1973, President Nixon sent him to Moscow to negotiate for the release of Soviet Jews to Israel. Chuck told Vasily Kuznetsov, the hard-nosed Soviet negotiator, that if the Soviets refused to release the Jews, Congress would refuse to pass the trade treaty, which the Soviets desperately wanted passed: they needed our grain. Kuznetsov was enraged; he pounded the table with his fist and shouted, "You have no right to interfere in our internal affairs!"

"These aren't your internal affairs," Chuck answered. "Human rights are not conferred by government; they cannot be denied by government. They are God-given. We call them 'inalienable.'"

In the end, the Soviets reluctantly agreed to release the Jews, Congress passed the trade treaty, and the Soviets got their grain.[8]

Sadly, sometimes our leaders seem to take exactly the opposite approach to hard-nosed dictators today. Whether it's the Chinese, the North Koreans, or somebody else, our approach is to send them food and aid money, or allow them to host the Olympic Games, if they *promise* to be nice to those they are persecuting. In the end, little changes.

Although I was disappointed that President Bush attended the Beijing Olympics, he did do some good things on the human rights front. He became the first sitting president to meet publicly with the Dalai Lama, in October of 2007. Adding insult to injury (from China's point of view), Bush awarded the spiritual leader the Congressional Gold Medal, the highest civilian honor America can bestow, and used the occasion to call for religious liberty and basic human rights in China. Chinese leaders scolded Bush, and the U.S. Congress, for once again "interfering in China's internal affairs."[9]

Bush also met with five Chinese dissidents in the White House, including Bob Fu, Harry Wu, Wei Jingsheng, and Sasha Gong. Bob later filled me in about the get-together: "The meeting with Mr.

Bush was warm and frank — perhaps, at times, a little more frank than the president expected. Wei Jingsheng told Mr. Bush bluntly to his face that it was a mistake for him to attend the Olympics. Mr. Bush seemed caught off guard by Wei's bluntness but replied, 'I happen to believe it is the right decision.'

"I was pretty blunt myself. I knew President Bush was a Christian, so I said, 'Mr. Bush, please don't forget that a fellow Christian, a lady seventy-nine years old, Ms. Shuang Shuying, is serving two years in a jail just eighteen miles away from the Bird's Nest stadium, where you plan to attend the opening show.' I also presented Mr. Bush with four Pray for China bands made by Chinese Christians, and urged him and his family to wear them during the Olympics. I'm not sure whether he did or not."

But President Bush's desire to court China as an economic partner meant he did not say, and do, as much as he might have. I believe that history will show a legacy of missed opportunities on human rights.

On our last day in China, Chris and I stepped into a packed Beijing internet café to find out if internet access was restricted by the government. Before we were allowed access to a computer, café employees asked to see our passports. We tried to access sites like those of the National Endowment for Democracy, Voice of America, and Reporters Without Borders, as well as sites devoted to the Dalai Lama. Every one came up with an error message — a message symbolic of China's attitude toward freedom.

• • •

In the aftermath of the Beijing Olympics, I've continued to work on behalf of Chinese prisoners of conscience and others who suffer under one of the most brutal regimes in the world. Tragically, their suffering has increased on Barack Obama's watch, because human rights are not a priority for his administration. Hillary Clinton made the administration's policy priorities crystal clear on her first trip to China as secretary of state in February of 2009. Mrs. Clinton bluntly stated that pressing the Chinese about human rights "can't interfere with the global economic crisis, the global climate change crisis, and the security crisis."[10]

In other words, peddling America's debt to China was more important than speaking out for pastors being tortured in Chinese prisons.

I was so disappointed that I sent Mrs. Clinton a letter telling her that her comment sent the wrong signal to every dictator and authoritarian regime that chooses repression over freedom. "America has always been a friend to the oppressed, the persecuted, the forgotten," I noted. "Has our allegiance changed?"

Chris Smith, Congressman Joe Pitts, and I held a joint news conference condemning Mrs. Clinton's comments and asking the Obama administration to take a much firmer stand on human rights offenses. Amnesty International was also dismayed by Clinton's comments, asking her to "repair the damage caused by her statement."[11]

I've kept after the Obama administration on this issue, writing letters to administration officials and speaking out on the House floor, chastising them for their failure to champion human rights as a central part of American foreign policy. On July 29, 2009, on the floor of the House, I criticized both Hillary Clinton and Treasury Secretary Timothy Geithner, who had just outlined in the *Wall Street Journal* topics they planned to discuss in upcoming talks with the Chinese government: "In Monday's Wall Street Journal, Secretary of State Hillary Clinton and Secretary of the Treasury Timothy Geithner co-authored an opinion piece outlining the issues to be discussed in the U.S.-China Strategic and Economic Dialogue."[12]

No mention of human rights.

No mention of the Chinese government's suppression of journalists.

No mention of the dozens of human rights lawyers across China who've been stripped of their licenses.

No mention of the thirty-five Catholic bishops who languish in Chinese prisons and slave labor camps.

No mention of the Chinese government's crackdown on the Chinese ethnic Uyghurs.

No mention of how China continues to repatriate North Korean refugees.

Human rights simply cannot be separated from economic policy.

The Obama administration has missed *yet another* opportunity to make human rights a fundamental component of U.S. foreign policy.

If I sounded angry — and I did — it was because I *was* angry over the lack of progress on human rights. I spoke out again during an October 29, 2009, hearing of the Tom Lantos Human Rights Commission, which I co-chair. Six Chinese human rights attorneys had flown to the U.S. to testify about how conditions had worsened that year, and they made it clear that any faint progress that had taken place prior to the Olympics had gone with the Games.

For example, Gao Zhisheng, a famous human rights attorney, had not been seen or heard from since he was taken from his home by Chinese authorities in February.[13] Four Tibetans had been executed in connection with the deadly riots in Lhasa the year before. And Human Rights Watch had recently released a report detailing the disappearances of forty-three Uyghur men and boys since the July uprising in Xinjiang.[14]

Life is especially difficult for Uyghur converts to Christianity, who are hated by both Muslims and Chinese authorities and are forced to gather in complete secrecy in groups of just two or three people. Their leader, Alimujiang Yimiti, was sentenced to fifteen years in prison on a fabricated charge of releasing state secrets to overseas organizations.[15]

It would help the cause of religious freedom if U.S. Embassy personnel and American officials — including President Obama —

made a point of attending services at house churches, the six Chinese lawyers told our commission, and they wanted Obama "to convey this religious persecution to the Chinese government during his visit to China."[16]

Following the hearing, Chris Smith and I sent letters to President Obama and Secretary of State Hillary Clinton asking them to ensure the safety of the lawyers once they returned to China, and, during a press conference, I warned both President Obama and Chinese leaders that if any of the lawyers were arrested or harassed when they returned to China, "I will do everything I can to just create the biggest problem possible for the Obama administration and for the Chinese government."

We subsequently heard that one of the lawyers did pay a high price for his testimony after his return home. As Jiang Tianyong and his wife attempted to take their seven-year-old daughter to school one morning, four Public Security Bureau officers showed up at their apartment building, grabbed Jiang, and forced him into a police car. Another officer threw Jiang's wife to the ground and beat her in front of the couple's terrified daughter.

Jiang was taken to a police station, where human rights attorneys swiftly gathered to demand his release. The U.S. Embassy (which was probably more alert to possible problems, assuming our State Department followed through and alerted them to potential difficulties when the lawyers returned home) was contacted about the arrest. The embassy called the Chinese Ministry of Foreign Affairs to register its concern. Jiang was released that evening after thirteen hours in custody.

The damage done early in the Obama administration, by Mrs. Clinton's careless comments and President Obama's apparent indifference, may be worse than either of them realize. Wei Jingshen, who spent years in prison and is referred to as the father of Chinese democracy and the Chinese Nelson Mandela, once told Chris Smith that when American leaders pander to Chinese dictators, they beat dissidents more in the prison camps. By contrast, when American leaders are tough, predictable, and transparent, "they beat us less."[17]

Human rights observers say the beatings have gone into overdrive during the Obama administration. Obama's entire human rights policy is to suggest that we agree to disagree. Dissidents who are thrown into slave labor camps, women who are forced to have abortions, North Koreans who are repatriated to prison and death, pastors and priests who are locked up, Buddhist monks who are tortured in Tibet — these things are at the bottom of Obama's priority list, and the Chinese know it.

President Obama, who is known to admire Abraham Lincoln, ought to acquaint himself with a campaign speech Lincoln made in July of 1858. As he prepared his notes, the man who would one day be known as the Great Emancipator had in his thoughts the Great Abolitionist, William Wilberforce.

"I have not allowed myself to forget," Lincoln said, "the abolition of the slave trade by Great Britain. School boys know that Wilberforce ... helped that cause forward, but who can now name a single man who labored to retard it?"[18]

Or, Lincoln might have added, remained indifferent.

As for the rest of us, we should regularly remind ourselves of something else Lincoln said in that speech delivered long ago: that "the abolition of the Slave-trade by Great Britain was agitated a hundred years before it was a final success."[19]

Wilberforce himself devoted some three decades to fighting the buying and selling of human beings. While he frequently despaired over the lack of progress — and over politicians who didn't much care about the plight of slaves — he never gave up.

We can't give up, either. We can't say that we didn't know. We must stand up and speak out for those who suffer around the globe — no matter how hard the battle, nor how long it takes.

CHAPTER THIRTEEN

OUR FISCAL TIME BOMB

For the United States' enemies in Iran and Iraq, it must be consoling to know that U.S. fiscal policy today is preprogrammed to reduce the resources available for all overseas military operations in the years ahead.

Niall Ferguson

ARE AMERICA'S BEST DAYS BEHIND HER?

It seems to be topic A at Washington dinner parties these days — and in Oregon churches and at Texas softball games.

I believe this foreboding national anxiety is born of certain realities: exploding debts and deficits, shuttered factories, rising unemployment, bloated government, and an acrimonious tenor to our national discourse. People fear that America's influence is waning and that our "shining city on a hill" is dimming.

As a father of five and grandfather of fifteen, I must admit to sharing these same anxieties. I have never been more concerned about my country's future. Yet I do not believe that the realization of these fears is inevitable. Sober-minded people believe that we must dramatically change course, especially as it relates to our ballooning national debt and deficit, and I agree. But is America — and are her leaders — willing to make the necessary tough decisions?

Within days of the report of President Obama's National Commission on Fiscal Responsibility and Reform in December of 2010 — one that warned of the dire consequences of failing to address growing mandatory spending — it was business as usual.

Congress merrily passed, and the Obama administration enthusiastically supported, a tax-and-spending bill with an $857 billion price tag — one that included a yearlong "payroll tax holiday," raiding the Social Security trust fund at a cost of $112 billion, without paying for it, thereby increasing the national debt.

Historically, Americans have shown themselves willing to sacrifice. The nation's future now falls to our generation. Will we step up to the plate — or will we fail to act?

For too long, routinely increasing the amount of money our government can borrow without taking any action to stem our country's growing debt has been standard operating procedure. But the storm warning signs have been posted.

Consider these grim realities: America is now more than $14 trillion in debt and accumulating a trillion-dollar deficit every year. Both Moody's Investment Service and Standard & Poor's cautioned the U.S. — again — that its coveted AAA credit rating was at risk if the country's deteriorating fiscal situation was not corrected.

The practical implications of a downgraded credit rating are severe. The cost to borrow money will rise. Everything from a home loan to a car loan to a student loan will increase.

Interest on the debt was $202 billion in 2010. That's nearly $4 billion a week. In 2021 interest on the debt is projected to be $1 trillion a year — or roughly $2.7 billion a day. Unsustainable debt in Europe and the resulting economic woes and austerity measures led to riots in the streets. Is it just a matter of time before we see that at home? If we are on the same trajectory as these countries, their unemployment numbers should give us pause.

Last year a report from the Congressional Budget Office revealed that for the first time in twenty-five years, Social Security was taking in less in taxes than it was spending on benefits. In addition, recent reports found that as 2011 opens, the first of the baby boomers will turn sixty-five, and baby boomers will continue to reach that age at the rate of ten thousand a day for the next nineteen years. Or consider that just over the past decade, foreign ownership of U.S. debt has increased significantly, from 5 percent forty years ago to 46 percent today.

If the U.S. does not begin to rein in spending, by 2028 every penny of the federal budget will go to interest on the debt and entitlement spending. This has grave implications for a host of national priorities, not to mention America's very survival. In 2007 then – U.S. comptroller general David Walker warned of "striking similarities" between America's current situation and the fall of the Roman Empire.[1]

But as America sinks deeper into debt, we seem satisfied to live utterly in the moment with no concern for the future. And as our own investments in the future lag, China is forging ahead, making significant gains in education while our children are left in their wake. Do we really want the twenty-first century, this century, to be the Chinese century?

Roughly half of America's outstanding publicly held debt is now foreign owned, with China and Saudi Arabia among the largest holders. Saudi Arabia, you may recall, was home to many of the 9/11 terrorists. A recent *New York Times* story reported that "Saudi donors remain the chief financiers of Sunni militant groups like Al Qaeda." Is this a country we want to be beholden to financially?[2]

Or what about Communist China? The U.S. intelligence community has thoroughly documented that China's attempts to spy on U.S. agencies are the most aggressive of all foreign intelligence organizations, and, according to the FBI, "pose a significant threat both to the national security and to the compromise of U.S. critical national assets."[3]

In 2006 I came to the floor of the House proposing an independent bipartisan commission to address unsustainable federal spending. It would put *everything* on the table: entitlements, all other spending, and tax policy. The SAFE Commission, short for Securing America's Future Economy, would operate in a transparent way, holding public meetings across the country to hear from the American people and give them a vested interest in the outcome. It would also require Congress to vote on the recommendations. I reintroduced this legislation, with Congressman Jim Cooper, in the 110th and 111th Congresses. Each time it gained more supporters, but each time it was voted down.

In 2010 Senators Kent Conrad and Judd Gregg introduced a similar bill calling for a deficit commission — one that became the blueprint for President Obama's National Commission on Fiscal Responsibility and Reform, or the Simpson-Bowles Commission.

While I didn't agree with every aspect of the commission's report, the commission's work was important in moving the national conversation forward. It put forth serious ideas rather than just kicking the can down the road, and had I been appointed to the commission, while supporting some changes, I would have voted for its final report.

The plan set forth by the Simpson-Bowles Commission, supported by a majority of the commission's eighteen members, makes clear that addressing the debt and the deficit isn't just a simple exercise in rooting out waste, fraud, and abuse. Yes, we should eliminate earmarks, waste, fraud, and abuse and rein in discretionary spending. But these actions alone won't come close to solving our debt and deficit problems.

The infamous bank robber Willie Sutton reportedly said he robbed banks "because that's where the money is." In our government, the money is in entitlements — Medicare, Medicaid, and Social Security — and that's where reform must begin. If we don't deal with Medicare, Medicaid, and Social Security, we cannot possibly solve our debt problem. We must resolve it in a way that really fixes the problem — for us and for the next generation. And we must do it in a way that strengthens America, creating economic growth and jobs.

This will be difficult, and at times controversial, but the longer we wait, the more certain it will be that the process will only become more difficult and more controversial.

The commission's forthright assessment about what's necessary to put us in good fiscal standing was a step in the right direction. The success of any such endeavor, however, is predicated on actively involving the American people and must require an up-or-down congressional vote. The president's commission came up short in that regard. We need to come up with a bipartisan solution — something that can pass and be enacted into law, as soon as possible.

If we neglect to do this, America will decline — and on our watch. We will have failed our children and grandchildren and broken faith with the Founding Fathers and past generations who sacrificed greatly to make this nation what it may soon no longer be: a shining city on a hill. Instead we will see tax increases, drastic entitlement reductions, and no money for important discretionary spending such as infrastructure, national security, medical research, and education. The longer we fail to address this problem, the more draconian the options will be when the nation is forced to change course, as it most assuredly will be.

If you're on Social Security or Medicare, you should insist that Congress take action. If you're a young adult, you should worry that your generation will be significantly less well off than your parents' generation. If you care about American global leadership, if you yearn for our country to have the resources to combat global scourges, if you hope for a cure for cancer and Alzheimer's, you should press Congress and the administration to step up to the plate now. If you belong to America's faith community, you should speak out about the moral component of the debt crisis; the poor will be hardest hit if we fail to act. And if we say we are passionate about justice, we must not be complicit in committing a massive generational injustice.

Finally, all of us, whatever our political views, must ask ourselves a vitally important question: do we want to make a point, or do we want to make a difference?

At his 1796 farewell address, George Washington admonished

his fellow countrymen to avoid "ungenerously throwing upon posterity the burden which we ourselves ought to bear."[4]

An apt charge for today's political leadership, for not only is our current course immoral; it is also un-American. Generations past have always passed the torch of the American dream to their children and grandchildren. Presently, we're poised to hand off the struggling flicker of a flame instead.

The implications of an America on the decline has ripple effects the world over. In the *Washington Post*, Robert Kaplan hauntingly writes, "America's ability to bring a modicum of order to the world is simply fading in slow motion."[5] Daily headlines remind us that the world is a much more dangerous place when our nation is perceived as weak, or worse yet, when that perception becomes reality.

If we summon the courage to act, I believe we will see a rebirth in America, marked by grand innovations in science and technology that will be the wonder of the world, advances in medical research that will save millions of lives, further exploration into the remaining frontier of space, and much more.

I was reminded of our unique American spirit on Election Day in 2010 when I stopped by the Snow White Grill in Winchester, Virginia. While I was there, a man enthusiastically told me, "We are ready! We are prepared to sacrifice. We're ready to do what's right." Several other diners echoed his words.

But the question remains, are America's *leaders* prepared to sacrifice? Are America's leaders prepared to do what's right? And are you and I willing to tell them we won't settle for anything less?

CHAPTER FOURTEEN

THE END OF THE ROAD — OR THE BEGINNING?

From everyone who has been given much, much will be demanded; and from the one who has been entrusted with much, much more will be asked.

Luke 12:48

A FEW MONTHS AGO Carolyn and I drove our eleven-year-old grandson, Howe, back to his home in Princeton, New Jersey. But first we made a detour to Independence Hall, home of the Liberty Bell. The Park Service guide took us first to the room where the Declaration of Independence was crafted, then across the hall to the room where the Constitution was hammered out in 1787 by the Constitutional Convention, presided over by George Washington.

Fifty-odd years ago, as a teenager working at the Curtis Publishing Company, I used to get off the trolley car, cut through Independence Hall, and run my fingers along the Liberty Bell. I knew its history, and touching it sent a shiver down my spine. I wish Howe could also have touched it, but now that old, cracked bell hangs behind glass.

Some people think our country is a bit cracked, too — including me. America is traveling in the wrong direction, and it's traveling there fast.

In 2005 members of the National Academies' Committee on Prospering in the Global Economy of the Twenty-first Century spoke before the U.S. House of Representatives Committee on

Science. Their findings, detailed in a report titled "Rising Above the Gathering Storm: Energizing and Employing America for a Brighter Economic Future," were ominous. America, it warned, was on a losing path and "in substantial danger of losing the economic leadership position and suffering a concomitant decline of the standard of living of its citizens because of a looming inability to compete for jobs in the global marketplace."[1] They made a number of recommendations — such as recruiting ten thousand new science and math teachers each year, strengthening our commitment to long-term basic research, and establishing scholarships in mathematics, engineering, technology, and competitive science. Our government funded some of these things, but five years later, in 2010, the committee asked where America stood. In a book titled *Rising Above the Gathering Storm, Revisited: Rapidly Approaching Category 5*, the authors write, "The unanimous view of the authors is that our nation's outlook has worsened."[2] For example,

- "The World Economic Forum ranks the United States 48th in quality of mathematics and science education."
- "Manufacturing employment in the U.S. computer industry is now lower than when the first personal computer was built in 1975."
- "China has now replaced the United States as the world's number one *high-technology* exporter."
- "No new nuclear plants and no new petroleum refineries have been built in the United States in a third of a century, a period characterized by intermittent energy-related crises."
- "Eight of the ten global companies with the largest R&D budgets have established R&D facilities in China, India or both."
- "Sixty-nine percent of United States public school students in fifth through eighth grade are taught mathematics by a teacher without a degree or certificate in mathematics."

British historian Niall Ferguson expands on this theme in an article in *Foreign Affairs* titled "Complexity and Collapse." While most historians see the collapse of empires in "cyclical and gradual terms," the reality is that they tend to collapse rapidly, he writes. "Great powers and empires are … complex systems, made up of a very large number of interacting components that are asymmetrically organized, which means their construction more resembles a termite hill than an Egyptian pyramid…. Such systems can appear to operate quite stably for some time…. But there comes a moment when complex systems 'go critical.' A very small trigger can set off a 'phase transition' from a benign equilibrium to a crisis — a single grain of sand causes a whole pile to collapse, or a butterfly flaps its wings in the Amazon and brings about a hurricane in southeastern England."[3]

The trigger for World War I was "a series of diplomatic miscalculations in the summer of 1914, the real origins of 9/11 lies in the politics of Saudi Arabia in the 1990s, and the financial crisis was principally due to errors in monetary policy by the U.S. Federal Reserve and to China's rapid accumulation of dollar reserves after 2001," Ferguson notes. Other empires from ancient Rome to the Ming Dynasty to the Bourbon monarchy to the former Soviet Union also suffered sudden collapses, Ferguson writes.[4]

All great empires collapse eventually, and, if the historians are correct, the same thing could eventually happen to the United States — which, while not an empire, has greater power and influence than any empire the world has ever known. Can we do anything to stave off the demise of our privileged place in the world, of our enviable standard of living, and, quite possibly, of our freedoms?

For many empires, collapse came as something of a surprise, but Americans can see the handwriting on the wall. At least, the handwriting is there to see, if we are willing to take a good look at the wall, if we understand the words, and if we are willing to act on the warnings being given to us.

I have already talked about the need to reduce America's debt, to encourage Americans to pursue careers in science and engineering, and to invest in medical research. But we must also invest in something even more important, if we want to avoid an event every bit as dire in its implications as economic collapse: moral collapse. We must ground our children and grandchildren in moral truth, cultivating both conscience and character.

My friend Chuck Colson talks a lot about worldview and how to determine if our personal outlook on the world is true. He constantly asks people probing questions about their beliefs, such as, "Is your belief system rational and defensible? Does it conform to reality?"

Some people have fallen into the postmodern belief that there's no such thing as good or bad, no difference between vice and virtue, no transcendent standards of right and wrong. If you've been to the places I've been, you wouldn't fall for that nonsense. Who could look into the eyes of a gang rape victim in Darfur, or of a young Thai girl who's been sold to a brothel, and tell her there's no such thing as right or wrong, good or evil? She knows better.

And so we need to seek a spiritual renaissance as well as an economic one, teaching our children that ultimate truth comes from God, passed on through the Judeo-Christian tradition. We must ground our children in moral truth, teaching them that good and evil both exist, and of the consequences of embracing one or the other.

The alternative to doing this is frightening. If we do everything the experts recommend to save our country — if we reduce debt, improve teaching, and increase the number of college graduates with degrees in science, engineering, and technology — but do not provide our children and grandchildren with moral truth, we may end up in a worse place than we are now. We will have a nation of highly educated citizens indifferent to morality — which is exactly where Germany found herself in the 1930s.

Today faulty ideas about right and wrong have led to doctors who pressure mothers to abort babies with Down syndrome or other disabilities, lest society be burdened with their care. It has led to a culture that encourages the sick elderly to "die and get out of the way," lest they become a burden to their relatives. But we must choose righteousness, both personally and as a society, encouraging our young to bring their faith into the public square, attempting to persuade their fellow citizens of the rightness of their cause.

Some people criticize the faithful for getting involved in politics, but it's important to remember that down through the centuries, people motivated by their faith have done many important things. Wilberforce — motivated by his faith — brought about an end to the slave trade. Bonhoeffer — motivated by his faith — stood up against the persecution of the Jews. Martin Luther King Jr. — motivated by his faith — brought about an end to segregation in our country. The Americans who fought child labor, opened orphanages, and worked for the abolition of slavery were mostly Christians, and the church should continue this noble tradition, speaking out against the evils of our own day.

For instance, we should not look the other way when America's children are trafficked at luxurious hotels and dingy truck stops. We should get angry when corporate executives steal from investors, or when we see hard-core pornography permeating every corner of our culture, twisting the minds of the men, women, and children exposed to it. We should respond to the destructive power of gambling, which undeniably causes crime and destroys families, spreading across the nation.

I've been disappointed that the church has neglected so many of these problems — even the persecution of their brethren overseas. I send letters to dozens of church leaders, imploring them for their help on such issues as the ongoing persecution of Coptic Christians in Egypt and the attacks on the ancient Christian community in Iraq. If I'm lucky, I receive a small handful of responses.

This is why I've appreciated the yeoman's work Chuck Colson, along with Robert George, professor of politics at Princeton University, and theologian Timothy George, have done in creating a document titled "The Manhattan Declaration: A Call of Christian

Conscience," with which the church speaks out with one voice on the need to protect religious freedom, traditional marriage, and the sanctity of human life at all stages.[5]

Christian leaders across the religious spectrum have signed it, including Bishop Harry Jackson Jr., His Eminence Justin Cardinal Rigali, the Reverend Tim Keller, Dr. Alveda King, Josh McDowell, the Most Reverend Donald W. Wuerl, and Ravi Zacharias. Close to half a million Americans have also signed it and committed themselves to working to achieve its goals.

We cannot even begin to solve America's massive problems unless we politicians recognize that we can no longer afford to have a government made up of Democrats and Republicans — in effect, enemy combatants — who refuse to talk to one another. For the good of the country, we need to reconcile — in some cases, to forgive or ask forgiveness.

In Matthew 5:23 – 24 Jesus says, "If you are offering your gift at the altar and there remember that your brother or sister has something against you, leave your gift there in front of the altar. First go and be reconciled to them; then come and offer your gift."

Some of the problems that could bring the Right and the Left together: human trafficking, world hunger, genocide, religious persecution, and the lack of medical care in the developing world. We could battle these things with the help of government — passing stronger laws to fight trafficking, for instance — or we could encourage volunteer efforts, such as inviting newly minted doctors and nurses to spend a year or two in Africa working among the poorest of the poor, perhaps forgiving some of their student loans if they do.

We are a nation of a hundred different races and religions. But we can and should find common ground with matters that ought to be important to all of us.

. . .

On the day Carolyn and I visited Independence Hall with our grandson, our guide told us a story I will never forget. She told us that in September of 1787, on the final day of the Constitutional Convention in Philadelphia, eighty-one-year-old Benjamin Franklin is said to have wept when he signed the document. As James Madison wrote in a letter to Thomas Jefferson, "Whilst the last members were signing it, Dr. Franklin looking towards the president's [Washington's] chair, at the back of which a rising sun happened to be painted, observed to a few members near him, that painters had found it difficult to distinguish in their art a rising from a setting sun."[6]

And then Franklin remarked that during the course of the session, "I have often looked at that picture behind the president without being able to tell whether it was a rising or setting sun. Now at length I have the happiness to know that it is indeed a rising, not a setting sun."[7]

Is the sun still rising over America? Or is it about to set?

Every politician loves to give speeches saying that the sun has barely begun to rise and that America's best days are ahead. But if we are indifferent to the signs of coming economic and moral collapse, then Niall Ferguson's prediction will come true: America will rapidly decline. And then we, and everyone else, will live in a more dangerous world.

During his farewell address, George Washington, whose exploits I loved to read about as a boy growing up in post – World War II Philadelphia, said, "Of all the dispositions and habits which lead to political prosperity, Religion and morality are indispensable supports."[8]

The old general was right. Will we remember and act on his warning?

If we come together to solve the problems of our nation — if we work for economic and moral rebirth — then America's best days will yet be ahead. And the sun will truly have just begun to rise on this country.

It's not too late. God is sovereign.

ACKNOWLEDGMENTS

I WANT TO EXPRESS MY THANKS to Anne Morse for her gifted way with words, making these chapters come to life in a way I never could. I also appreciate the great amount of time she spent interviewing people for the book and doing research. A person who urged me to write this book and recommended Anne to me is Chuck Colson, who is a friend and has given me wise counsel many times over the years.

Many people generously arranged time for interviews, sent information by email and some read the relevant chapters, commented on them, and corrected any errors. I want to express my gratitude to my longtime friends, colleagues, and sometime traveling companions, Congressman Chris Smith and former Congressman and Ambassador Tony Hall. Thanks also go to Senator Dan Coats, Fred Van Gorkum, Ion Mihai (Mike) Pacepa, Dana Damaceanu Bart, Richard Stephenson, Mikhail Kasakov, Alexandr Goldovich, Vladimir Potashov, the late Daja Meston, Mary Beth Markey, Dick Foth, Steve Saint, Blaine Harden, Roger Winter, Dr. Elizabeth Morgan, David Holdridge, Bob Fu, Harry Wu, and three lifelong friends — Bill and Buddy Pepe and John Federico. I also want to recognize Renee and Bill Brohard, who put my photos in a usable format, the folks at Zondervan for their editing and design work, and my agent from Alive Communications, Joel Kneedler. Assisting Anne in transcribing conversations and interviews were Martha Anderson and Travis Morse.

My wife, Carolyn, discussed every chapter with me, helped jog my memory for details, and spent hours on the computer communicating my thoughts, text changes, and corrections to Anne. Carolyn has been my helpmate and encourager for fifty years.

Through the years my small Bible study group has been a source of great support, starting in the early 1980s with our first group: Tony Hall, Dan Coats, and Bob McEwen. Over the years the participants have changed with Tony and myself being the constants. Today our group also includes another colleague, Joe Pitts. Other friends who have encouraged me have been Doug Coe, Dick Foth, and David Boyd.

Many excellent people have worked for me throughout my time in Congress. My former Chief of Staff, the late Charlie White, and my current Chief of Staff, Dan Scandling, traveled with me on many trips to troubled places. They, along with my Legislative Director, Janet Shaffron, and my Director of Constituent Services, Judy McCary, represent all the fine and dedicated people on my congressional staff, past and present, who have made my work possible and who have helped tirelessly with the issues addressed in this book and with a thousand other issues.

I want to express gratitude to my former political consultants, Ed DeBolt and Bob Chase. They supported me, against odds, from my very first campaign and remain friends. Although retired from politics, Ed is someone I still count on for sage advice.

I am also appreciative of the many people who have helped me in my election campaigns, and I want to thank the constituents of my congressional district who have given me the opportunity to serve.

Finally, I want to thank my family. My parents, Frank and Virginia Wolf, provided a loving home and taught me strong moral values, a good work ethic, and perseverance. My brother, Joe, is my hero; I don't know a more faithful and caring person. My wife, Carolyn, and my five children have given me all the love, encouragement, and support any husband and father could want. So, thank you to my son, Frank, his wife, Enida, my daughters and their husbands: Virginia and Derrick Max, Anne and Andrew Fredbeck, Brenda and Howe Whitman, and Rebecca and Dan DiBiase. I am also thankful to them for fifteen (and counting?) grandchildren who give joy beyond measure: Adam, Ben, Caleb, Hannah, Sarah, Rebekah, Lucas, Daniel, Wilson, Howe, Clara, Annie, Virginia, Noah, and Josephine.

And most especially, I am grateful to the God who made me.

NOTES

Foreword

1. Kevin Belmonte, *William Wilberforce: A Hero for Humanity* (Grand Rapids, Mich.: Zondervan, 2007).
2. Blaine Harden, "A One-Man Human-Rights Crusade," *Washington Post* (July 16, 1995).

Chapter One

1. Tony Hall with Tom Price, *Changing the Face of Hunger* (Nashville: Nelson, 2007).
2. Blaine Harden, "Politicians, Actors Gather in Ethiopia; Drama of Famine Victims Draws Celebrities," *Washington Post* (December 9, 1984).
3. Meron Tesfa Michael, "Ethiopia: Famine Threat," March 2003, *Worldpress.org*: *www.worldpress.org/africa/948.cfm*.
4. Hall, *Changing the Face of Hunger.*
5. The communist dictatorship had been overthrown in 1991.
6. Dale Petrosky, president of the National Baseball Hall of Fame and Museum, said he was concerned that Sarandon and Robbins would exploit the occasion to further publicize their views and perhaps further endanger U.S. troops.
7. Personal conversation with Fred Van Gorkom.
8. Dambisa Moyo, *Dead Aid: Why Aid Is Not Working and How There Is a Better Way for Africa* (Toronto: Douglas & McIntyre, 2010), 72.

9. Bill O'Reilly, "Giving Money to Poor Africans," June 8, 2005, *Fox News*: *www.foxnews.com/story/0,2933,158902,00.html*. Also: Mary Fitzgerald, "Ethiopia: Will Charity Scandals Starve Aid Donations?" May 1, 2010, *Irish Times*: *www.irish-times.com/newspaper/weekend/2010/0501/1224269451759. html* and Mary Fitzgerald, "Irish Aid Rejects Claim Ethiopia Uses Help as a Political Tool," October 27, 2010, *Irish Times*: *www.irishtimes.com/newspaper/world/2010/1027/1224282071786.html*.

10. Moyo, *Dead Aid*, xix.

Chapter Two

1. Tony Hall served in the House of Representatives from 1978 until 2002, leaving when President George W. Bush nominated him to serve as U.S. ambassador to the United Nations Agencies for Food and Agriculture. He is now director of the Alliance to End Hunger.

2. Richard Wurmbrand, *Tortured for Christ* (London: Hodder & Stoughton, 2004).

3. Voice of the Martyrs, *Persecution.com*: *www.persecution. com*.

4. In 1991, two years after the revolution, one of my other daughters, Brenda, went over to be a teacher at Emanuel College of the Second Baptist Church of Oradea in Transylvania and also taught at the secular University of Oradia.

5. Genocide in Transylvania website, *www.hungarian-history. hu/lib/genoci/genoci08.htm*.

6. Details about the Bibles being turned into toilet paper, Father Geza Palfi's murder, and other abuses may be found in an opinion piece by *Wall Street Journal* staff writer Peter K. Keresztes, published in the *WSJ* on June 14, 1985.

7. Patricia Sullivan, "Anti-Communist Priest Gheorghe Calciu-Dumitresa," *Washington Post* (November 26, 2006).

8. Ibid.

9. "Human Rights in Romania and Its Implications for U.S. Policy and Most Favored Nation Status." Hearing before the Subcommittee on Human Rights and International Organizations of the Committee on Foreign Affairs, House of Representatives, One Hundredth Congress, First Session, June 24, 1987.

10. Ibid.

11. Ibid.

12. See "The American Presidency Project," *www.presidency. ucsb.edu/ws/index.php?pid=30660*.

13. Ion Mihai Pacepa, *Red Horizons: The True Story of Nicolae & Elena Ceausescus' Crimes, Lifestyle, and Corruption* (Washington, D.C.: Regnery Gateway, 1987).

14. Roger Kirk and Mircea Raceanu, *Romania Versus the United States: Diplomacy of the Absurd, 1985–1989* (Washington, D.C.: Institute for the Study of Diplomacy, 1994), 155.

15. "Human Rights in Romania and Its Implications for U.S. Policy and Most Favored Nation Status." Hearing before the Subcommittee on Human Rights and International Organizations of the Committee on Foreign Affairs, House of Representatives, One Hundredth Congress, First Session, June 24, 1987.

16. Douglas Brinkley, ed., *The Reagan Diaries* (New York: Harper Collins, 2007), 547.

17. Ibid., 548.

18. The speech, delivered on May 31, 1988, may be found at *www.reagan.utexas.edu/archives/speeches/1988/053188b. htm*.

19. Reagan's remarks and a question-and-answer session with the students and faculty at Moscow State University, May 31, 1988, *www.reagan.utexas.edu/archives/ speeches/1988/053188b.htm*.

20. Natan Sharansky, "The Prisoner's Conscience [Natan Sharansky Eulogizes President Reagan]," *Jerusalem Post* (June 6, 2004), *www.freerepublic.com/focus/f-news/1148749/posts*.

21. Congressional Record, 1988.
22. Hall, *Changing the Face of Hunger*.
23. Arnaud de Borchgrave, "Red Past in Romania's Present," *Washington Times* (January 13, 2004).
24. Pacepa, *Red Horizons*.
25. Personal conversation with Anne Morse.
26. Ibid.
27. An account of Dana's arrival can be found at *http://articles.latimes.com/1990–01–28/news/mn–1248_1_ranking-official*.

Chapter Three

1. Mary Anne Mobley and Lynda Lee Mead.

Chapter Four

1. I was also a member of the executive committee of the Congressional Human Rights Caucus, an organization that works to keep members of Congress informed on human rights issues and assist people around the world who have been wrongly denied their basic freedoms.
2. Michael Kilian, "All in the Game," *Chicago Tribune* (March 7, 1997).
3. Associated Press, "10 Freed from Notorious Gulag," *Los Angeles Times* (February 8, 1992), *http://articles.latimes.com/1992–02–08/news/mn–1386_1_soviet-gulag*.

Chapter Five

1. *http://en.wikipedia.org/wiki/Tiananmen_Square_protests_of_1989*.
2. Harry Wu and George Vecsey, *Troublemaker* (NewsMax.com, December 13, 2002).
3. Ibid.
4. Aleksandr Solzhenitsyn, *The Gulag Archipelago, 1918–1956: An Experiment in Literary Investigation*, vol. 1 (New York: Basic, 1997).

5. A. M. Rosenthal, "On My Mind: Sixteen Million Slaves," *New York Times* (June 19, 1992), *www.nytimes.com/1992/06/19/opinion/on-my-mind-sixteen-million-slaves.html.*

6. Wu and Vecsey, *Troublemaker.*

7. When I returned to the U.S., I asked the U.S. Customs Service to begin an investigation into this matter.

8. Extension of Most-Favored-Nation Treatment to the People's Republic of China, House of Representatives, October 18, 1990.

9. Farhad Manjoo, "The iPad Suicides," June 1, 2010, *Slate*: *www.slate.com.*

10. The testimony of "Wujian" can be viewed at the website of Women's Rights Without Frontiers, *www.womensrightswithoutfrontiers.org/index.php?nav=wujian.*

11. *www.womensrightswithoutfrontiers.org/index.php?nav=wujian.*

12. Ibid.

13. Ibid.

14. Ibid.

15. Wu and Vecsey, *Troublemaker.*

16. Carol Divjak, "China Admits to Organ Trade from Executed Prisoners," December 29, 2006, *World Socialist Web Site*: *www.wsws.org.*

17. *http://laogai.org/.*

18. Wu and Vecsey, *Troublemaker.*

19. Guoqi Wang, "Habeas Corpus," *Harper's* (February 2000).

20. The Congressional Research Service *(www.fas.org/sgp/crs/index.html)* does not make its reports available to the public.

21. Brian Grow, Keith Epstein, and Chi-Chu Tschang, "The New E-spionage Threat," *Business Week* (April 10, 2008).

22. Ibid.

23. Shane Harris, "China's Cyber-Militia," *National Journal* (May 31, 2008).

24. Ted Bridis, "Laptop Tampering in China Alleged," Associated Press (May 30, 2008).

25. Associated Press, "China Denies Hacking into U.S. Computer," *USA Today* (June 12, 2008).

26. United States Government Accountability Office, "Cybercrime," 2007, *www.gao.gov/new.items/d07705.pdf*.

27. Ellen Nakashima, Steven Mufson, and John Pomfret, "Google Threatens to Leave China after Attacks on Activists' Email," *Washington Post* (January 13, 2010).

28. Ibid.

29. Ibid.

30. Ibid.

31. Tini Tran, "China Confirmed It Renewed Google's Operating License," July 13, 2010, *Guardian.co.uk*: *www.guardian.co/uk*.

32. Sarah Lyall, "Winner's Chair Remains Empty at Nobel Event," *New York Times* (December 10, 2010).

33. *www.pbs.org/newshour/bb/international/july-dec10/nobel_12 – 10.html?print*.

34. Ronald Reagan, Constitution Day Speech, Philadelphia, Pennsylvania, September 17, 1987, *www.reagan.utexas.edu/archives/speeches/1987/091787a.htm*.

35. David Aikman, *Jesus in Beijing: How Christianity Is Transforming China and Changing the Global Balance of Power* (Washington, D.C.: Regnery, 2006).

Chapter Six

1. Daja Meston died in 2010.

2. Details about Daja Meston's childhood in Nepal and his encounters with the Chinese government can be found in his autobiography: Daja Meston with Clare Ansberry, *Comes the Peace: My Journey to Forgiveness* (New York: Free Press, 2007).

3. Ewen MacAskill and Tania Branigan, "Barack Obama Risks China's Ire with Human Rights Remarks," January 19, 2011, *Guardian.co.uk*: *www.guardian.co.uk/world/2011/jan/19/barack-obama-china-human-rights*.

4. Photographs of the shooting, taken by Romanian camera-man Sergiu Matei of Romania's Pro-TV, who happened to be engaged in a climbing trip to Cho Oyu, can be viewed by visiting *http://sftcanada.wordpress.com/2006/10/14/nang-pa-la-pass-killings-picture-video/.*
5. MacAskill and Branigan, "Barack Obama Risks China's Ire."

Chapter Seven

1. Elisabeth Elliot, *Through Gates of Splendor: The Event That Shocked the World, Changed a People, and Inspired a Nation* (Peabody, Mass.: Hendrickson, 2010).
2. I-TEC (Indigenous People's Technology and Education Center), *www.itecusa.org/.*
3. Dick Foth paid his own way to Ecuador.
4. Dambisa Moyo, *Dead Aid: Why Aid Is Not Working and How There Is a Better Way for Africa* (Toronto: Douglas & Mcintyre, 2010).
5. Ibid.
6. Muhammad Yunnus, *Banker to the Poor: Micro-Lending and the Battle against World Poverty* (New York: Public Affairs, 2003).
7. William Jefferson Clinton, speech to the National Prayer Breakfast, February 4, 1999.
8. *End of the Spear*, Twentieth Century Fox, 2006.

Chapter Eight

1. Nicolas D. Kristof, "Obama Backs Down on Sudan," *New York Times* (April 21, 2010).
2. Desmond Butler, "Promises, Promises: US Fails to Punish Sudan," Associated Press (July 13, 2010).
3. Dave Eggers and John Prendergast, "In Sudan, War Is around the Corner," *New York Times* (July 12, 2010).
4. Michael Abramovich and Lawrence Woocher, "How Genocide Became a National Security Threat," *Foreign Policy* (February 26, 2010).

Chapter Nine

1. Paula Chin, Jane Sims Podesta, and Linda Kramer, "Vowing to Protect Her Child from Rape, Elizabeth Morgan Faces Her Twenty-third Month in Jail," *People* (June 12, 1989), *www.people.com/people/archive/article/0,,20120524,00.html.*
2. Ibid.
3. June Carbone and Leslie J. Harris, "Family Law Armageddon: The Story of Morgan v. Foretich," Family Law Stories, Forthcoming. Available at SSRN (Social Science Research Network), *http://ssrn.com/abstract=983770.*
4. Emily Henry, "Morgan vs. Foretich, Twenty Years Later," *LA Weekly* (February 4, 2009), *www.laweekly.com/2009 – 02 – 05/ news/morgan-vs-foretich-twenty-years-later/.*
5. Jane Sims Podesta and Paula Chin, "A Mother's First Taste of Freedom," *People* (October 16, 1989), *www.people.com/ people/archive/article/0,,20121427,00.html.*
6. Carbone and Harris, "Family Law Armageddon."
7. In response, Professor Doug Rendleman of Washington and Lee University School of Law and an expert on injunctions said it was appropriate for Congress to involve itself in the Morgan case "because the checks within the judicial system failed." Marcia Coyle, "A Question of Contempt," *National Law Journal* (October 30, 1989), *www. uiowa.edu/~030116/153/articles/coyle.htm.* And in *Time* magazine, law professor Robert Martineau notes, "If you refuse to comply with the order of the court after a certain period of time, you've clearly indicated that you are not going to comply. Keeping a person in jail after that simply becomes punishment." John Elson, Steven Holmes, and Andrea Sachs, "Ethics: A Hard Case of Contempt," *Time* (September 18, 1989), *www.time.com/time/magazine/print-out/0,8816,958575,00.html.*
8. Carbone and Harris, "Family Law Armageddon."

Chapter Ten

1. Lyndsey Layton, "The Story behind the Iraq Study Group," *Washington Post* (November 21, 2006).
2. Frank Wolf, "Fresh Eyes on Iraq," *Washington Post* (September 24, 2005).
3. Co-chairs Baker and Hamilton chose the rest of the members, who were a pretty diverse group: Lawrence Eagleburger, Vernon Jordan Jr., Ed Meese, Sandra Day O'Connor, Leon Panetta, William Perry, Charles Robb, and Alan Simpson. Bob Gates and Rudy Giuliani were in the group originally. Gates stepped down when he became secretary of defense, and Giuliani stepped down because other commitments kept him from attending meetings.
4. Peter Baker, Robin Wright, and Dafna Linzer, "From Hundreds of Sources, Panel Forged Consensus," *Washington Post* (December 7, 2006).
5. John Mueller, "The Iraq Syndrome," *Foreign Affairs* (November/December 2005).
6. Steven R. Weisman, "What Civil War Could Look Like," *New York Times* (February 26, 2006).
7. Excerpted with permission from army chaplain J. D. Moore's "Chronicles of Pastor J.D.," *www.unionbaptistchurch.net/*.

Chapter Eleven

1. Transcript, Senator John Edwards, house party remarks at the home of Chris and Kristin Sullivan, Concord, N.H., February 2, 2002, *www.gwu.edu/~action/2004/edwards/0202nhtrip/conctransc020202.html*.
2. Stephanie Condon, "Most Americans Want Afghanistan Withdrawal Timeline," *CBS News*: *www.cbsnews.com/8301–503544_162–20010459–503544.html*.
3. Bob Woodward, "Military Thwarted President Seeking Choice in Afghanistan," *Washington Post* (September 27, 2010).

Chapter Twelve

1. *http://en.wikipedia.org/wiki/Wang_Weilin.*
2. Jill Drew and Edward Cody, "China Blocks Dissident Lawyers from Beijing Dinner Hosted by Congressmen," *Washington Post* (July 1, 2008).
3. *www.cardinalkungfoundation.org/prisoners/index.htm.* This information is also contained in my trip report, available at *http://wolf.house.gov/uploads/China2008TripReport-Enews. pdf.*
4. According to CHINAaid's Bob Fu, the Chinese Foreign Ministry warned journalists that certain topics were not to be covered, threatening journalists with the loss of their annual credential renewal, which allows foreign journalists to stay in Beijing, if they covered off-limits topics. More about Chinese repression of the press may be found at *www.ifex.org/ china/2010/12/09/ifj campaign bulletin/.*
5. Martin Lee, "China's Olympic Opportunity," *Wall Street Journal* (October 17, 2007).
6. Steven Lee Myers, "Bush Praises China but Continues Rebuke during Embassy Dedication in Beijing," *New York Times* (August 7, 2008).
7. Ibid.
8. This story may be found at *http://thepoint.breakpoint.org/ commentaries/4508-sanctioning-persecution.*
9. Tim Reid, "Bush Medal for Dalai Lama Alarms China," *Times/Sunday Times* (October 15, 2007), *www.timesonline. co.uk/tol/news/world/us_and_americas/article2658653.ece.*
10. Richard Spencer, "Hillary Clinton: Human Rights Secondary to Economic Survival," *The Telegraph* (February 20, 2009).
11. "Amnesty International Shocked, Dismayed, by U.S. Secretary's Comments That Human Rights Will Not Top Her China Agenda," Amnesty International press release, February 20, 2009, *www.amnestyusa.org/document.php?id=ENGU SA20090220001&lang=e.*

12. Hillary Clinton and Timothy Geithner, "A New Strategic and Economic Dialogue with China," *Wall Street Journal* (July 27, 2009).

13. As I write, Gao is still missing. In March of 2011, his wife, Geng He, said, "Our children and I [live] with worry and anxiety. Gao's disappearance, in the past, has sychronised with brutality and shocking torture by the state. My husband's case is a true presentation of China's on-going human rights crisis."

14. "We Are Afraid to Even Look for Them," Human Rights Watch report, October 20, 2009, *www.hrw.org/en/reports/2009/10/22/we-are-afraid-even-look-them*.

15. Tom Lantos Human Rights Commission report (October 29, 2009).

16. "Chinese Pastor Sentenced to Fifteen Years in Prison," December 11, 2009, *Crosswalk.com: www.crosswalk.com*.

17. "Human Rights Not 'Interference' in U.S.-China Relations, Critics Say," February 25, 2009, *Catholic News Agency: www.catholicnewsagency.com/news/human_rights_not_interference_in_u.s.china_relations_critics_say/*.

18. "Abraham Lincoln and Power," review of *Abraham Lincoln: A Life* by Michael Burlingame (Baltimore: John Hopkins Univ. Press, 2008), *Abraham Lincoln's Classroom, www.abrahamlincolnsclassroom.org/Library/newsletter.asp?ID=145&CRLI=202*.

19. Ibid.

Chapter Thirteen

1. David Walker, "Transforming Government to Meet the Demands of the 21st Century," August 7, 2007, *www.gao.gov/cghome/d071188cg.pdf*.

2. Scott Shane and Andrew W. Lehren, "Leaked Cables Offer Raw Look at U.S. Diplomacy," *New York Times* (November 28, 2010).

3. Joby Warrick and Carrie Johnson, "Chinese Spy 'Slept' in U.S. for Two Decades," *Washington Post* (April 3, 2008).

4. From Washington's Farewell Address, quoted at the Eagle Forum website, *www.eagleforum.org/educate/washington/advice.html.*

5. Robert D. Kaplan, "Where's the American Empire When We Need It?" *Washington Post* (December 3, 2010).

Chapter Fourteen

1. Norman R. Augustine et al. "Rising Above the Gathering Storm: Energizing and Employing America for a Brighter Economic Future," *National Academies* (October 20, 2005).

2. *Rising Above the Gathering Storm, Revisited: Rapidly Approaching Category 5*, ebook available at the website of the National Academies, *www.nap.edu/catalog.php?record_id=12999.*

3. Niall Ferguson, "Complexity and Collapse," *Foreign Affairs* (March/April 2010).

4. Ibid.

5. "The Manhattan Declaration: A Call of Christian Conscience" may be found at *www.manhattandeclaration.org/the-declaration/read.aspx.*

6. This quotation may be found at *www.academicamerican.com/revolution/documents/franklin.htm.*

7. This quotation may be found at *http://library.thinkquest.org/22254/biopenn3.htm.*

8. This quotation may be found at *www.propheticroundtable.org/ForeFathers/GeorgeWashington/Quote.htm.*

Share Your Thoughts

With the Author: Your comments will be forwarded to the author when you send them to *zauthor@zondervan.com*.

With Zondervan: Submit your review of this book by writing to *zreview@zondervan.com*.

Free Online Resources at

www.zondervan.com

Zondervan AuthorTracker: Be notified whenever your favorite authors publish new books, go on tour, or post an update about what's happening in their lives at www.zondervan.com/authortracker.

Daily Bible Verses and Devotions: Enrich your life with daily Bible verses or devotions that help you start every morning focused on God. Visit www.zondervan.com/newsletters.

Free Email Publications: Sign up for newsletters on Christian living, academic resources, church ministry, fiction, children's resources, and more. Visit www.zondervan.com/newsletters.

Zondervan Bible Search: Find and compare Bible passages in a variety of translations at www.zondervanbiblesearch.com.

Other Benefits: Register yourself to receive online benefits like coupons and special offers, or to participate in research.

ZONDERVAN®

ZONDERVAN.com/
AUTHORTRACKER
follow your favorite authors